Making Vintage 1950s *Clothes for Women*

Making Vintage 1950s Clothes for Women

THERESA PARKER

THE CROWOOD PRESS

First published in 2018 by
The Crowood Press Ltd
Ramsbury, Marlborough
Wiltshire SN8 2HR

www.crowood.com

© Theresa Parker 2018

All rights reserved. No part of this publication may be reproduced or transmitted in any form or by any means, electronic or mechanical, including photocopy, recording, or any information storage and retrieval system, without permission in writing from the publishers.

British Library Cataloguing-in-Publication Data
A catalogue record for this book is available from the British Library.

ISBN 978 1 78500 435 3

Typeset by Sharon Dainton Design.
Printed and bound in India by Replika Press Pvt Ltd

Contents

Introduction		7
1	Tools and Materials	17
2	Measuring and Fitting	23
3	The Bra and Girdle (Belt) Set	27
4	The Petticoat	43
5	The Strapless Cocktail Dress	51
6	The Town Suit: The Soft Tailored Jacket	59
7	The Town Suit: The Chalk Line Skirt	69
8	The Bow Tie Blouse	77
9	The Housewife's Kimono Shirt with Detachable Collar and Cuffs	85
10	The Self-Neatening Gathered Skirt	95
11	The Manteau	103
12	Creating the Look	113
Stockists and Suppliers		124
Suggested Reading and Information Sources		125
Acknowledgements		126
Index		127

Introduction

Paris has two profiles – wide, out-flowing: 'l ampleur douce – and slim, self-contained: 'le droit-fil .
UK *Woman's Journal,* February 1952

In this book I have tried to identify what I think are the key silhouettes for the decade. I have applied the same research process as I would employ when designing a wardrobe for a character in a film or creating a fashion collection. The inspiration for the projects has come from a variety of different sources with some elements that are completely true to the originals and some that have required a degree of interpretation to figure out. This is normal when all the information needed cannot come from one source alone. For example I have frequently referred to my own collection of vintage magazines, especially the British and American editions of *Vogue* and *Woman's Journal,* to identify the fit of key looks for the period, even though I could not always see the construction processes in the photographs. I have also used museum archives to examine garments at first hand for a more tactile investigation into construction and fabrication but as they are of historical interest and need to be conserved I could not try them on to see the fit. I have also referred to a variety of original 1950s paper patterns, which did not always come with markings or instructions, and so half toiles frequently had to be made to identify fit or order of manufacture stages ('toile' is the French term for a test garment and a half toile is literally one half, or slice, of that garment). I also frequently had my nose in vintage instruction manuals for pattern drafting, construction and finishing techniques, which I also tested in calico before committing anything to the real fabrics.

I have been inspired by the ingenuity of garments made by both couturiers and home dressmakers. The quality of manufacture is incredibly varied and obviously down to the skill and competency of the seamstress and her experience with the equipment at her disposal. For some women that was only a needle and thread, whilst others would have used hand sewing machines or treadle versions and some

Two silhouettes from UK *Woman's Journal,* June 1952. (Author's own collection)

had treadle machines converted into electric models.

I had extensive access to the archives at Worthing Museum and Art Gallery, which has influenced the projects selected for the book. The focus of the archive is specifically on maker/owner pieces, catalogue buys and garments made by local tailors and less about pieces made by well-known designers of the time. That is not to say that the latter's aesthetic did not influence what women chose to make or buy as the garments effectively fell into two key silhouettes already identified in *Vogue* as the Paris profiles most of us already associated with clothing of that era. The looks have clearly been inspired by

Cover of UK *Woman's Journal* showing a painting of the Duchess of Haddington in a Dior gown, June 1952. (Author's own collection)

Behind the scenes at the Worthing Museum and Art Gallery.

Vintage pattern. (Author's own collection)

Pattern manual. (Worthing Museum and Art Gallery)

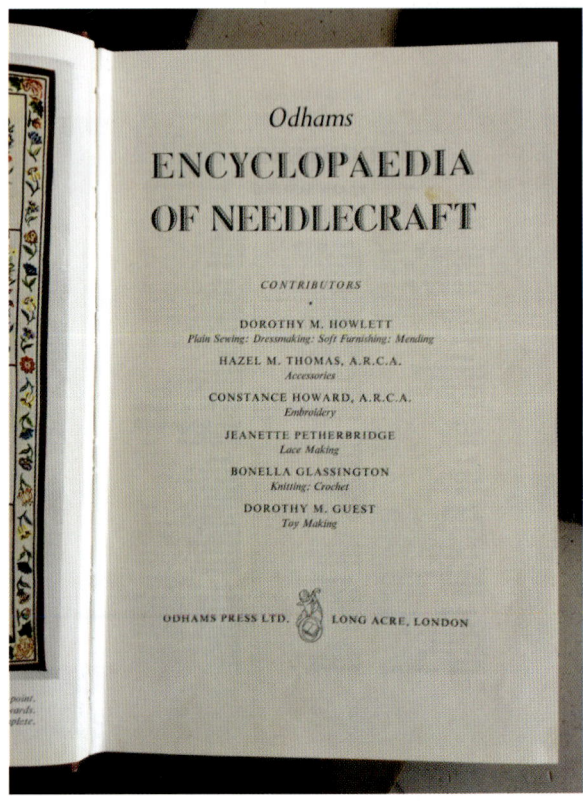

Instruction manual. (Author's own collection)

Introduction

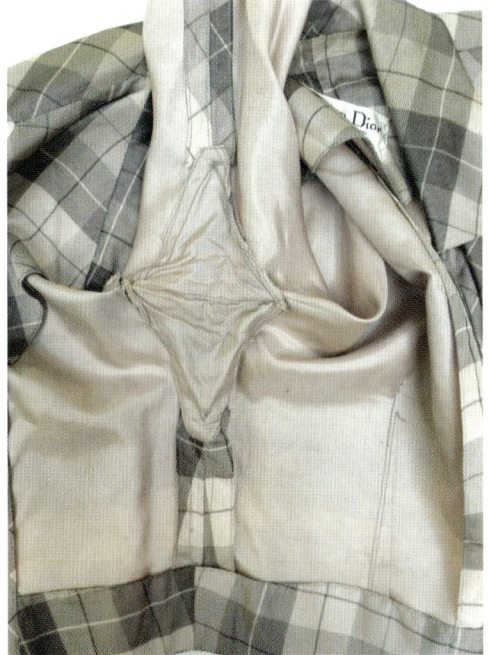
House of Youth/Dior kimono jacket lining. (Worthing Museum and Art Gallery collection)

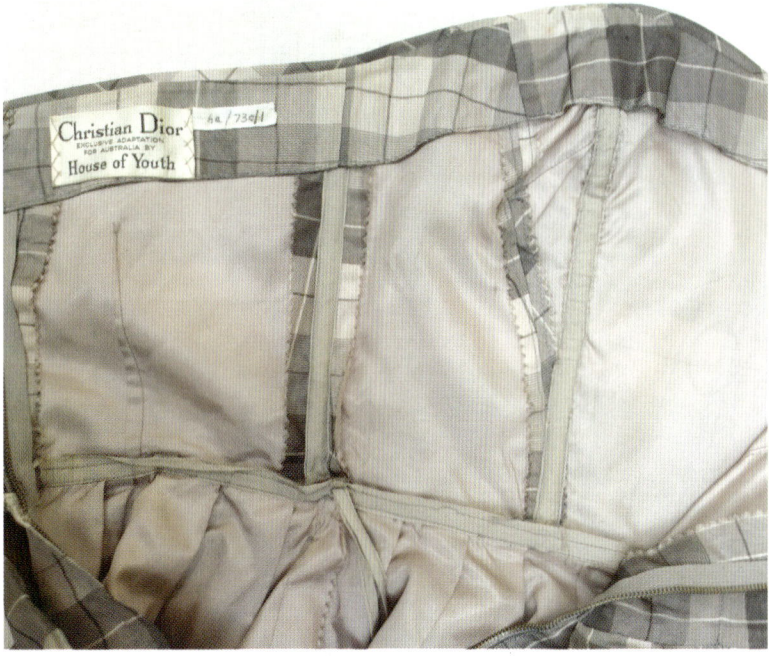
House of Youth dress with pinked finish on seam. (Worthing Museum and Art Gallery collection)

the work of couturiers as have the frequently sophisticated quality of finishing; for example, many of the garments are fully lined and turned through at the shoulders. This construction method enables raw seams to be covered and encompasses a neat way of completing tiny shoulder straps. Archive pieces from the late fifties have sometimes incorporated a zigzag stitch, no doubt speeding up the neatening processes and allowing women to machine their own buttonholes for the first time. It has also been interesting to see examples of pinking employed both by the home dressmaker and couturiers.

The New Look

The overriding silhouettes of the decade originated in Paris with the couture house of Christian Dior being particularly influential. Dior constructed his dresses based on his observations of the female body and the desire to idealize its proportions. The names he chose for his lines reflected the dominant silhouette from each show, such as the Corolla, the Zigzag, the Oblique and the Sinueuse, to name but a few. The lines were described in great detail in press kits, providing journalists with a commentary on the latest fashion innovations.

The name of Dior's first collection for his own fashion house was La Ligne Corolle. Dior was very much inspired by nature and the name was actually a botanical term referring to a circlet of flower petals, a concept he endeavoured to capture with his designs. Carmel Snow, editor-in-chief of *Harper's Bazaar,* cried out in delight when she saw it, declaring 'It's quite a revolution, dear Christian ... It's such a New Look!' The style became pivotal to the way women dressed during the decade and changed very little throughout that timespan. Set against a background of shortages of food, materials and fuel in war-torn Paris, Dior took the softer feminine shape of a round sloping shoulder line, narrow waist and spreading skirts to the extreme. *Harper's Bazaar* published detailed line drawings of the New Look's construction, demonstrating how skirts with 23 metres (25 yards) of fabric were supported inside. The style lines were also illustrated in *Vogue* and *L'Officiel*. The Bar Suit was one of the most popular and most frequently copied models in Dior's La Ligne Corolle collection.

The ateliers were, and still are, the cornerstone of the House of Dior. The atelier's role has always been to turn ideas into reality, using the designer's sketches as a starting point. From 1947, Marguerite Carré was the technical director at the House of Dior and she was the person to whom Dior's sketches were first given. In turn the sketches were distributed to two other colleagues – the head of flou (dressmaking) and the head of tailleur (tailoring). The ateliers created toiles (test garments) based on the drawings and Madame Marguerite would present them to Dior, famously enquiring each time, 'Have I correctly expressed your vision?' The toiles deemed worthy were kept, fabrics for the season attributed, embroideries placed and accessories chosen during the numerous fittings, not as an add-on at the end of the process. It is still done like this today, even with the current creative director Maria Grazia Chiuri. It was and is still common practice for seamstresses to put in over a thousand hours of work to perfect one design. The garments are incredibly labour-intensive, but this is considered normal

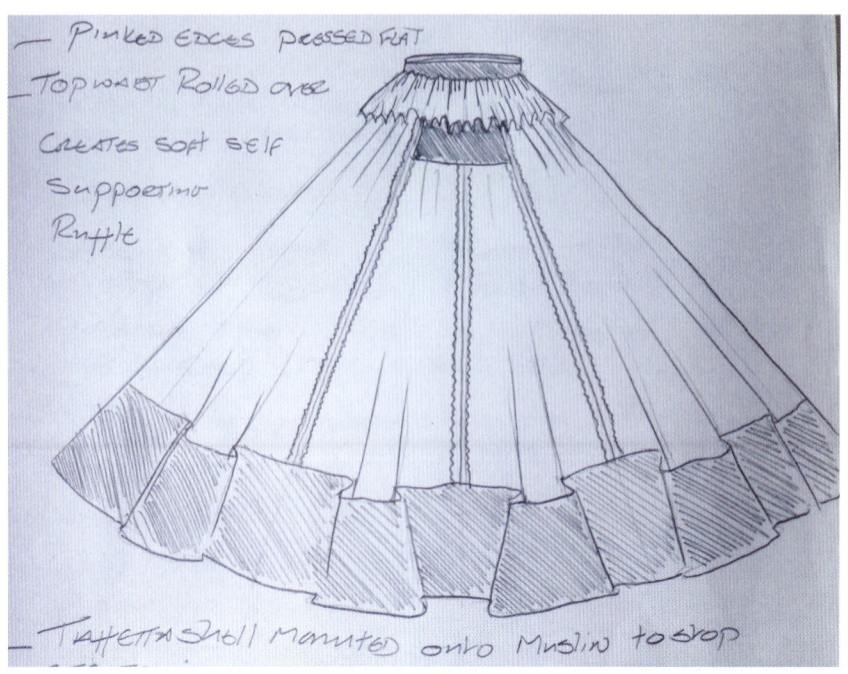

Author's sketch of the New Look skirt turned inside-out.

practice in the world of haute couture. It is really not surprising, then, that only the wealthy social elite have ever been able to afford it.

The scope of the New Look was staggering and impacted uncompromisingly across the Western fashion world for a decade. Age, size and body type made no difference as the look trickled down from the couturiers through department stores and patterns for dressmakers all over Europe and the US. The fashion commentator Peter York is famously quoted as saying, 'There was no alternative'. This element of conformity is very different from what we know and see in our more pluralistic society today. For example, regardless of budget, the bodice was always darted and close-fitting to show off a tiny waist. This new nipped-in waistline was raised to its natural position – a significant change to the more austere fashions during World War II – and accentuated with a full skirt, often bolstered with layers of petticoats or small hip pads. The prominent tight waist was often accentuated with belts, and the skirt, depending on the occasion for which it was being worn, had varying degrees of flare or was very straight and stopped mid-calf. Luckily for the home dressmaker and her tight budget, the two skirt silhouettes could frequently be bought in the same pattern envelope and styled with a duster coat or box jacket over the top.

Fashion involves change, novelty and the context of the time, place and wearer. That change is truly effective when ideas can be disseminated widely and understood easily by a large consumer audience. The fifties saw significant advances in technology as a direct result of the war: among these were more sophisticated colour printing presses for publications and advertising, improved techniques for printing cloth and the introduction of TVs and electric sewing machines in many households. Parallel with these was the burgeoning film industry which drew huge numbers of people to the cinema, and all of these impacted on how fashion products were distributed and consumed. American culture was dominant in Europe, with prominent film stars such as Audrey Hepburn setting fashions in etiquette, make-up, hair and clothing. Hepburn had a very specific relationship with the French couturier Hubert de Givenchy who was responsible for many of her key film looks. Although it was still unlike today's immediate online access to high fashion catwalks, the general public had wider visual access to this imagery for the first time. The fifties was also the golden age of fashion photography. Dior's spectacular and highly photogenic style attracted magazines and top photographers like Irvine Penn, Horst P. Horst and Richard Avedon who

Magazine advertisements from UK *Vogue*, November 1952.
(Author's own collection)

consistently created stylish and sophisticated imagery with models in awkward and uncompromising poses. In Britain, the royal family were popular stylistic influencers and bucked this trend. In 1951 Princess Margaret's official twenty-first birthday portrait was taken by Cecil Beaton: she chose to pose for a series of photographs in a bespoke New Look Dior gown that had a tightly fitted bodice and layers of tulle for its full skirts. She was a devoted customer and helped to cement the label's popularity and style amongst the wealthy British elite of the time. The iconic images went global in a commemorative hard and paperback book, easily obtainable from bookshops and department stores.

The Importance of the Paper Pattern in the Fifties

Anthropometry, or the science of recording human measurements, had been developed in the US to create a standardized measurement system for the garment industry before World War II. This became more finely tuned in the 1950s, allowing more garments to be successfully sold in stores or by mail order without customers trying them on first. Many women's technical skills, or at least their confidence in them, greatly increased as a result of their war efforts either with 'make do and mend' or from making uniforms in factories, and a new type of more innovative and demanding consumer emerged to reflect the zeitgeist. This highlighted the critical contribution made by the humble paper pattern and dressmakers' ability to interpret and adapt it to the styles of the decade.

Vogue patterns had been available from department stores since 1916 throughout the US, Canada and the UK, with special editions being produced for publication in Vogue magazine – a tradition that had been running in the US since at least 1899. Although this went against the grain of the editorial ethos of exclusivity of the publication, it sowed the seed of fashion for the masses in the years to come. Vogue licensing reached Australia in the 1920s and ownership of high-quality printing equipment made it possible for the Condé Nast group to publish the Vogue Pattern Book six times a year, each issue featuring around 350 uncut printed paper patterns.

Through the Utility Clothing scheme (1942–52) high-end European fashion designers/couture houses produced styles for the masses for the first time

Vintage Vogue pattern. (Worthing Museum and Art Gallery collection)

Re-issued and updated copy of Butterick's Walkaway dress. (Author's own collection)

and rose to the challenge of creating desirable looks that complied with civilian rationing and the safeguarding of raw materials. Vogue bought out the 'Couturier' line in 1931 and by 1949 Mr Nast of Condé Nast – Vogue's owner – became the first and only licensee authorized to duplicate and sell 'Paris Original' patterns from eight famous French couturiers including Schiaparelli, Paquin, Balmain, Fath, Molyneux, Lanvin and Heim. By 1956 Vogue had incorporated the international designer pattern into their Couturier lines along with millinery and accessories and included patterns from Yves St Laurent, Hubert de Givenchy and Emilio Pucci.

Not surprisingly Vogue patterns were frequently criticized for being too complex for the average home dressmaker to follow properly. In response, dressmaking pattern manufacturers such as Butterick, McCall's and Simplicity, along with magazines such as Woman's Journal, Woman's Own and Woman's Weekly, began creating stylish and more accessible dress patterns that retained the essence of the looks created by the couturiers in Europe but promised a New Look silhouette in under three hours for even the least experienced dressmakers. Butterick's famous Walkaway dress was so popular that production stopped on all other patterns to meet demand for this one.

The Haslam System of Dress Cutting

This method of dress cutting was designed by Grace Haslam in Bolton for women who wanted to draft their own patterns from scratch rather than use and adapt existing ones. The system was trend-driven and provided women with over eighty books of draftings throughout the forties and fifties. To use it you first had to invest in the Foundation drafting book which taught women how to measure themselves properly, how to make accommodations for different body types and how to use the accompanying Haslam Chart – a sort

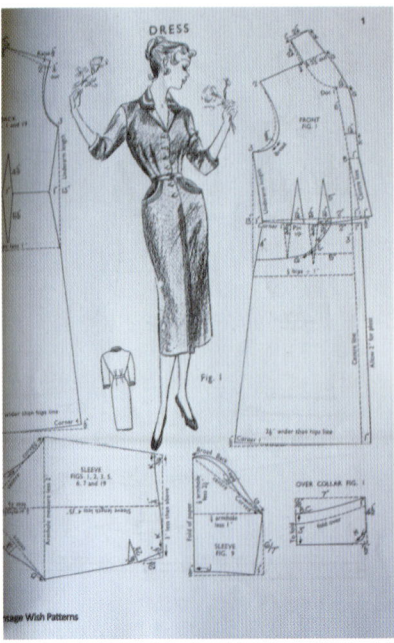
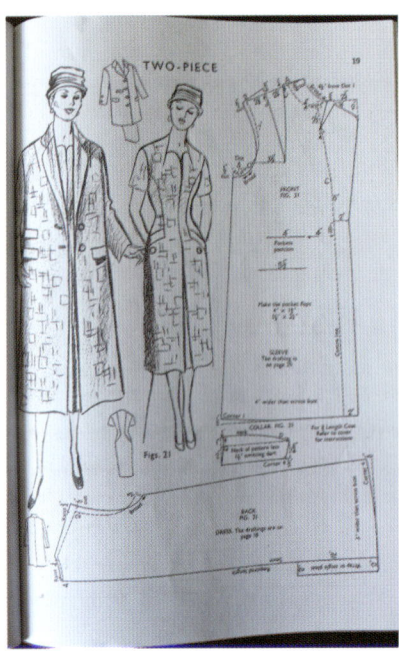

Pages from *The Haslam System for Dress Cutting*, reproduced with permission from My Vintage Wish.

Author's parents' wedding photo, March 1953.

of vintage pattern master or elaborate set square – to draft a set of personal basic blocks or 'base' drafts specific to your own measurements. The drafting books could then be used as an instruction manual to manipulate the base draft into a variety of designs and different garment types starting with underwear for women and children. The system more or less guaranteed a bespoke fit regardless of your body type. The instructions for construction were not that detailed – more pointers in the right direction – but the visual instructions were communicated clearly. She also toured the country teaching her system of dressmaking, which is how my mother, an enthusiastic home dressmaker, used a Miss Haslam book to draft a pattern and make her own wedding dress.

Working with Vintage Patterns

The photos and illustrations of the fifties we see in magazines and on film, as with all advertising, are designed to show a product at its optimum. Models were cinched in with shape wear and then padded out within an inch of their lives posing in unrealistic positions to get the right shot. The majority of women didn't live or dress this way and they too were frequently seduced by the cover of a designer pattern only to discover that it didn't fit without significant adjustment and the right underwear. For the woman of today it is frustratingly hard to get a good fit from an original vintage pattern or garments even though they are very easy to get hold of.

Vintage patterns are generally cut slightly smaller and tighter than modern-day patterns to reflect the average female physique of the day. There is plenty of research on this subject, especially by mannequin manufacturers, showing that the women of today are significantly bigger than our female counterparts of the fifties. Vintage bra specialist What Katie Did says the average vital statistics in the fifties were 37-27-39 by comparison to 38-34-40 today. Obviously these are only mean averages, but there is no denying that over the last sixty years women have got bigger! Women ate roughly the same number of calories as we do today, but only around one-third of it was from refined sugars and processed food. Effectively we carry more belly, boob and back fat as a result of our modern diet! Women in the fifties were also less sedentary than women today and could easily burn off up to 1,000 calories going about their daily chores, which were significantly more physical, such as putting their washing through a mangle or managing wet sheets in and out of a twin tub, walking to the shops, and so on. It is better to accept our differences and look for ways we can achieve the look without drastically changing our lifestyles.

Moulage and Pattern Drafting

Most costume designers and cutters I know will take a pattern from an existing garment if it is relevant. It will involve pricking along all the seams with a tracing wheel and then toiling up and making minor adjustments to the garment on the stand. As much of my source material has been museum artefacts this technique is obviously not an option. Working with museum pieces requires careful handling and

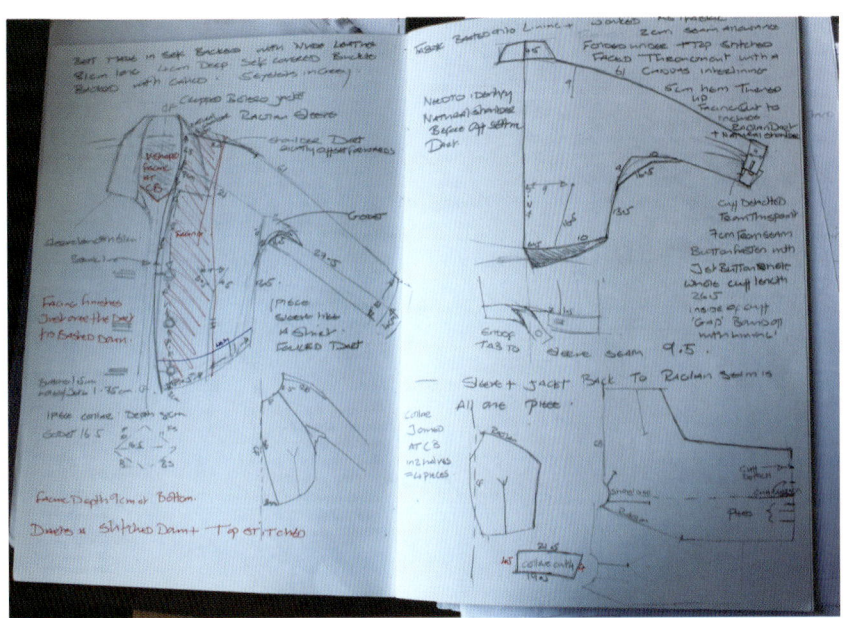

Sketchbook pages with notes for the House of Youth Kimono jacket.

the wearing of white cotton gloves to prevent the transference of grease from hands to the textiles. The research has been done with the garments laid flat, usually on a table covered by tissue paper, and photographed. I have kept meticulous notes on each garment and made sketches that include as many measurements as possible. Where I can, I have stuck to these proportions for the patterns in the book. With regards to conservation, archive pieces are often delicate and can not withstand much manipulation handling. As with many pieces in museum archives they only fit the wearer so putting them on a mannequin is not an option. As a result I was not able to see any of the source material on a body before I started the patterns. With the vintage patterns that belonged to me, I photocopied the pieces and joined them together to test them out in calico rather than risking ripping 65-year-old tissue paper, and I would actually recommend this method to anyone who has vintage patterns themselves. With the patterns from the museum archive I photographed the front and back of the envelopes so that I had an illustration and technical drawing and whatever instructions, if any, that came with the pattern piece. I am used to developing patterns from a

garment design or sketch so to me this has seemed the most logical approach, regardless of whether or not it was my sketch.

Pattern making for fashion is normally based on a flat drafting system using a series of basic blocks derived from a series of measurements standard to industry. These are then graded up and down into different dress sizes. Initially I could not visualize the impact the use of a conical bustline would have on a flat pattern block or see how it would then impact on the shape or position of darts through the waist. Likewise I could not visualize how steep the curve from the waist to hip might become to accommodate hip pads. Instead I used a 3D technique used by couturiers called moulage to develop the patterns. This process allows patterns to be developed by directly draping fabric onto a mannequin, adjusting the fit and then transferring the information from fabric (usually calico or muslin) to paper. This creates a master pattern for a first toile in calico, which can be made up and tried on a fit model or back on the mannequin. This pink Dior gown worn by Madonna for the film *Evita*, where she played the part of Eva Peron, is a good example of the technique in practice. The foundation garments were made first to create the desired shape of the body then the fabric was draped in a continuous piece on the bias over the foundations to create the silhouette of the dress. In this instance the original was modified to fit her specific measurements and new duplicates made in her size using this traditional method. It is likely that the dress stand used would also have had to be modified to accurately reflect her size and create the right silhouette for draping at the outset.

My career in film and TV has very much been about interpreting the style and fit of an era as accurately as possible, whilst adapting it to suit a modern physique. For the purpose of this book I have worked directly to a modern industry size 12 mannequin in a remodelled B cup bullet bra to accommodate the bigger bust waist and hip. When I was satisfied with the fit and silhouette, I draped the outer garments over the bras, girdles and petticoats, allowing me to see how the fabric moulded over such a conical bust shape or from a tiny waist to a more curvaceous hip line. I could also see the effect gravity had on the hang of the fabric before committing to the final pattern. I also only draped on the wearer's right as half toiles, only transferring to the left half when I was happy with the pattern. I appreciate not everyone is a standard size 12 but the patterns in the book can be graded up or down to increase or decrease the size as desired. I have listed some excellent resources for this in the final section of the book and there is a chart for basic alterations to lengthen or shorten and add or reduce width in Chapter 2.

Pattern Abbreviations and Terminology

The scale used for each pattern is indicated next to the pattern. There is no seam allowance included; everything is nett. The following abbreviated terms have been used:

CF – centre front
CB – centre back
SS – side seam
SG/Straight of grain – the direction of the selvedge edge
Selvedge – the finished edge of your fabric (usually more tightly woven than the body of cloth so might need cutting off to avoid distortion)
RS – right side of the fabric
WS – wrong side or back of the fabric
Notches – denoted by a small bar on the edge of the pattern pieces so that you can match them together – you can add more if you wish
Darts – denoted by a broken line, each dart is an area of suppression that shapes the garment over the contours of the body
Fold – where the pattern piece should be placed along a folded edge of the fabric.

Pink Christian Dior ball gown, made in England by C.D. Models (London) Ltd, No 07929. (The Cosprop Archive)

 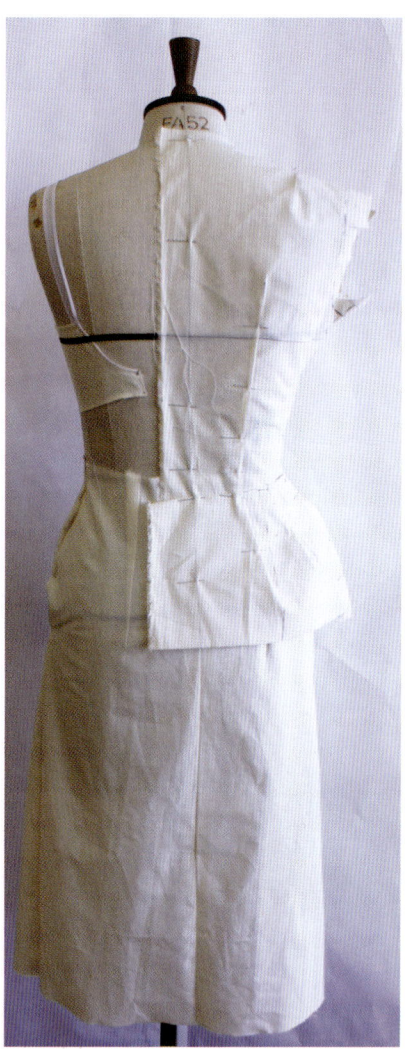 

Moulage and pattern development for projects in this book.

Tools and Materials

1

It is important to have the best tools for the job. Most of the tools only need to be very basic but make sure they are the best quality you can afford, especially your scissors. I have split this chapter into categories based sequentially on the processes where you are likely to need the tools and have included my favourite suppliers in the Stockists and Suppliers section at the end of the book.

Pattern Making and Alterations

These will be needed if you want to adapt or amend one of the existing patterns.

Propelling (mechanical) pencil: the lead must always be kept sharp. Sharpies (fine-tipped permanent marker pens): have two different colours in case you want to re-mark style lines.

A tracing wheel allows you to mark off (on paper only) any seam or style lines. Note that you can use it in conjunction with carbon paper if you want to trace lines directly onto cloth.

A pattern master is a clear plastic template with both curved and straight calibrated edges. It is really useful for perfecting your armholes and bra cups or any curved hems and necklines, especially after making alterations. The pattern master also has the advantage of having measurements and right angles for marking off grain lines and for seam allowances.

Pattern drafting tools.

Scotch® Magic™ tape or equivalent matt finish adhesive tape: if you are making alterations this keeps any cutting and sticking neat and accurate and you can draw over the top of it with your propelling pencil.

Tailor's chalk is really useful for drawing on fabric, marking off darts, buttonholes, etc. It brushes out easily without leaving a residue and can be sharpened with a scalpel to produce a fine line.

Measuring

The tape measure: this may be in centimetres on one side and inches on the other: stick to one or the other. Tapes are prone to stretching so replace yours every few years.

A 20cm/8in ruler for redrawing fiddly bits; it is more manageable than a yardstick.

Tape measure

Cutting

Scissors/shears: anything with blades over 15cm/6in long are called shears; select what is comfortable for you to hold. As a standard 'go to' I would suggest 23cm/9in blades. I still have my first-ever pair of cutting shears because it was drummed into me at university to look after them properly. I bought the best pair I could afford from Morplan in 1986 and have only ever cut cloth with them. I keep the screw oiled and clean the blades regularly. I also have a small blade sharpener for them. Be aware that if you drop your scissors or shears they will be permanently damaged. I also recommend a second cheap pair (pound shop shopping) for cutting paper and, if you can afford it, a pair for cutting tough fabrics like horsehair interlinings and canvas.

17

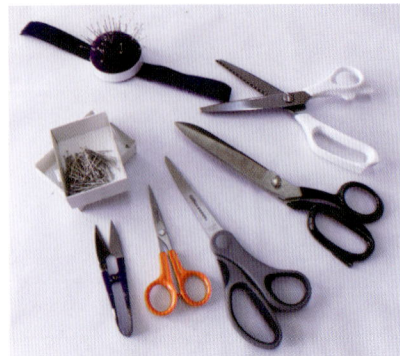

Scissors and shears.

A rotary cutter is a useful alternative to scissors depending on how steady your hand is. It is useful for cutting on the bias: the cutting is more accurate because the fabric is not being lifted off the cutting surface. Replace the blade so it doesn't get blunt, otherwise it will ruin your cloth.

Small scissors approximately 10–13cm/4–5in long are really useful provided they are kept sharp. You will be able to snip right into corners to create a crisp mitre as well as trimming threads or cutting buttonholes.

Pins should be steel without glass beads on the head (which are impossible to push in if you are using a thimble). They should be fine so as not to damage your cloth and at least 3cm/$1^{1}/_{4}$ in long. Prym is a good brand. Get a magnet so you can collect them all up after you have finished working and reuse them.

The seam ripper is useful for the home dressmaker but non-existent in a couture workroom. Instead they pull out the thread from alternate sides to undo a seam rather than cutting in case the fabric on the stitch line gets cut by mistake

Pattern weights: you can make your own weights in whatever substance is suitable but make sure they are covered in something soft to avoid catching your main fabric. The weights are used to secure your pattern on the fabric before cutting.

Tissue paper or brown paper can act as a temporary stabilizer when trying to cut sheer and slippery fabrics. Place it under the fabric then put the pattern on top of the fabric. Use lots of pins to secure the layers and then cut out. Your cut edges will be straight.

Sewing

The sewing machine: many people spend a lot of money on a sewing machine and that is fine if you are going to use its computerized fancy functions regularly. All you really need is a good-quality basic domestic (or industrial) machine like a Bernina or a Singer that is operated by a foot pedal and sews straight stitches forwards and backwards. Blow the budget on your scissors instead. If you really must go crazy, get a machine with a buttonhole function and zigzag stitch and practise using it on scraps of fabric before you commit to a real garment. Make sure you have spare bobbins and spare bobbin case.

A variety of different-sized machine needles: a no. 80 is a good all-rounder that will sew most medium-weight fabrics but I would also keep no. 70s for silks and fine fabrics and no. 90s or no. 100s for thicker coat weights. You may need ballpoint needles for knitted fabrics like the power mesh used in the girdle.

A variety of different sewing machine feet: the ones I find useful are the straight stitch foot for sewing pretty much everything: it is assumed that you will have this to hand for all the projects in this book so only additional feet are mentioned in the lists of materials and equipment. Other attachments include the zip foot or single foot which allows you to stitch directly next to bulk (such as zip teeth or piping); the concealed zip foot specifically for putting in concealed zips; and a walking foot or Teflon foot for stretch fabrics, leather and multiple layers You may also find a gathering foot useful for some of the projects in this book.

The overlocker is a sewing machine with three or four threads and a blade that cuts, hems and neatens all at once. This is a really sound investment and will allow you to finish all fabrics with a professional touch; it is especially good for neatening and finishing stretch and knitted fabrics. Make sure you keep a good pair of long tweezers with it and regularly clear the fluff away from the cutting blade.

A selection of hand sewing needles will be needed, depending on the weight of the cloth you are sewing. Make sure the end with the eye is not thicker than the needle itself as it is harder to push through the fabric.

The thimble: tailors use an open-topped one as they use the side of the finger to push the needle through but dressmakers tend to have a closed one

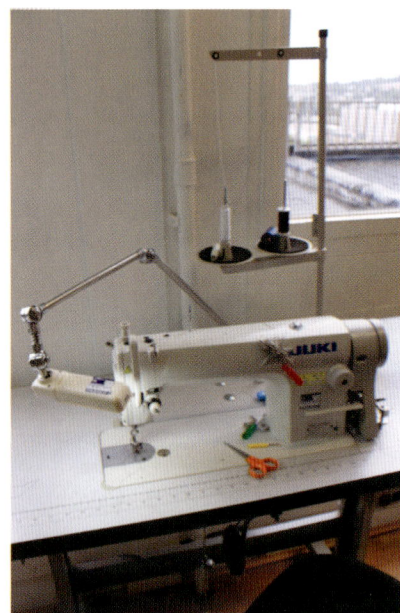

Industrial sewing machine. (UCA Fashion Atelier workshop)

Industrial overlocker. (UCA Fashion Atelier workshop)

Chapter 1 / Tools and Materials

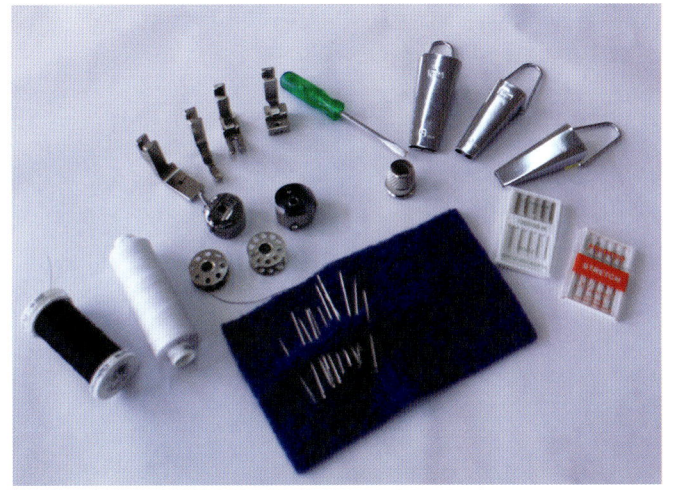

Hand sewing kit.

and push the needle through with the tip of the finger. The side of the finger is stronger for pushing a needle through tough tailoring canvases. They come in different sizes so get a steel one that fits your middle finger properly.

Thread comes in a variety of weights so pick one that is appropriate for your cloth. Always match the colour unless it is a feature: a bad sewing line in a mismatched colour will be very obvious. A regular cotton or poly-cotton thread is suitable for most types of work but you would need specific threads for buttonholes, very heavy fabrics like denim, darning or embroideries and a stretch thread for working with knitted and stretch fabrics. Don't waste money on cheap threads because they snap and are not durable enough: the only situation where they are permissible is where you are tacking (basting) and they are likely to be removed afterwards. Always test your machine tension and thread on a scrap of the actual fabric first and adjust the stitch length accordingly.

A bias binding maker is a small device that enables you to fold strips of fabric evenly to make your own bias binding and tapes for an authentic finish. Various sizes are available.

Pressing

A steam iron is important, and a heavier-weight one is always best. The average for a domestic iron is 1.5kg/3lb, which is good for light fabrics like silks and cottons, but you need something more robust for heavier-weight cloth. It is also worth checking the highest temperature on your iron before you buy because sometimes the temperature even on the hottest setting is not enough for some cloth such as heavy wools or worsteds. You won't always need to use steam but if you can afford it a tabletop steam iron with its own tank is a good purchase, especially as you don't have to fill up the tank so often.

A pressing table: ideally we would all be in our own workrooms with this constantly set up. As some of these projects use a lot of yardage, a larger flat table rather than a domestic ironing board would be really helpful. Cover a table top with a layer of coat wool and put a layer of calico over the top of that: this will create a padded base similar to an ironing board but on a larger scale and you can fold it away when you are done. It is better to press as you go; it is too late to flatten puckers or folds once the garment is constructed.

A sleeve board is a narrow padded board used to press long straight seams and rounded sleeve heads.

A tailor's ham is a firmly stuffed cushion that will help to press round shapes or seams on a garment (for example, over the bust). They come in different sizes and are easy to make.

Using a pressing cloth will enable you to put your iron up to an even hotter setting and get a sharp press without scorching. For example, if you are pressing wool or silk you can use the setting for cotton. Well-laundered linen tea towels are good for this if you have one handy.

A point pressing block is a small wooden device that looks like a handle: it is extremely useful for pressing small sharply angled areas such as collars and cuffs.

A needle board has fine bristles/needles set very close together and can be used to press fabrics with a pile or nap, such as velvet or corduroy.

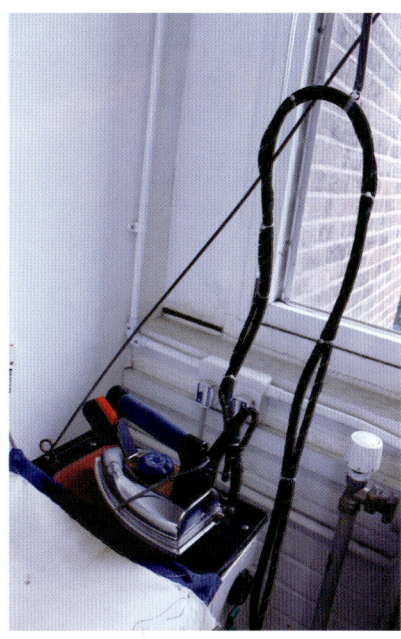

Industrial steam iron. (UCA Fashion Atelier workshop)

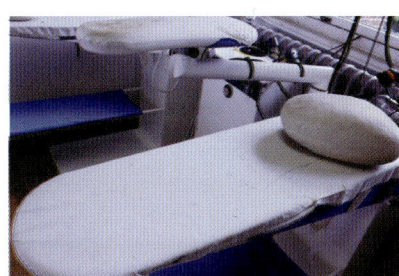

Pressing board and hams. (UCA Fashion Atelier workshop)

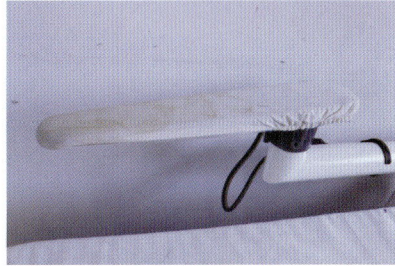

Sleeve board. (UCA Fashion Atelier workshop)

19

Alternatively, you can press the reverse of the fabric using a spare piece of the same fabric turned nap upwards on the ironing board.

Fitting

The stand, mannequin or dummy is used for checking the fit and hang of a garment. Each manufacturer has their own different systems of standard measurements for different sizes, dependent on which different aspect of the industry's clientele they are representing: for example, a stand for outerwear has different body proportions from that of a lingerie stand which will also have a crotch and a thigh. The dress stand is also there to represent the fashionable silhouette and aspirational physique of the time: for instance, one from the fifties would have a smaller waist, fuller hips and a higher bust than one designed for today's tall lean aesthetic. A professional dress stand is a serious investment financially – Kennett & Lindsell are excellent suppliers. It is much cheaper to look for second-hand stands on eBay and pad out and/or re-cover as required. A lot of the projects in this book are tight-fitting so ideally you also need a stand with collapsible shoulders to get garments on and off more easily. Please remember that whatever dress stand you have is standardized and is not a true representation of a real body. To achieve that, certain areas will always need padding from the outset. It will also be useful to make a calico arm that has a bicep and wrist girth to match yours (or your clients') that can be pinned onto the mannequin's shoulder.

Appropriate undergarments and shoes: if you are fitting the patterns to yourself always wear the underwear you intend to use for that garment and fit over the top of them. Wear shoes that are ideally the style and height of the shoe you intend to wear with the outfit. Heel height can really influence the hang of your garment and definitely affects the length of the hem.

Fabrics and Haberdashery

My fabric choices for this book have been influenced by the garments I saw at Worthing Museum and Art Gallery, many of which were nylon or rayon, not cotton or silk as one would imagine. As a result I have used quite a few synthetics for the projects. Post-World War II only around 30 per cent of households had a washing machine and most laundering was done by hand. However, this period also saw a flood of synthetic fabrics and easy-care processes arrive on the market. These fabrics were wrinkle-resistant, easily washable at high temperatures and held creases and pleats well, even after laundering. 'Drip-dry' nylon

Magazine advertisement for nylon, *Women's Journal,* June 1953. (Author's own collection)

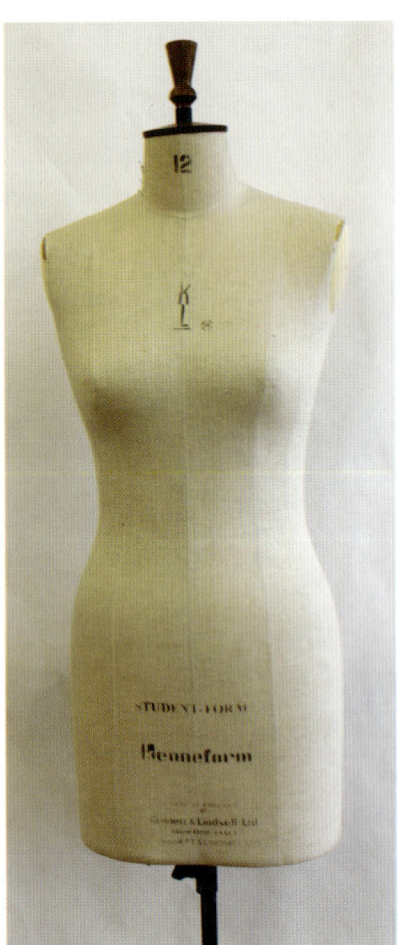

Size 12 dress mannequin.

Magazine advertisement for fabric, UK *Vogue,* June 1953. (Author's own collection)

Chapter 1 / Tools and Materials

Assorted fabric swatches from a range of stockists.

Assorted vintage and new haberdashery from a range of stockists.

became immensely popular for overgarments and acrylic, polyester, triacetate and spandex (later also known as Elastane and Lycra) were all introduced for underwear.

I collected a lot of fabric swatches first before buying anything. The synthetics in my research were often springy to touch so I have chosen fabrics for their handle, colour or texture and as a personal preference avoided anything with flowery prints. That does not mean you have to do the same; the patterns will work just as well in wools, cottons and silks with spots and florals too. Be aware of the width of your cloth as some garments utilize the full width of the fabric from selvedge edge to selvedge edge. Effectively, the wider the fabric, the fuller the skirt!

Fabrics like nylon, rayon and rubber, which were in development in the 1930s, became embedded into the design of new control garments. The support garments we commonly see today owe a lot to the panty girdle and bullet bra of the fifties. Foundation garments of this era were often made of heavy layers of thick non-stretch nylon, rayon and rubber which had to be perforated because the wearer perspired so much. It did mean that steel boning and corsetry fastenings were no longer required. Elastanes were more prevalent by the late fifties and whilst this gave fantastic control and was much easier to wash, undergarments were frequently so solid that they could stand up on their own and had to be rolled on and off. I have used specialist satins and power meshes for the underwear from a specialist supplier, as these types of fabric are hard to find on the high street, and the fabric for the soft tailoring is vintage tie silk. (Power mesh is a finely knitted fabric that is light, soft and stretchy yet strong.) Very few of the original garments are fully lined, even the tailored items – a direct result of rationing long after the war had ended. I have used linings as similar to the originals as possible but have again considered their properties and effect on the hang of the final garment. For example, the Dior House of Youth original has a synthetic taffeta lining but when I tried it the skirt became very limp. Instead I lined the shell with synthetic organza, which gave it the volume and bounce of the original almost immediately.

The haberdashery is also a mixture of new and vintage with specialist notions for the bras and girdles. With fifties garments what you don't see is as important to the silhouette as what you do see so a variety of woven non-fusible canvases and interlinings have been used; these have been listed for each project. The finishing touches like cover buttons and belts have all been made by a specialist company (via mail order) in my own fabrics to match the garments.

In the past some women would have done this and some would have made them themselves but would not have had such variety or choice in what they could use. Again, these touches aren't available on the high street but are definitely worth the investment if you can afford them.

All suppliers have been listed in the Stockists and Suppliers section.

Bespoke cover buttons.

Fabric-covered belts.

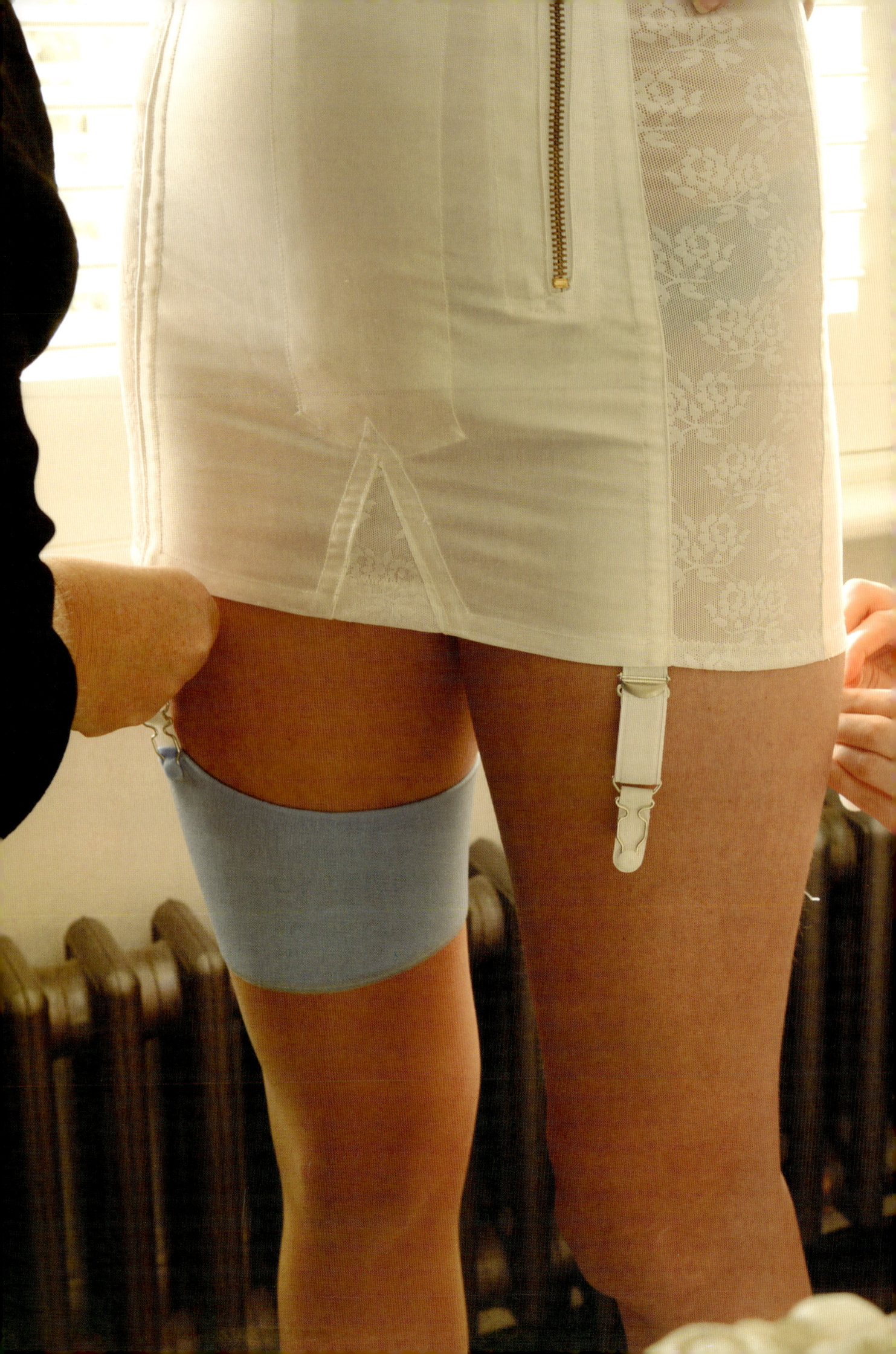

Measuring and Fitting

2

How to Measure

Read the instructions for measuring yourself before you embark on any dressmaking project. The diagram and chart show you where to measure and record the information. I have also included an additional column for any notes about pattern adjustments you might need to make. Think about the style of the garment you want and whether or not you need specialist shape wear to achieve it: this usually involves identifying and wearing the right foundation garments, which might be different from your normal underwear. For projects in this book the bare minimum would be using the conical bra fillers or falsies from What Katie Did inside a soft bra (not moulded cups) regardless of how odd it looks to begin with. Once you are happy with your temporary body shape then take your measurements. I quite like doing a 'before and after' so I can see how my vital statistics change if, for example, I wear a corset and push-up bra rather than my natural body. Always stand in front of a mirror so you can see what you are doing properly. Measure with the tape held closely to but not tightly round the body (I was taught to keep two fingers between the tape measure and the body).

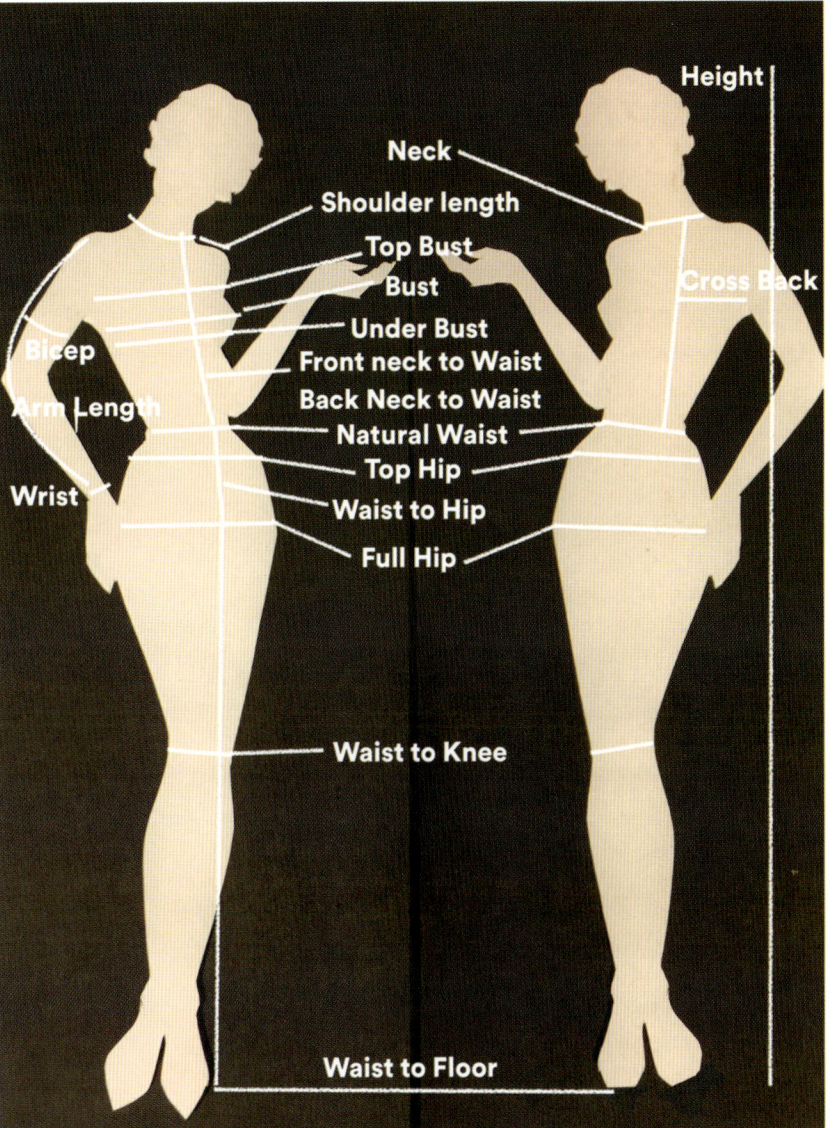

Personal template.

	Your measurements	Pattern measurements	Adjustments + or –
Height			
Shoulder width			
Top bust/chest			
Bust			
Under bust			
Bust point to bust point			
Cross back			
Natural waist			
Front neck to waist			
Back neck/nape to waist			
Front shoulder to waist			
Back shoulder to waist			
Waist to hip			
Full hip			
High hip or top hip			
Waist to knee			
Waist to floor			
Inside leg			
Arm length			
Bicep			
Wrist			
Neck			

Personal measurement chart.

Height: stand erect without shoes and with your back against the wall. Place a ruler flat on top of your head and lightly mark the point where it touches the wall. Measure from the mark to the floor.
Shoulder width: base of neck to shoulder bone.
Top bust: measure your chest horizontally around the body above the bust and under the arm.
Bust: measure around the fullest part of the bust. If you have fillers this might also be the pointiest.
Under bust: measure horizontally around the ribcage.
Bust point to bust point: measure horizontally from one nipple to the other.
Waist: tie a cord around your natural waist and measure the circumference along the cord. Leave the cord in place while you take other measurements.
Front neck to waist: centre of base of neck above the collar bone to the centre of the waist cord.
Back neck to waist: top of the spine/nape of the neck to the centre of the waistline cord.
Front shoulder to waistline: from the shoulder over the bust to the waistline cord.
Back shoulder to waistline: from the back of the shoulder to the waistline cord.
Waist to hip: measure from the side of the waistline cord to the fullest part of the hips – usually 18–23cm/7–9in down.
Full hip: measure horizontally around the fullest part of the hips.
High hip girth: measure horizontally at the abdomen or top of your hip bone 8–10cm/3–4in down.
Waist to knee: from the waistline cord to the knee cap.
Waist to floor/outside leg: from the waistline cord to the ground or to the ankle bone.
Inside leg: crotch to floor or ankle.
Arm length: bend the elbow slightly and measure from the shoulder bone to the wrist bone.
Bicep: measure horizontally around the widest part of the top of your arm.
Wrist: measure horizontally around the full wrist at the bone.
Neck: the base of the neckline.

Notes on Fitting Your Bra

Originals can obviously be found at vintage fairs and stores listed in the Stockists and Suppliers section. The fit can be hit-and-miss and originals are difficult to alter. Excellent replicas can be bought from specialist shops like What Katie Did: such stores sell new or faux vintage pieces where there are clear guidelines for sizing and fit with a bit more comfort. The traditional way to fit a bra means that the under bust measurement doesn't equal the band size. Unlike a modern bra, there is no stretch in a vintage band. To find your band size, measure the ribcage firmly under the bust. Traditionally you would then add 10–13cm/4–5in to get the band size. Some modern-day faux vintage fit bras recommend 7.5–10cm/3–4in, as it is believed that in the past we have worn our bras too loose. Traditionally bras have always been designed to be cross-graded, meaning that the same cup is used across several different sizes, so if the band is too tight you can go up a band size and down a cup size. When fitting a bullet bra it is important to fill as much of the cone as possible with your own breast by lifting from the side and moving into the front of the cup then adjusting the strap to be as tight as possible. If you are still between cups then you will need a conical pad or falsie to do the rest!

Fittings

You will need to check the fit of your garment and make alterations, particularly as you will be scaling up the patterns in this book, which can lead to some inaccuracy. Generally it is normal to do at least two fittings, one in toile form and one in the real fabric. Always do this in front of a mirror wearing the right underwear and shoes – heel height does affect your posture and therefore the way the fabric hangs. For toiles, make as much of the garment as possible without the finishings (hems, etc.) but obviously include all suppression like darts, etc. Make sure you use a calico that reflects the weight of your actual fabric. It is also worth tacking the lines of centre front and centre back so that you can check they hang perfectly straight. The side seam generally hangs in a vertical line perpendicular to the floor. Fit the right half of the figure then transfer the alterations to the left later. Check the ease at bust and hip so that it is not too tight. If you are fitting a sleeve do not insert it until after alterations have been made to the bodice. If it is long-sleeved then obviously make sure you can bend your arms before setting the sleeve in.

Making Alterations

Once you have pinned or tacked alterations trace them from the calico onto the right side of the pattern. Fold the pattern in half and transfer the alterations from the right to the left side so the pattern is symmetrical. You will need to refit in the real fabric for any final tweaks before finishing. There are instructions for a variety of alterations on most patterns and the ones included here were actually pages of a supplement of some kind on pattern tissue that were being used as bookmarks and thus preserved among the pages of my *Encyclopaedia of Needlecraft*: this is probably why they still look pristine. The basic alterations for lengthening, shortening, widening and reducing patterns are fine to use with the patterns in this book.

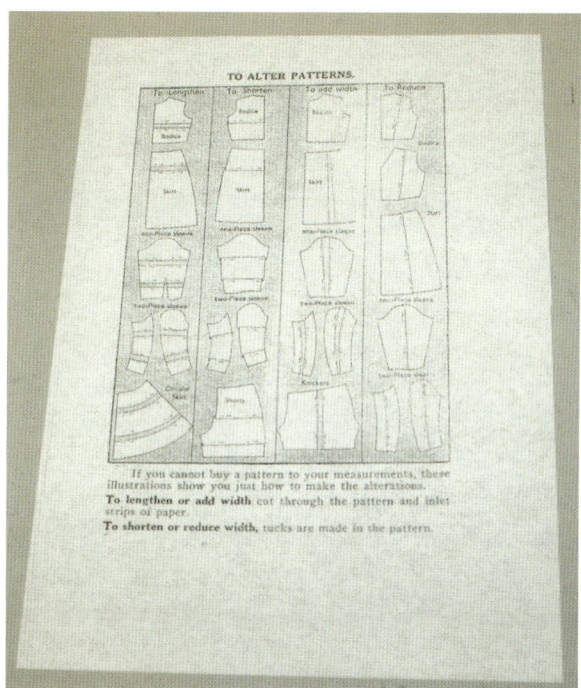

Pattern alteration supplements on pattern-making tissue, origins unknown. (Author's own collection)

The Bra and Girdle (Belt) Set

3

Bras

First impressions of an outfit are based on its silhouette before we see any other qualities such as fabric or detail. Dior's New Look was in fact far from new, as it revisited the corseted bodice and large skirts of the Victorian era, but its strong feminine shape with cinched-in waist and curving hips was viewed as an antidote to the wartime styles and therefore new for the time. It would be impossible to create the fifties look authentically without the right foundation garments to cinch the waist, give the torso a smoother line and lift and separate the breasts. Naturally this couldn't be achieved without help and foundation garments suddenly became a booming industry in that period. Corsets, controllers and bustiers were standard beauty fare for all women, along with latex and nylon 'slimmers'. Bras and bust paddings that helped achieve that defined and almost cone-like shape for busts were also in abundance and advertised everywhere.

Women with larger breasts had the choice of long-line bras, built-up backs, wedge-shaped inserts between the cups, wider straps, power Lastex, firm bands under the cup, and even light boning. In 1937, companies like

Lingerie advertisements, UK *Vogue*, November 1954. (Author's own collection)

Twilfit bra circa 1952. (Author's own collection)

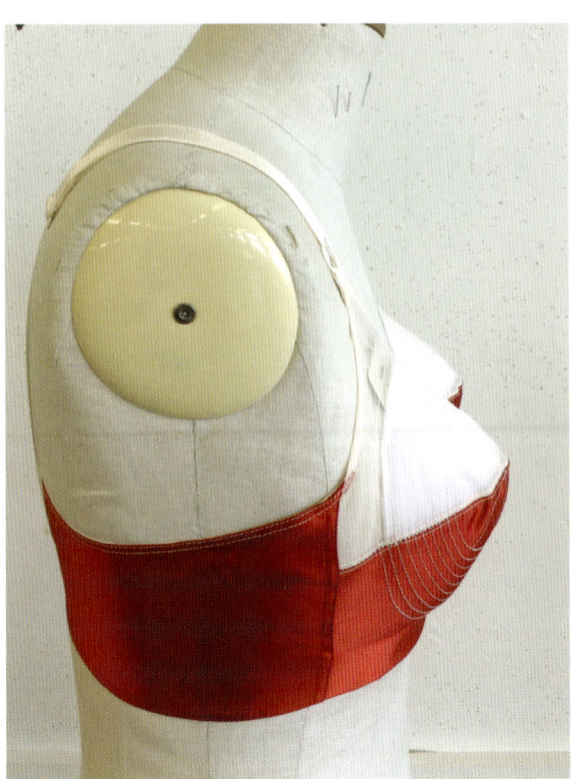
What Katie Did modern bullet bra. (Author's own collection)

Warner and Twilfit had begun to feature cup sizing in their product lines and this became very widely popularized in the fifties. Unfortunately, the sizing for the masses neglected to go any higher than a C cup for almost another forty years, making the industry that we know today that caters for significantly fuller cup sizes relatively new. The Twilfit bra shown on the mannequin is a 34B cup with a filler.

The bullet bra, popularized by actresses like Lana Turner and Marilyn Monroe, was actually available from 1939, but World War II put plans on hold for widespread manufacture until the 1950s when its shape became much more extreme than that of the forties. The spiral stitching on it accentuated the pointiness of the cone shape. Padded versions or falsies, developed by Warners in the 1930s, were also popular, allowing women to go up a bust size. Maidenform was the first brand to reach the masses in the US with its now infamous 'I dreamed ...' advertising campaign which ran successfully for twenty years and showed lifestyle images of confident women in its bras who had beautiful homes, handsome husbands, exciting dream jobs and were overtly sexy. The ads, mainly featuring the Chansonette bullet bra, could be seen on billboards all over the US, often opposite the department stores that stocked them, and in full-page ads in *Vogue* and *Vanity Fair*. The controversial campaign was so successful it made Maidenform a brand leader on the mid-range lingerie market. When the company launched the Maisonette bullet bra in the UK in 1955 it was with a more pragmatic but less risqué strapline: 'What makes it so special? Spiral stitched to round as it accentuates'. This was more in line with the conservative approach to lingerie advertising and attitudes to modesty in the UK at the time but it resulted in a significantly less successful campaign. Nowadays the bullet bra and its belt or girdle is viewed as a niche piece, but the set would have been viewed at the time as the ultimate in achieving a 'pin-up girl' silhouette.

Girdles (Belts)

Historically, the girdle or belt was an outer item worn by both women and men to gather in garment fullness at or just below the waist; in the times before integral pockets, the girdle could also carry a pouch for everyday necessities. However, when women discarded the bust-to-thigh corset and began using two separate undergarments, the term 'girdle' or 'belt' was applied to the lower one. The modern girdle of the fifties was constructed of thick elastic or rubber and designed to enhance a woman's figure. It was considered an essential foundation garment regardless of shape or physique. Lingerie companies like Berlei were quick to respond to their consumers' demands as the concept of using 'stretch' and flexible fastenings more effectively in lingerie became more

Chapter 3 / The Bra and Girdle (Belt) Set

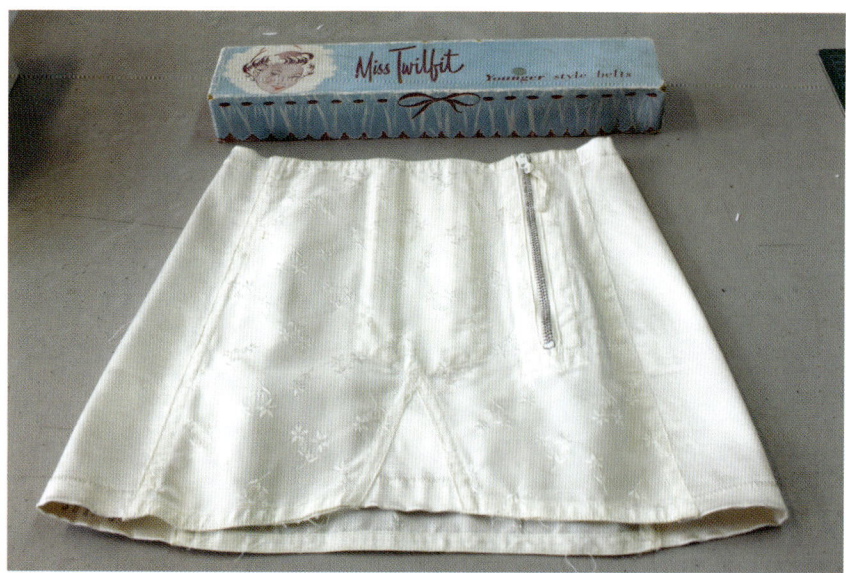

Original Twilfit girdle and box. (Author's own collection)

prevalent over the decade. But these fabrics were challenging to wear and had to be effectively 'rolled' on and off. Compared to the smooth shape wear of today it seems remarkable that these thick heavy garments with bulky metal zips and hooks and eyes (as seen here in the Twilfit example) would be used under close-fitting clothing. The metal shortages of World War II had encouraged the demise of the corset with all of its metal boning and busks. This made way for new materials and fastenings to be used in innovative ways. For example, the zipper, named onomatopoeically for the sound it made, was originally made for boots and its potential in the fashion industry was overlooked until the 1930s when it was adopted for men's fly front trousers.

Companies like Twilfit experimented with putting zips in either the centre front or centre back of their girdles or belts although these were expensive, and heavy metal zip fastenings were often at the side or back of the garment. Adjustable bands were also introduced using multiple eye and hook positions across the back with extenders for larger women, putting the lingerie industry at the forefront for using new technology for fashion at that time.

The patterns here are based on a combination of original pieces and vintage patterns from my own collection. There are three different bra types varying in complexity from a construction and fit point of view and they have been used for projects depending on the style of garment they are being worn under. None of them has underwires but the corsetry satin used is very robust and provides a lot of support. Although the idea is to fill the bra cup with as much of your own breast as possible I have used fillers from What Katie Did to get a firm point. The girdle or belt is made with a very sturdy power mesh combined with the corsetry satin to keep it as authentic as possible.

Cutting Out

Once the pattern has been enlarged and graded it is advisable to toile it first to check the cup is full enough. The grain lines are marked on the pattern pieces so lay them out and pin them down with the straight of grain parallel to the selvedge edge. Pin in place and add seam allowance: I used 1cm metric but if you are being a traditionalist you will want to use ⅝in and trim the excess away later. Mark your notches with a snip. If you don't it is very

MATERIALS AND EQUIPMENT

Cotton-backed corsetry satin (this is firmer than dress satin)

Stretch power mesh/wide elastic for girdle panelling

Coutil (a specialized corsetry fabric which is densely woven, non-stretch and very strong)

Sealed set of bra hook and eye fastenings with corresponding width elastic for the back bra straps

Satin-finish elastic for CF of bra

Ribbon for bra straps or ready-made elasticated straps

Narrow cotton or satin bias binding

One pair of 4-bar G hooks or one pair of rings and one pair of sliders per bra

Hook and eye tape for the longline bra and girdle

Pre-made suspender straps (two pairs)

Fillers (optional)

Boning casing or wider bias binding

Ridgelene (plastic boning) and/or steel boning

Metal-toothed skirt zip

Sewing machine with a zigzag setting and a zip foot or single foot

Pattern paper or tissue paper

Pins (plentiful supply)

These notions and fabrics will have to come from a specialist supplier so don't waste time looking on the high street. I recommend two online stores:
www.bramakerssupply.com and **www.venacavadesign.co.uk**.

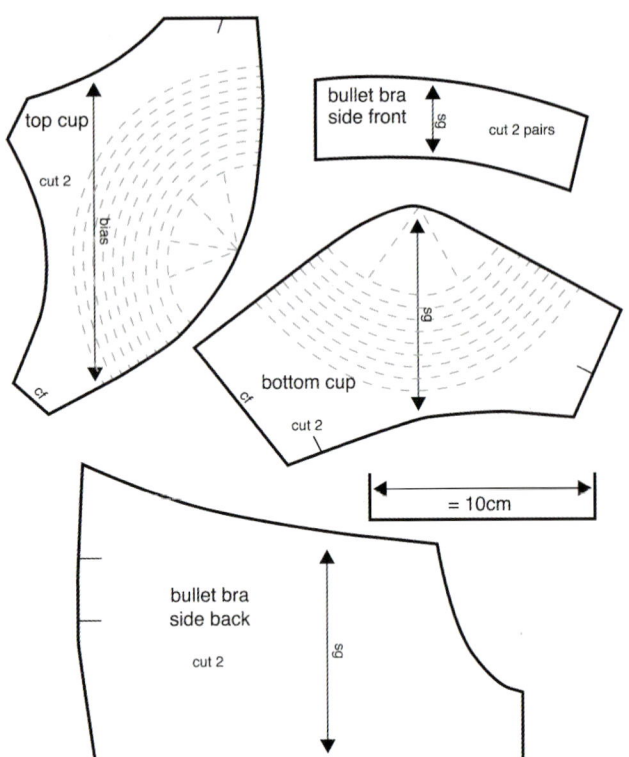
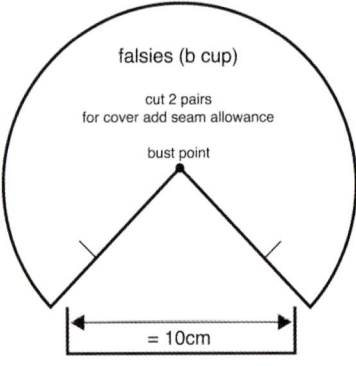

Bullet Bra

Falsies

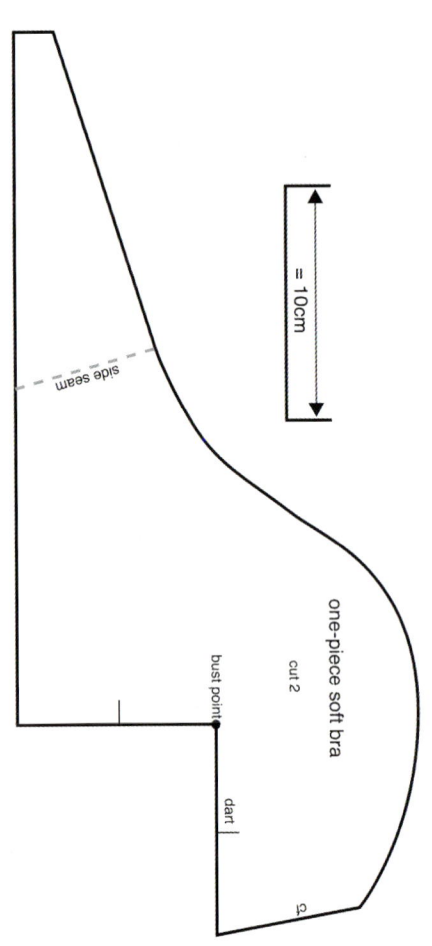
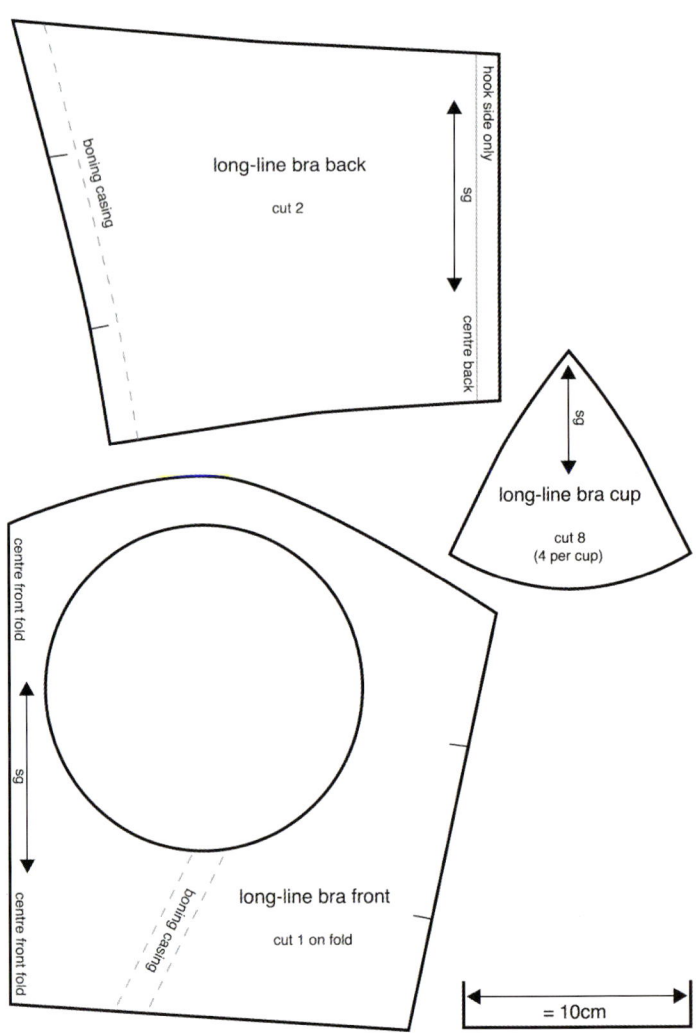

Soft Bra

Longline Bra

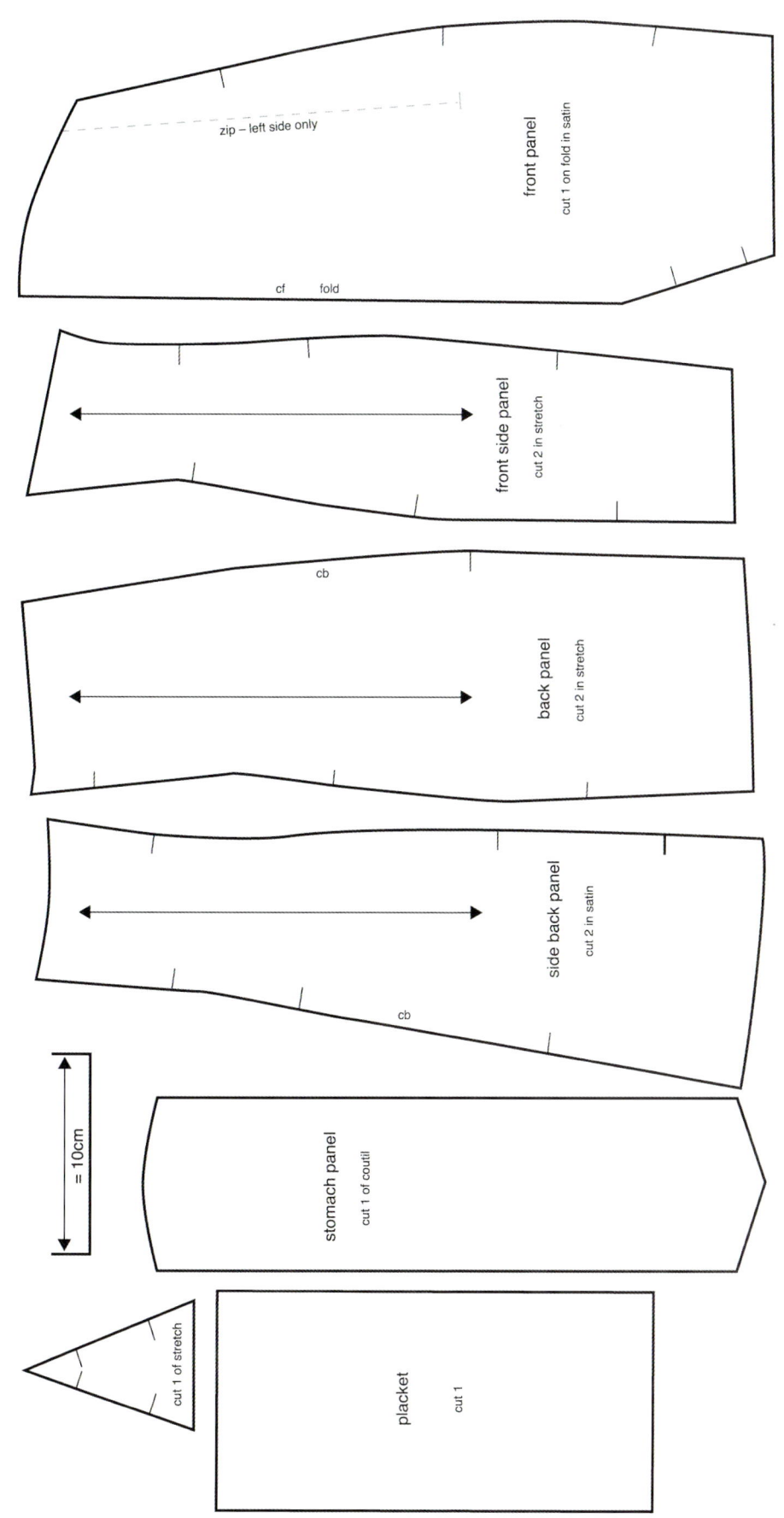

difficult to get the cups to line up properly for the bras or for the stretch to line up accurately to the woven on the girdle.

The Bullet Bra

1. Trace off the centre of both halves of the cups twice to the first circular stitch line to make a template/stitch guide. Pin onto the fabric and sew over the paper to position the first target lines radiating out from the bust point. Sew round the edge of the template to create the first circle of the spiral. The subsequent lines are a machine foot's width apart so once you have topstitched the first you can do the rest. You will probably have to pivot the machine foot for the first two as the circles are small. Remove the paper template by pulling gently away from the stitching. Do not attempt to make the cups then topstitch the spirals – the cup is too pointy for you to do this properly so prepare the cups before construction starts. (1,2,3)

2. Line up the bust point notches and sew the top cups to the bottom cups to make a pair. There is a little ease over the bust point so the notches are important.

3. Using a small ham, press the bust seams open. Cut away excess seam allowance; the finished width should be approximately 3mm/⅛in with a raw edge which you will later conceal with your covered filler. (4)

4. Sew the two completed cups together at CF, press the seam open and cut down to 6mm/ in.

Creating the template for the bullet bra cup.

Sewing with the template in place.

Removing the template to reveal the topstitching.

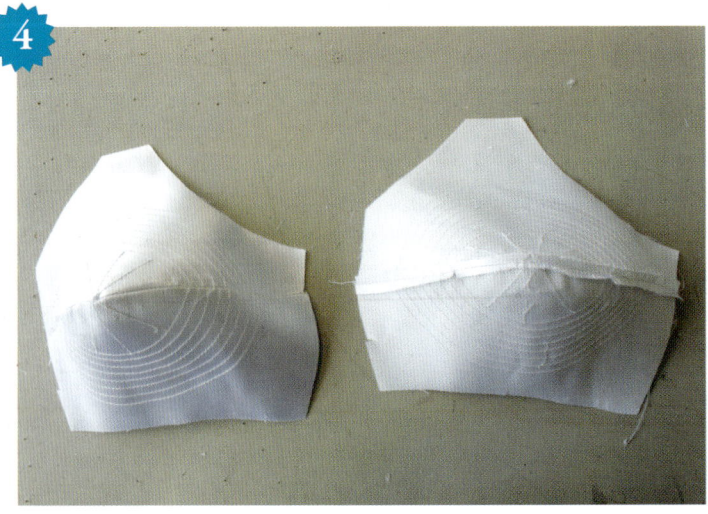

Making the cups and trimming the seam allowance.

Chapter 3 / The Bra and Girdle (Belt) Set

There are two notches on the bottom of the cups by the CF. Snip into these to the depth of your seam allowance and turn the CF part upwards into the cups. Finish the seam by putting binding over the raw CF seam and topstitching down. Place another piece of binding over the small turn-up and catch down by hand to neaten. The remains of the seam allowance turns down and will be inserted into the bra band. (5)

5. Prepare the bottom band for the bra front; note that it curves upwards slightly. You do not need an interlining for the corsetry satin but if you are using a lighter-weight fabric you will need a non-fusible interlining tacked (basted) to the front pieces before you start. Stitch the bottom seams on the wrong side. To attach the elastic line it up to the bottom seam and sandwich it right side to right side. Make sure it is lined up to the vertical raw edge and machine down on the wrong side. Trim the seam allowance down, also the bulk from the corners, and turn through. Repeat on the other side and press.

6. Pin the band to the cups right sides together and machine-stitch along both sides of the band starting from the band end nearest the centre.

7. Fold the back of the band upwards and tuck the raw edge in so that the top fold meets the stitch line and the seam allowance is enclosed. Pin or tack to the cups from the front and topstitch closed. The corners near the CF with the elastic will be bulky so trim away what you can before closing. (6,7)

8. Use bias tape to make tabs for the G hooks or rings. Position the rings on the top edge of the bra and machine-tack down. Finger-press the seam allowance inwards beforehand and refold to get the right width corresponding with your rings and mounts, particularly where there is a lot of shaping. (8)

9. Sew the side seams together, press the seams open towards the CB and trim down. Finger-fold the seam allowance on the bottom of the back pieces upwards and trim down a little.

10. Cover with bias binding to finish. Place the tape along the SS downwards along the bottom of the back and up the CB. Take your time to mitre the corners to reduce the bulk. Pin or tack before sewing

Sewing the CF and binding the seam to neaten.

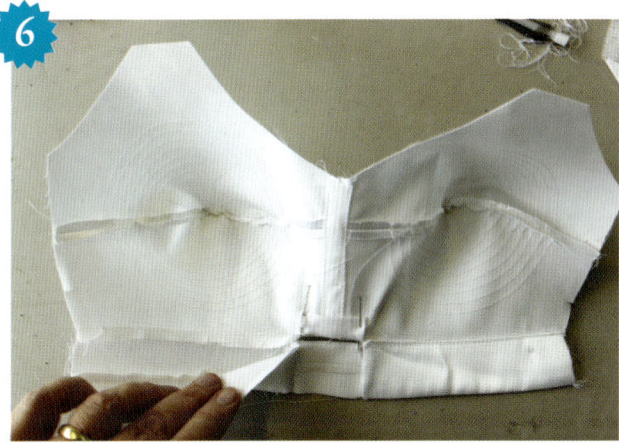

Attaching the band to the wrong side of the bra front.

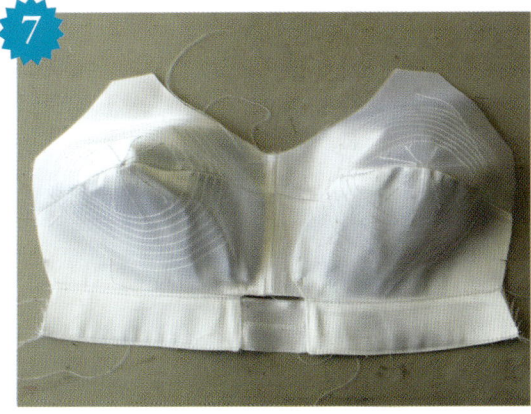

Finished band from the right side.

Mounting the rings on bias tape.

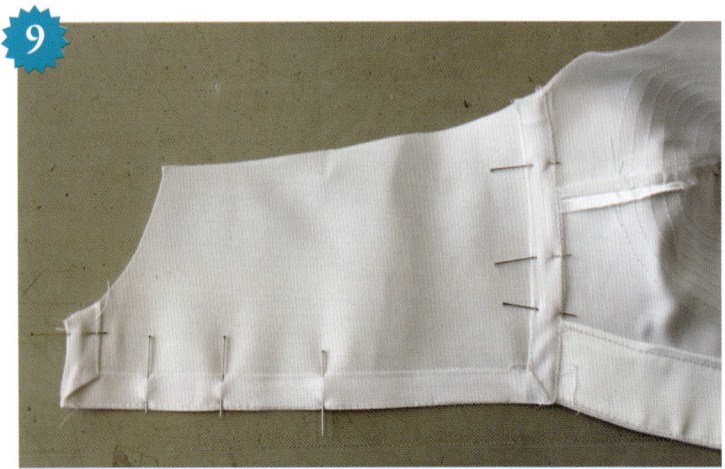

Bias binding the side seam and back.

Finished bra with fastening.

if necessary. Topstitch both edges of the tape down to neaten. (9)

11. Prepare the back fastenings but do not insert them until the straps have gone in. I used a pre-made hook and eye kit here. The eyes will go on the left-hand side and as they are already neatened they can just be topstitched onto the wrong side of the back strap. For the right side, face the hooks downwards and line the raw edge of the elastic (about 4cm/1$^9/_{16}$in long and the same depth as the hook and eye set) up to the back of the hooks. Flip over and topstitch using a zip foot. Fold the outer edge of the hook mount over so the hooks are underneath and topstitch the outer edge of the hook mount on the wrong side.

12. To prepare the shoulder straps, thread one end of the ribbon or elastic through the bra slider, turn the raw edge under and topstitch down. Feed the other end through the ring at the front of the bra and pull up through the other two bars of the slider. Pin this end into position on the back of the bra and machine-tack ready to be bound off.

13. To finish, bind the top edge as per the bottom edge. Pin the binding flat on top of the turned seam allowance, mitring the corners as you go. Stitch the outside edge first and then the inside edge.

14. Attach the bra hooks and elastic by lining up the raw edges on the right side with the hooks facing upwards. Stitch along the seam allowance then turn the elastic over so the hooks face downwards and topstitch the elastic to the main back strap of the bra. (10)

The Soft Bra with Overwire and Darted Cups

This is a simple two-piece bra that suits a smaller bust. Please note there is no band; it is the bias tape that keeps the cups anchored together at the CF and also conceals the overwire for this bra. I used white thread for the top and cream for the bobbin so that the stitching shows up better in the photos.

1. Close the darts in each cup. Reverse-stitch at the bust point to ensure it doesn't re-open. I used 1cm/⅜in seam allowance and needed to snip into the allowance at the point of the dart to press it flat. Press into shape on the ham. Topstitch down on the right side

One-piece bra with overwire.

Chapter 3 / The Bra and Girdle (Belt) Set

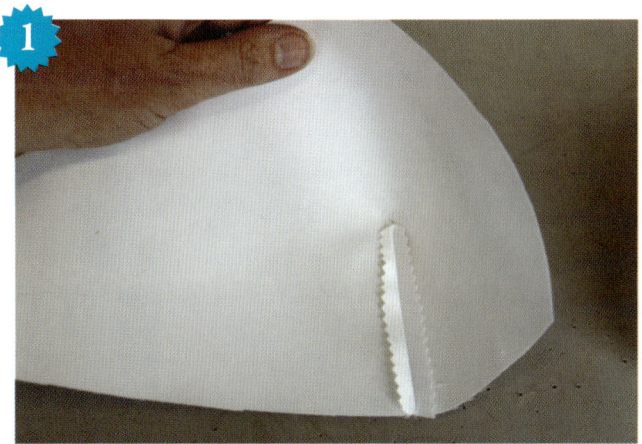

Closing the dart on the wrong side.

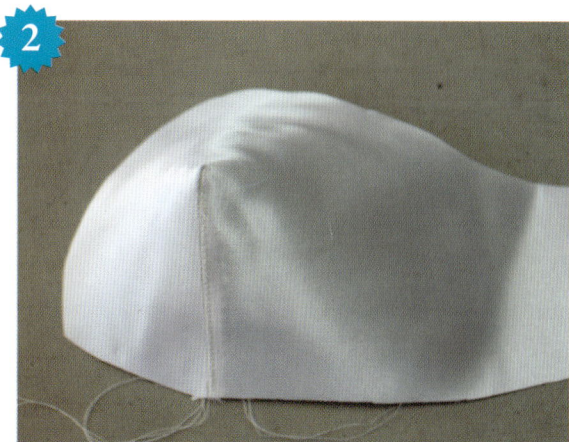

Topstitching the closed dart on the right side.

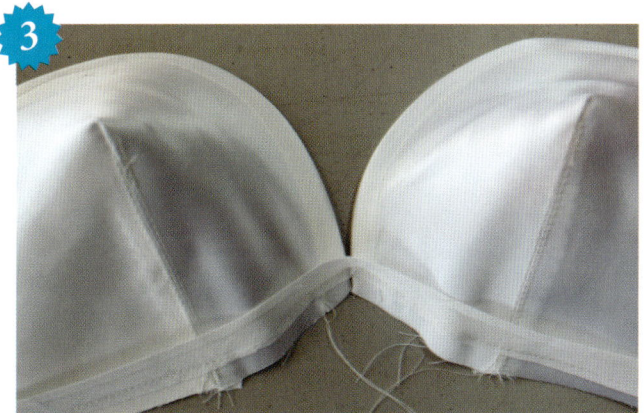

Adding bias binding to neaten.

Twilfit bra back strap.

and trim away the excess seam allowance on the wrong side: straight blades or pinking shears will do.(1,2)

2. Use bias tape to make tabs for the G hooks or rings. Finger-press the seam allowance so you know where the stitch line will be and tack or pin the ring and tabs at the notches on the right side of the fabric so they point towards and not away from the cups. Position the back of the straps at the back of the cups. Sew bias binding along the top edge of both cups on the stitch line on the right side of the fabric with the straps and rings sandwiched inside. Trim the cup seam allowance down to 6mm/$^1/_4$ in. Then roll the bias binding downwards onto the wrong side inside the cups. Finger-press or pin downwards and topstitch the other side of the binding down to the cup. Press.

3. Butt the two cups together at the bottom of the CF only. Tack a holding stitch into them if you need to. Stitch bias binding along the whole of the bottom edge on the right side. Turn the bias binding up into the cups and topstitch. The cups are curved so you will need to pivot them at the bottom of the CF to keep the binding even. Lift the machine foot up whilst the needle is positioned dead centre of the two cups and move them round slightly to reposition, put the foot down again and carry on sewing. (3)

4. Turn the bra over and sew the bra elastic to the right cup on the wrong side. How long your elastic is depends on its stretch but I used a piece 5cm/2in long. I used the vintage Twilfit bra as reference: the fastening closes to the left and not on the CB. Stitch the pre-made hook tape to the elastic on the back right. Bind the raw edge with bias binding using a strip longer than the seam so that the ends can be tucked under and neatened off by hand. The original was zigzagged but this is quite itchy to wear. (4,5)

5. Stitch the pre-made eye tape to the back left and bias bind as per the right side. (6)

6. Unpick the bias tape at CF and roll back slightly allowing access to the channel created by the bias binding over the top of the cup. Insert the overwire into both cups. (7,8)

7. The CF at the bottom of the band

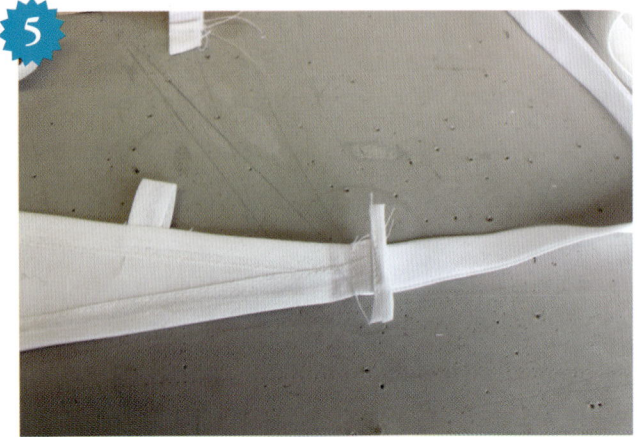
Binding the raw edges.

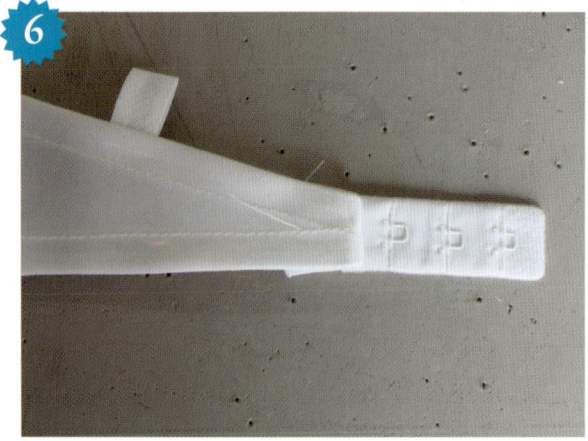
Attaching pre-made bra eyes.

Inserting the overwire.

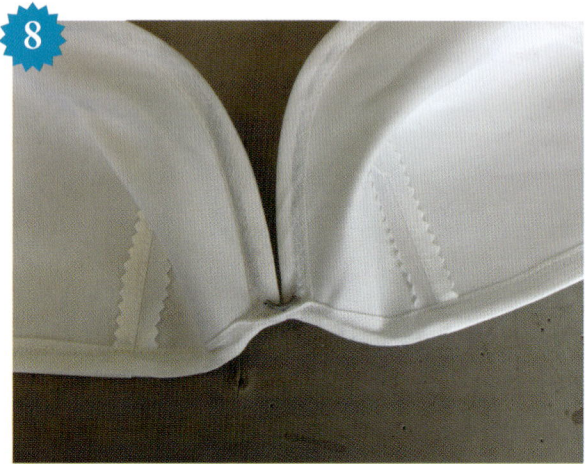
8. Overwire inserted at the CF.

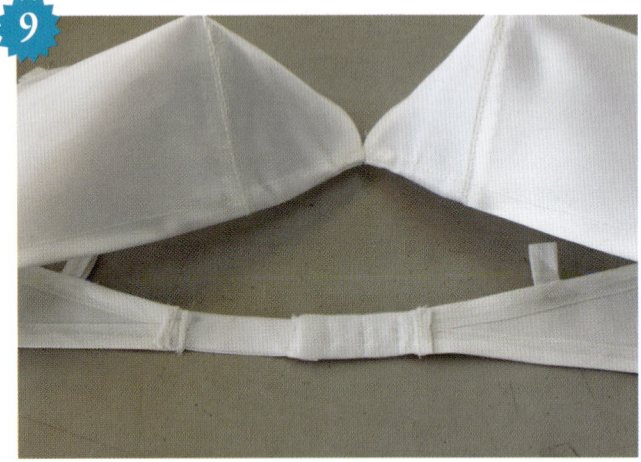
Completed bra band, wrong side.

can either be reinforced with a piece of bias tape or closed by hand.

8. Sew the bra elastic and fastenings at the CB. (9)

Chapter 3 / The Bra and Girdle (Belt) Set

The Longline Bra

This is a good bra for a fuller figure as the bra band extends downwards like a small corset. When worn with the girdle the whole body is covered. It is adapted from an original French pattern; unfortunately it had no accompanying picture on the envelope for me to include so I didn't know how it would look until I toiled it. It is very firm in the corsetry satin and uses a little bit of boning.

1. Sew the quarters of each cup together to make four pairs, then sew the halves together to make a pair of full cups. You may need to snip into the seam allowance to the stitch line to release the tension and get a smoother curve. Press the seams open on the ham. On the wrong side, topstitch and trim away any excess seam allowance to 3mm/$^1/_8$ in. (1)
2. Sew the boning casing on. I have used a specialist casing which has a double layer to sandwich the boning inside and a groove which acts as a stitch line, making positioning easier. You could also use bias binding. (2)
3. Using the notches, line the cups up to the cup holes and pin into position. You will need to ease the cups into position to ensure the circumference is evenly distributed, so it is better to tack them in position before machine-stitching. Check the cups are actually round and alter if necessary. Trim the excess seam allowance from the cups down to 3mm/$^1/_8$in and 6mm/$^1/_4$ in on the bodice. The cup seams can be finished in a variety of ways (for example, felling, overlocking, leaving raw) but decide how you are going to do it and use the right seam allowance before you cut the pieces out. I have pushed the raw edge up into the cup and on the right side of the fabric I have topstitched just inside the seam line. (3,4)
4. Machine-stitch the CF and press the seams open. Trim the seam allowance away and position the bone casing directly over the top. Pin or tack in place before machine-stitching either side of the CF seam.
5. Sew the front to the back at the side seams; press the seams open and then towards the back. Trim the seam allowance and position the bone casing as marked on the pattern. Pin or tack to check the position and machine-stitch into place. If you are using a falsie or filler, try it in your bra cup while the body of the bra is assembled but still soft and flexible enough to handle without the boning in. (5)
6. Insert boning into the channels. I used a synthetic boning called

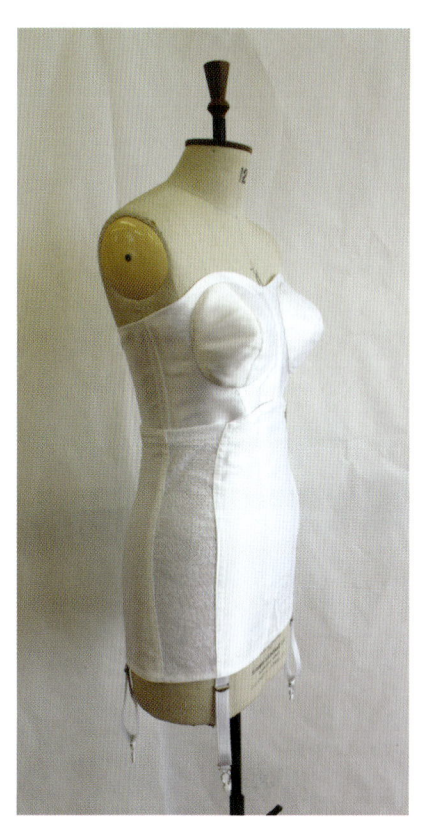

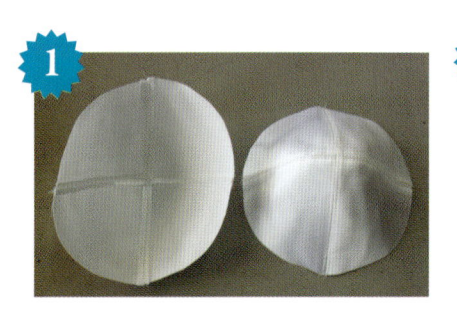

Longline bra and girdle, front and side views.

The bra cups inside and out.

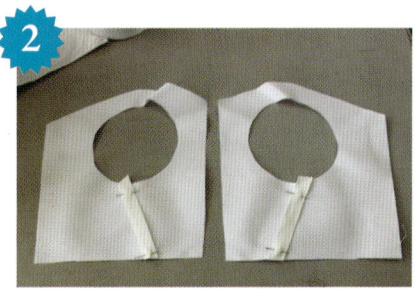

Positioning the boning casing.

Inserting the cup into the bodice, wrong side.

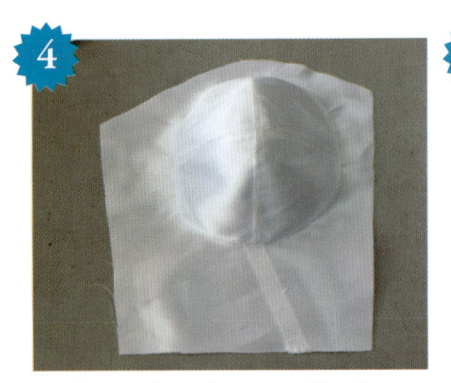

4 Topstitching the cup, right side.

5 Boning casings are stitched to CF and side seams. A covered filler is put in the bra cup.

6 Inserting Ridgelene into the boning casings.

7 Vintage hook and eye tape cut to size.

8 Topstitching the hook tape to the CB on the right side.

9 Topstitching the tape again on the wrong side.

10 Neatening the raw edges.

Ridgelene that was narrower than the width of the casing. Make sure it is 2cm/$^3/_4$ in shorter than the channel so that it doesn't go into the seam allowance and you are not stitching over it when you turn over the edge and tape to finish the garment. (6)

7. Turn the edges of the CB under and machine-stitch the hook tape to the right and the bar tape to the left; I used pre-made tapes for ease. Make sure that your top hook is set below the seam allowance and doesn't interfere with your finishing. Topstitch on the right side first to fix in place using a zip foot or single foot so that you don't break needles sewing over the hooks themselves. Then turn the bra over and fold the hook and eye tapes inwards. Topstitch the loose edge down from the wrong side. (7,8,9)

8. Bias bind the top and bottom edges to finish. Leave extra at the CB so that you can turn it under and hand-stitch down to neaten. (10)

Chapter 3 / The Bra and Girdle (Belt) Set

Fillers and Falsies

These were usually lightweight foam rubber or felt covered with rayon satin or crepe to be inserted into the bra cup. Some bras had pockets to accommodate them. One size fitted all regardless of your natural body shape. Some garments just required a small bust enhancer placed at the bust point as seen in the Liberty wedding dress foundation where the cup also has a half filler or 'cookie'.

1. Cut one pair in foam with no seam allowance and two pairs in fabric with a large seam allowance of at least 2.5cm/1in.
2. For the foam cut the whole dart out and close the dart with the edges flush to each other. Hand-stitch the edges closed.
3. Machine-stitch the darts into the fabric covers and press flat.
4. Sandwich the foam between two layers of the fabric with the darts aligned and pin into position.
5. Tack around the outside edge of the foam then machine-stitch round it.
6. Trim away the excess fabric with pinking shears so that you are left with an allowance of 1cm/$^5/_8$in.
7. Alternatively use the covering technique for an existing set from What Katie Did.

Bust enhancer for the Liberty of London wedding dress foundation, 1950s.

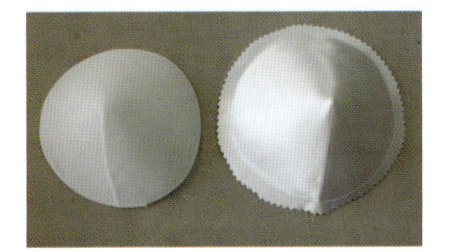

Uncovered and covered fillers.

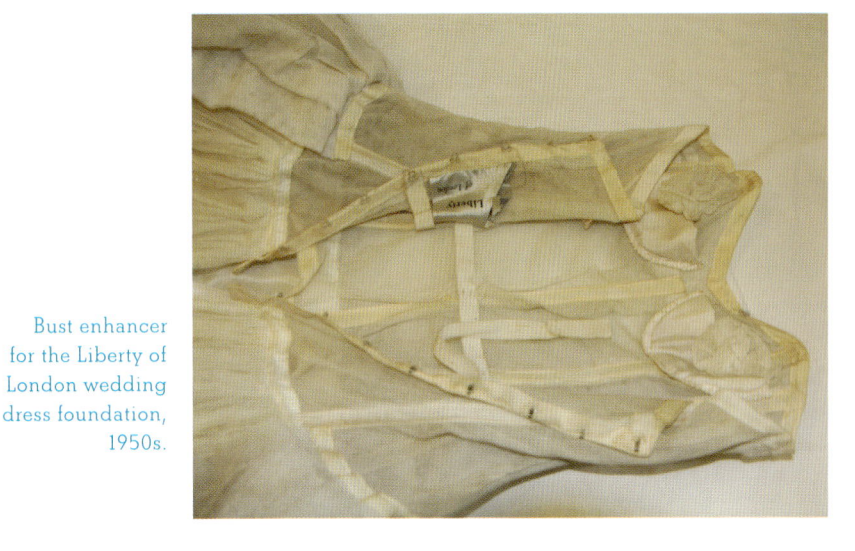

The Girdle (Belt)

You will be using a variety of woven and knitted fabrics for the girdle so it is useful to do some test pieces to check the tension on your sewing machine first. If you have never worked with stretch fabrics then you could toile with an offcut to practise before making the real one. Use a ballpoint machine needle if you can.

1. Prepare the front by inserting the triangle of power mesh into the corsetry satin. Match up the notches and sew one side of the triangle right side to right side. Turn it through and stitch the other side on the wrong side. Press flat.
2. Using a straight stitch, machine-stitch the side front panels to the front panel, pressing the seams towards the CF. Attach the side back panels to the side seams. The power mesh is very stable so can be treated like a non-stretch woven when it is being sewn to the satin.

Finished girdle, front view.

Finished girdle, back view.

1. Stitching one side of the triangle on the right side.
2. Stitching the other side of the triangle on the wrong side.
3. Machining the side front panels to the CF panel.
4. Overlocked CB seam.
5. CB seam zigzagged flat.
6. All panels joined together.
7. Zigzagging the folded edge of the mesh.
8. Positioning the suspenders.
9. Binding the bottom edge and mitring the mitring the tape around the triangular insert.
10. Positioning the boning casings on the coutil.
11. Inserting steel boning into the casings.
12. Attaching the boned panel to the CF.
13. Folding back the seam allowance on the zip opening.
14. Machining the hooks to the back of the zip tape.
15. Machining the zip and hooks to the opening on the inside of the girdle.

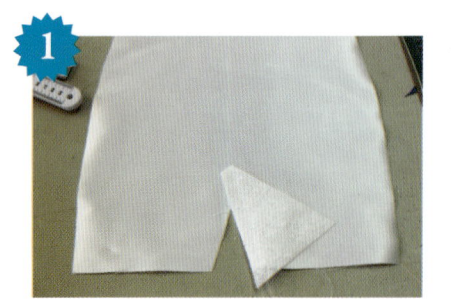

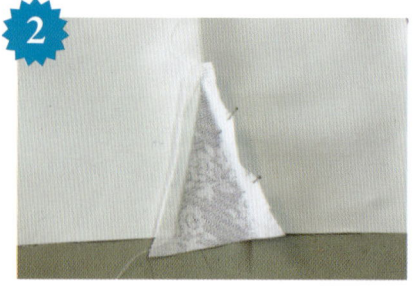

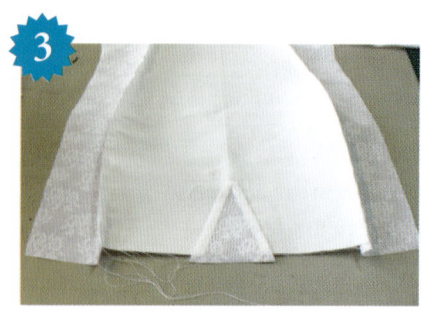

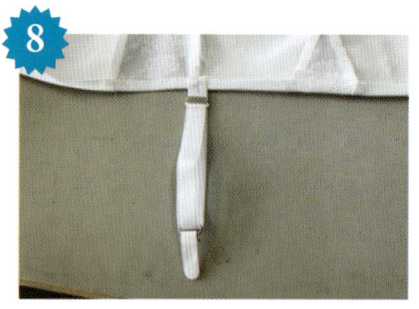

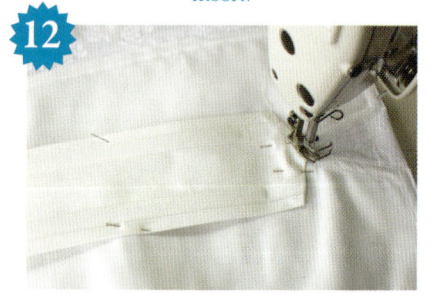

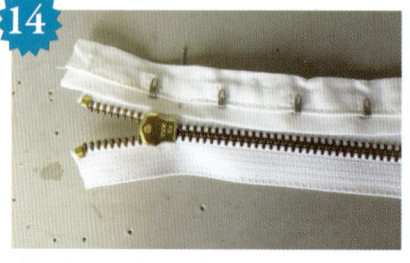

Chapter 3 / The Bra and Girdle (Belt) Set

I would recommend using Swan Stretch Thread or if your power mesh is a lighter weight you might want to sew using a Teflon foot or with tissue paper underneath to prevent it from stretching or being pulled into the bobbin chamber by the feeder teeth. (1,2,3)

3. Overlock the CB seam then press to one side and use zigzag stitch to secure. Attach one side only of the CB panel to one of the side back panels. It doesn't matter which but you need to be able to lay the whole garment flat at this stage.(4,5,6)

4. You will need to finish the waist and hem edges before closing the garment. Turn them in on the top and bottom edges and finger-press the satin. Pin down or tack. Finish the mesh edges only with a zigzag stitch. Finish the woven satin edges only using bias binding. This will involve a lot of stopping and starting again so zigzag all the mesh first then go back and straight-stitch all the satin afterwards. Use the flat binding technique and ensure that the edges are tucked under and kept neat at the beginning and end of each panel. For the bottom edge you will need to position the suspenders first and machine-tack before you bind; I used a pre-made suspender set which you can buy in pairs. The binding tape is mitred round the insert to create a smooth, neat, flat finish and reinforce the seam. (7,8,9)

5. The CF has a coutil-boned panel that will ensure the wearer's posture is kept in check. Machine-sew the boning channels into position 1cm/$^5/_8$ in in from the side edge of the stomach panel; I used the pre-made tape, but bias binding is just as good. To prevent the boning from moving in the casing, sew across the channels 3cm/$1^1/_4$ in from the bottom of the panel. Press the seam allowance under and insert the boning; I used flat steels as they are rigid but you could use Ridgelene for more mobility. Attach the stomach piece on the wrong side of the CF panel and topstitch round the outside edge. The bottom of the stomach panel should reach the tip of the mesh triangle. (10,11,12)

6. The girdle is fastened with hooks and eyes and a zip. The zip is topstitched directly into the zip opening once the seam allowance has been folded back. Place the zip face down and attach the hook tape to the back of the zip tape. Turn the zip and hooks over and insert into the opening with the hooks visible on the wrong side of the girdle. If the top hook and eye falls within the seam allowance then just unpick it. The teeth of the zip will be left visible from the front. Fold the placket in half and sew the seam. Turn it right side out and pink the raw edges. Pin the hook tape to the centre of the placket and machine-stitch on.

Close the hooks and eyes and line up the side of the placket along the zip edge. Pin the placket and hook tape to the other side of the zip opening and undo the eyes to sew from the wrong side. Machine-stitch along the pre-stitched line on the hook tape. Use a zip foot or walk the machine slowly over the hooks by turning the machine wheel by hand. Refasten the hooks and turn the garment to the right side. The hooks placket and zip tape should all be on the wrong side. Topstitch the tape to the outside edge of the zip and front panel. (13,14,15)

Suggested Adaptations

Make the bra and girdle in the same fabrics or colours to create matching sets. The top cups of the bullet bra could be in a power mesh or even a softer bobbinet (a hexagonally constructed tulle with minimal stretch) or you could use a patterned fabric. The straps for the bra could be in a variety of ribbons or coloured elastics for a more glamorous look. The longline bra and one-piece bra have been made so that you could include a detachable strap which you can either make yourself or use a pre-made kit (which is what I have done). There is no stretch in the back of any of the bras so the power mesh could easily have been used again here but I would recommend a stretch thread for sewing.

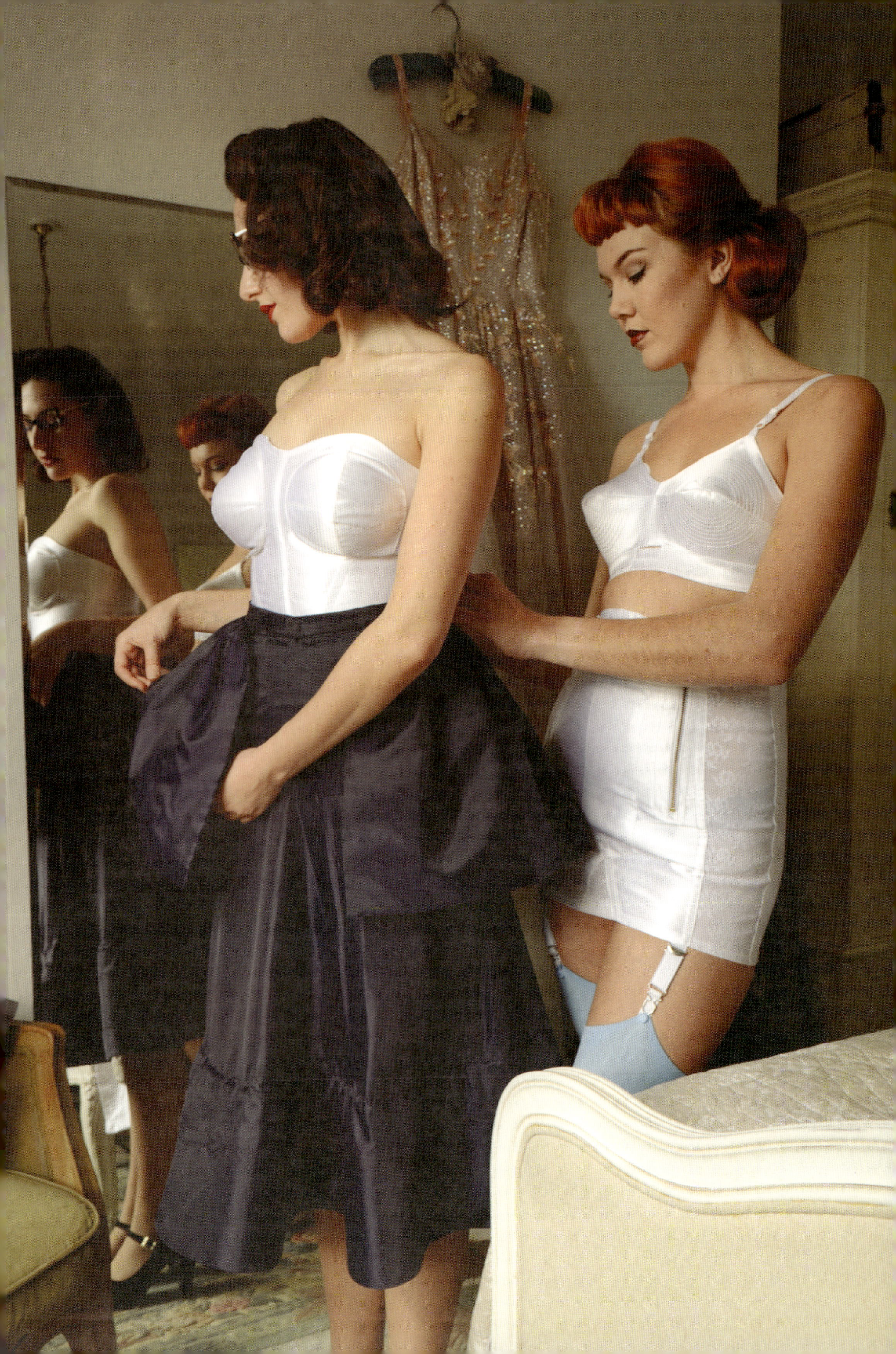

The Petticoat

4

The petite cote (little coat) was originally a padded coat worn by men under their armour to prevent chafing. The term was adopted in the mid-fifteenth century to describe an under-layer worn under a full-length dress and the name was anglicized to 'petticoat'. The New Look bought a resurgence of interest in it as a garment where Dior's full skirts required layers of voluminous petticoats to keep their shape. A 4.5m/5yd skirt required the same length of net petticoat. In couture, for garments that require volume it is traditional to see the volume built into the design; for example, the pink Dior dress with its tiered ruffles illustrated here. To some extent, with fast fashion we can also see examples of this on the high street today where it is cost-effective to do so. In the 1950s a couture approach would have been out of the reach of most women and separate mass-produced patterns would have been available for the dressmaker to adapt based on the length and volume of the dress it was intended to enhance.

The couture examples I researched were made of copious quantities of taffeta, silk tulle and cotton organdie. Cotton and broderie anglaise were sometimes used as they could be boiled white again and didn't yellow during the drying process, but most mass-produced petticoats would have been made of nylon for easier laundering. Nylon net was a relatively new invention that was adopted more widely in the mid-fifties and its stiffness meant that fewer layers were needed.

Petticoat without ruffle.

However, it did get flat quickly and needed frequent re-starching. Starch could be bought by the gallon and women's magazines offered endless advice on tactical starching that would

Petticoat with detachable ruffle.

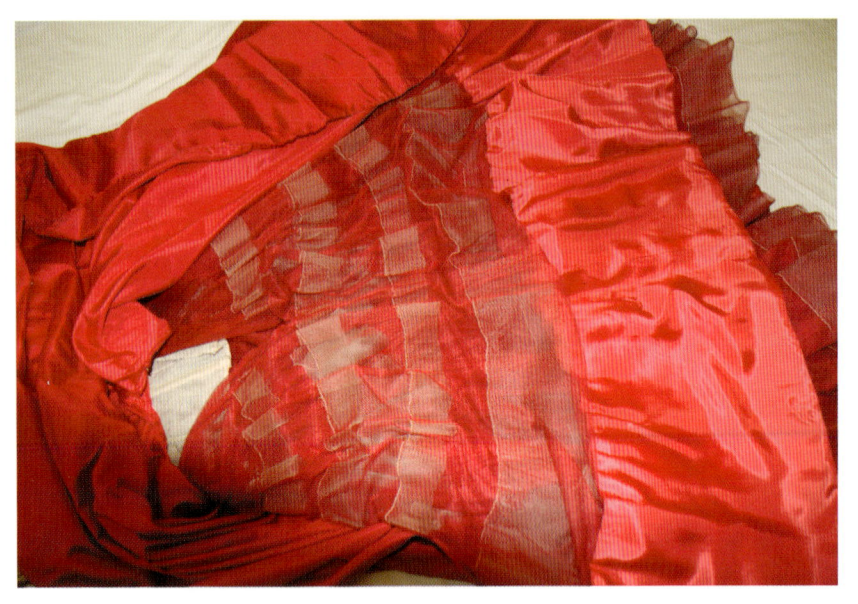

Petticoat of the Dior gown worn by Madonna in Evita. It is made almost entirely of horsehair braid and tulle with silk ruffles. (Cosprop Archive Collection)

give the most stiffness with the least amount of scratchiness on the wearers' legs. In keeping with that I have made this petticoat in a nylon taffeta with a nylon horsehair braid or crinoline to stiffen and, yes, I have already had to spray-starch it, which highlighted another drawback – with so many nylon layers a significant amount of static can be generated so, depending on your cloth, you may need an anti-static spray too.

The pattern here is based on an old French pattern from a brocante (second-hand shop) in Normandy. It had the pattern pieces in an envelope but no pictures, instructions or labelling so I had to half toile to see what it was. The horizontal dart at the side rather than a vertical one at the waist gives a tighter fit at the hip and a flatter stomach and may originally have been intended for a specific style of dress or skirt. This pattern is not complex but it is time-consuming because of the quantity of fabric to be gathered into the ruffle. You could speed this process up a little by investing in a gathering foot for your machine. Again I would also recommend vintage specialist stores from the Stockists and Suppliers section for ready-made petticoats to

MATERIALS AND EQUIPMENT

Fabric

Threads

Gathering foot for sewing machine (optional)

Crinoline/horsehair braid

Waistband canvas

Scissors

Pinking shears

Pins

Zip

Button

Anti-static spray and spray starch for long-term laundering

create the look; if you don't want to make it yourself then all you need to make is the hip ruffle for the cocktail dress in Chapter 5.

Cutting Out

Ensure your grain lines are parallel to the selvedge edge before pinning the pattern pieces down or marking them out with chalk. The ruffle pattern pieces are big so you will not be able to cut them on the fold unless your fabric is very wide. I used 1cm seam allowance for the ruffle seams and all joining seams and 2cm for the side seams; if you are using inches then make seam allowances $5/8$ in and side seams $25/32$ in.

Order of Construction

1. Prepare the hem ruffle by joining all the pieces together. Pink the seam edges and press open. If your fabric frays then use pinking shears to trim the gathered edge, otherwise you can leave it raw and it should only fray to the first row of machine stitching. As a last resort you can stitch the gathering onto a bias tape first to make it more stable then stitch it onto the petticoat. (1)
2. To gather, set your machine to a long stitch length such as a size 5. Sew two rows of stitching parallel to each other, the first on the seam line and the second in the seam allowance a machine foot's width from the first. Do not reverse-stitch at the ends as you need to be able to move the fabric along the threads. Leave long threads at either end so that you do not pull the fabric off altogether. Separate the threads and gently pull the fabric along either the two top threads or the two bottom threads but not both. If one breaks, don't worry – the gathering will still be on the second. The circumference of the ruffle is big so it is better to build in breaks rather than gathering too much at a time: I split this one into quarters. (2)
3. Construct the main body of the petticoat. Sew the darts into the yoke pieces and press. Sew the front of the yoke to the back of the yoke, leaving an opening for the zip.

Chapter 4 / The Petticoat

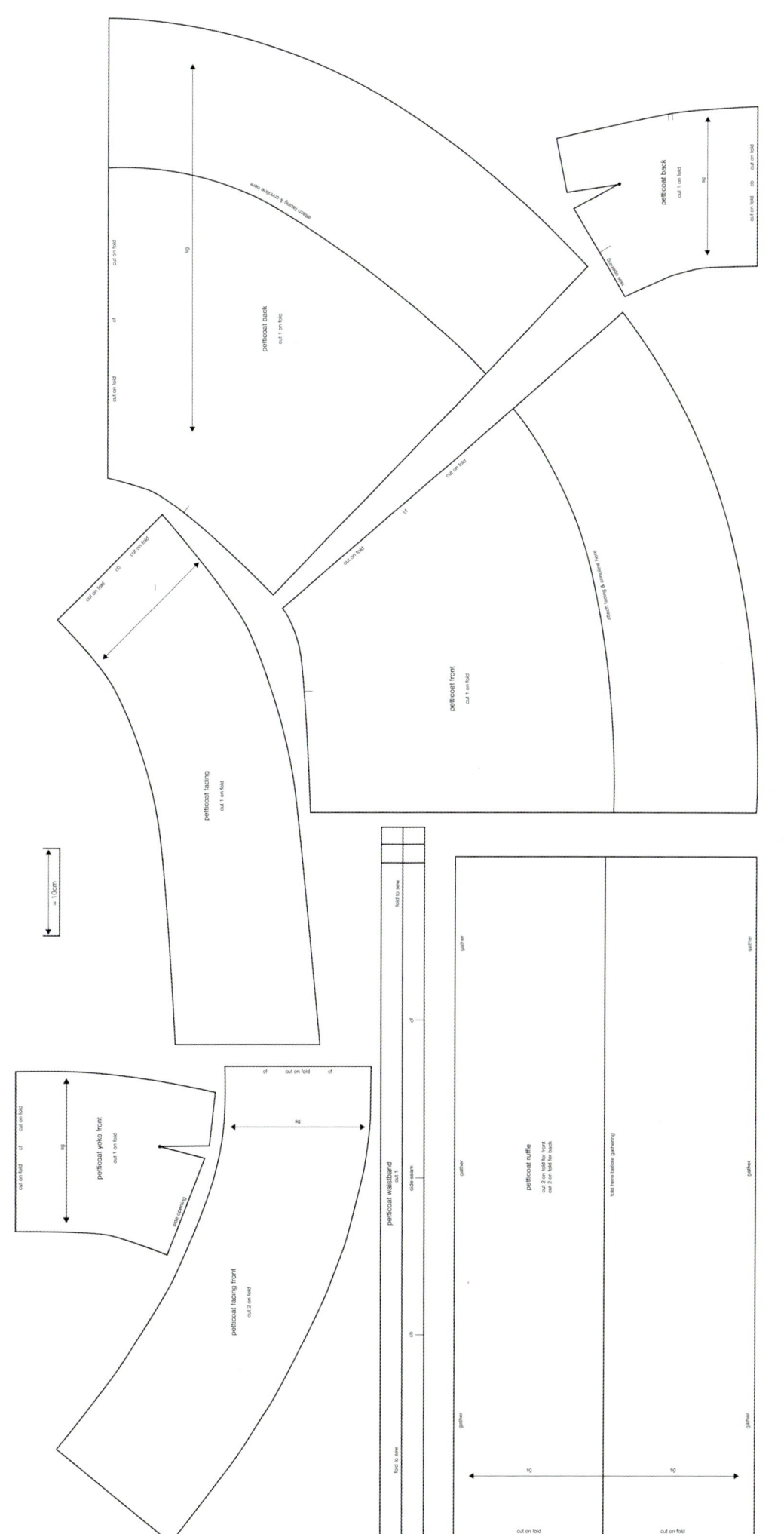

1. Machining the pinked seams of the ruffle.

2. Making a double row of machine stitching ready for gathering.

3. Manipulating the crinoline onto the petticoat hem and pinning it down.

4. Machining the crinoline once it lies flat to the petticoat hem.

5. Machining the ruffle on flush to the hem.

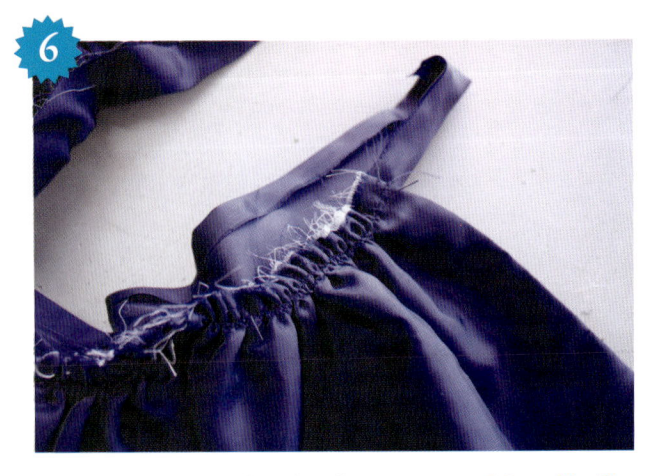

6. Waist band being machined to the waist waist of the ruffle. The same method is used to attach the waistband to the yoke of the petticoat.

Chapter 4 / The Petticoat

Inserting the canvas into the waistband.

4. Machine-sew the side seams and the CB seam. Line up the notches and attach the skirt to the yoke. Use chalk or a tacking stitch to mark the position of the stitch line for the ruffle on the wrong side.
5. The skirt hem is stiffened on the wrong side with a crinoline or horsehair braid, giving it solidity and shape. The crinoline is a folded nylon mesh with a row of stitching running through one edge. Tack the hem facing right side to right side with the petticoat shell. Put the crinoline on top and manipulate the crinoline to follow the curve of the hem on the right side of the skirt. Pin the folded edge in place along the hemline of both the skirt and facing and machine-stitch together. Turn through and lightly press the hem flat with the crinoline sandwiched between the facing and the shell of the petticoat. (3,4)
6. Gently pull the thread in the crinoline edge to ease the topside onto the stitch line. Pin or tack the crinoline and facing into place and machine-stitch closed.
7. In this version the ruffle is placed on the inside of the skirt. Place the gathering along the stitch line on top of the facing. Pin or tack into position and machine-stitch on. The bottom of the ruffle should be flush to the bottom of the hem (5).
8. The zip is inserted in the right side using the same method as for the chalk line skirt in Chapter 7.
9. The waistband is a straight one with self-facing and is stiffened with some lightweight canvas. The same method has been used for the ruffle. The waistband is cut twice the width of the canvas plus two lots of seam allowance. Fold your seam allowance over and press before you start. Line up the notches and machine-stitch the underlap of the waistband to the yoke waist starting at the front edge of the zip opening. Press seams open and then up into the waistband. Lap the canvas over the seam allowances with the main width of the canvas away from the garment. Sew along the edge of the canvas through both seam allowances. Sew the ends of the waistband while it is inside out then turn through and gently pull the corners square. Push out the corners with the end of the scissors. Turn under the seam allowance along the unstitched edge and press in place. Pin the folded edge to the waistband and slip-stitch closed. The stitching should not be visible from the right side of the fabric. Sew the fastenings onto the end by hand. (6,7)

The Detachable Hip Ruffle

This simple belt-like piece adds optional shaping and volume over the hip and is made in the same fabric as the petticoat. It is fastened at the front with a press-stud or hook and bar. It plays the same role as the fixed ruffle in the Liberty wedding dress foundation without the extra cost involved. You will need a left and a right to make up the pair.

1. Mount the fabric onto organza to give the ruffle more volume unless you are already working with a stiffened or starched fabric.
2. Fold the fabric in half on the wrong side and sew down both

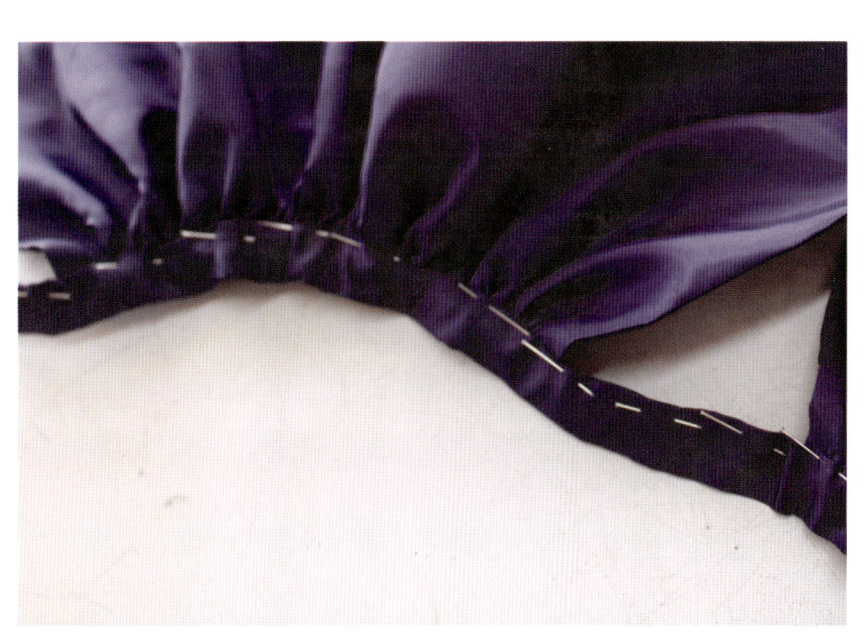

Pinning both the front and back of the waist band closed before stitching by hand.

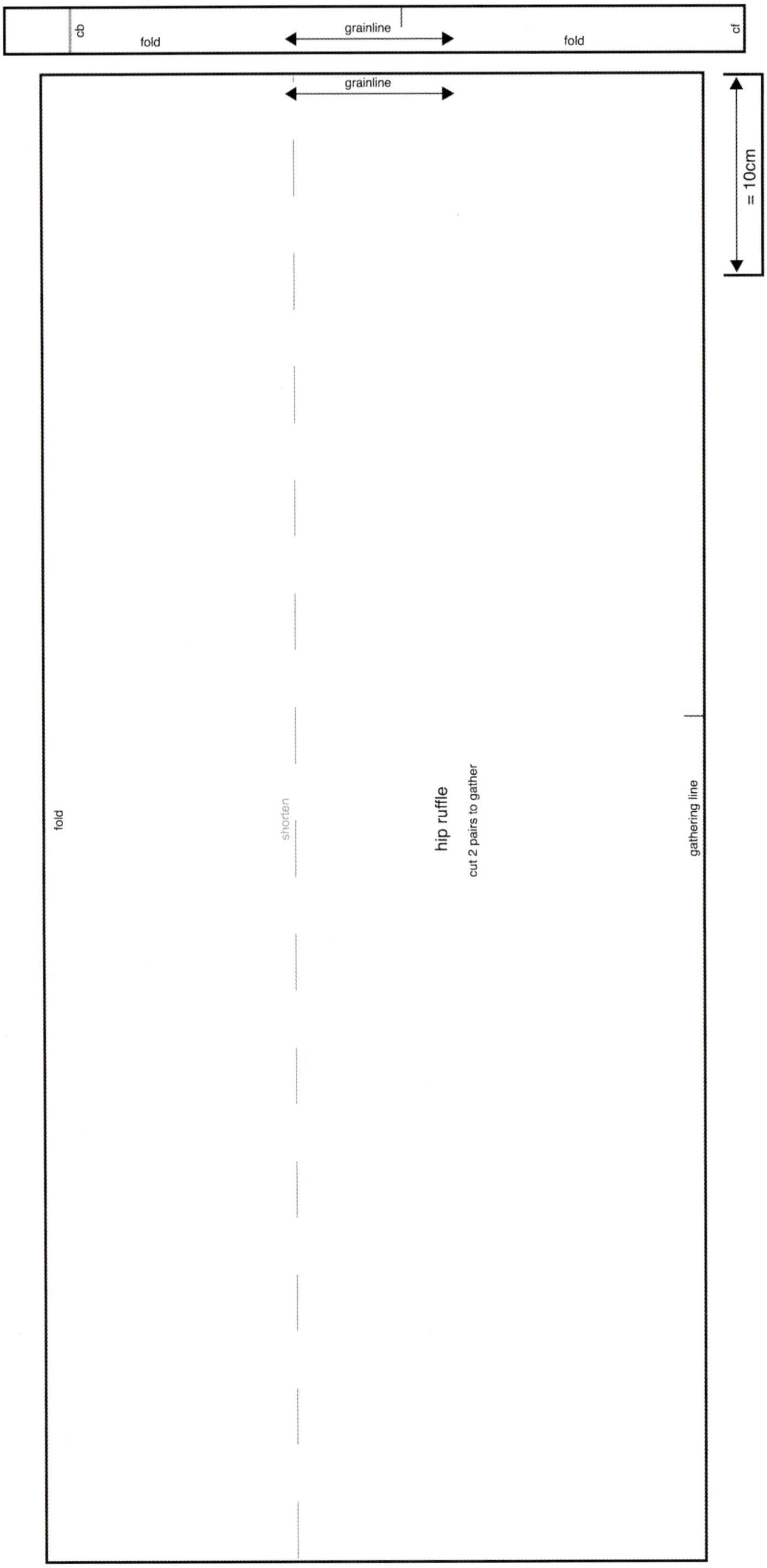

| cb | fold | ←grainline→ | fold | cf |

←grainline→

= 10cm

fold

shorten

hip ruffle
cut 2 pairs to gather

gathering line

Hip Ruffle

sides. Trim the bottom corners and turn through. Reshape the corners and press.
3. Use the gathering technique described for the petticoat to gather both pieces.
4. Prepare the waistband by pressing the underlap. Position the ruffles by using the notches; they should be equidistant to the CF and sit directly over the side seam. Machine-stitch them into place.

Use the same technique as the petticoat to inset the canvas then turn through and close by hand. Sew the fasteners on by hand.

Suggested Adaptations

The ruffle can also be sewn onto the outside of the skirt; alternatively the ruffle could be detachable and held in place with poppers. The hip ruffle is only one layer but it could be done with multiple layers, graduating the lengths to create more fullness or to control it in a specific position depending on the style of your garment. You could also increase the volume by slashing into the pattern from the hem all the way up to the yoke and opening it out at the bottom only: this technique is called 'slash and spread'. If you do this, remember to increase the length of the fabric for your ruffle or it will look mean.

The Liberty wedding dress foundation with its integral hip ruffle. (Cosprop Archive Collection)

49

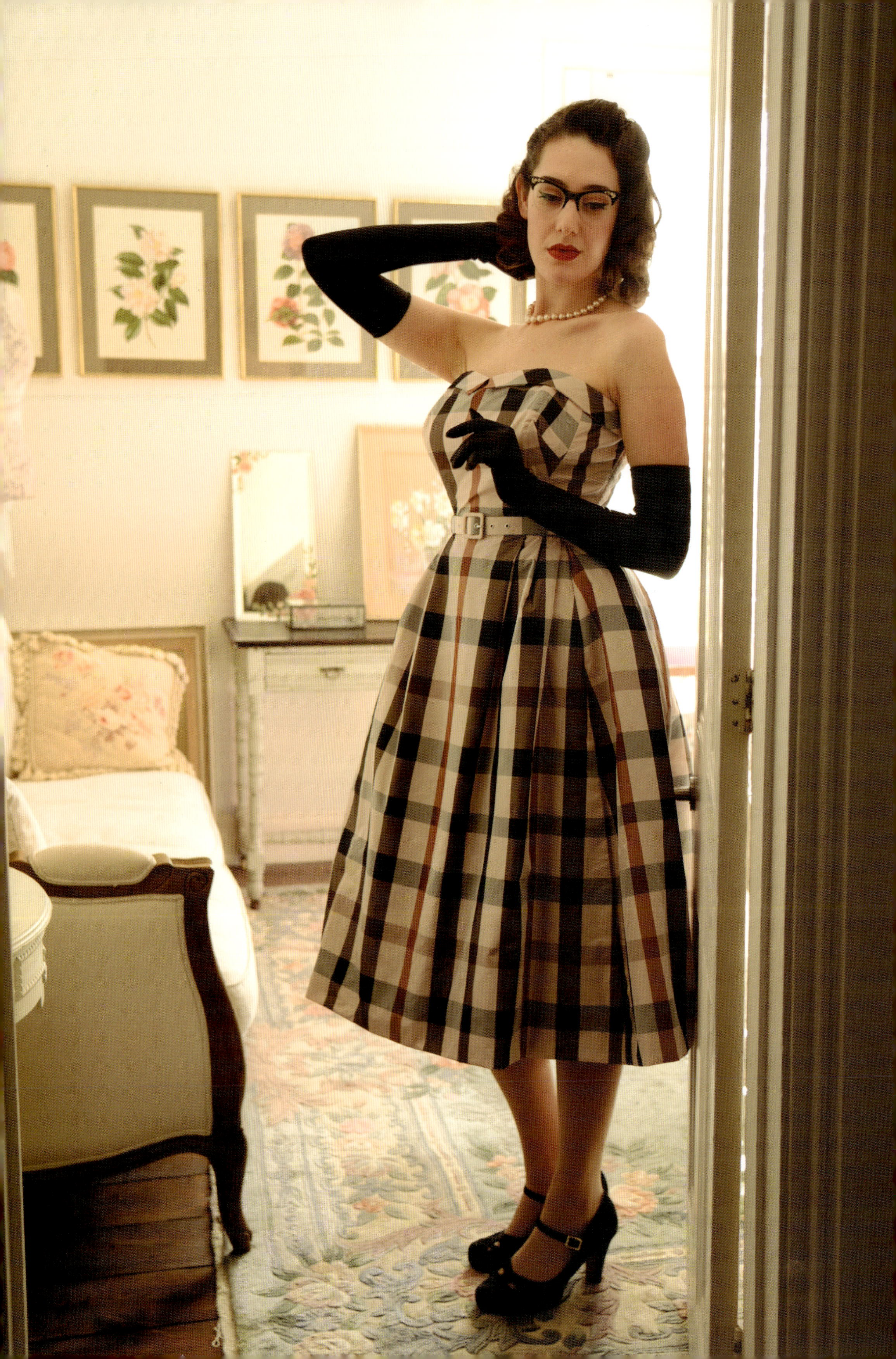

The Strapless Cocktail Dress

5

In 1949, the Australian couturier Douglas Cox travelled from Melbourne to Paris to meet Christian Dior to discuss the possibility of licensing Dior pieces for the Australian market. They signed a contract for Dior to produce original designs and for Douglas Cox to create them in his Flinders Lane workshop. The label was called House of Youth. The agreement between Dior and Douglas Cox really put Australian dressmaking on the global stage with licences for sixty Dior models to be produced. The first complete Dior collection to be shown outside of Paris toured Sydney, Melbourne and Adelaide in 1948, with the last collection being presented in 1957. It is believed that Dior influenced Australian fashion and in return Dior named some of his looks Australie and targeted that export market specifically.

Sadly, many of the designs proved to be too avant-garde for a more conservative Australian taste, making it hard for Cox to continue the contract in the long term. As a result this makes House of Youth pieces some of the most rare collector's items in Australian couture. As part of the House of Dior seventieth anniversary in 2017, Dior celebrated its Australian connection and influence with a large exhibition at the National Gallery of Victoria in Melbourne. Aside from Paris and New York this is the only other city where the

The strapless cocktail dress.

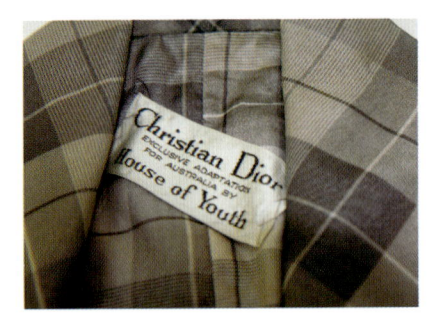

House of Youth label. (Worthing Museum and Art Gallery collection)

House of Youth cropped jacket. (Worthing Museum and Art Gallery collection)

House of Youth cocktail dress. (Worthing Museum and Art Gallery collection)

MATERIALS AND EQUIPMENT

Shell fabric

Lining fabric

Threads and tacking thread

Zip

Zip foot for sewing machine

Boning tape

Boning

Bias tape

Pinking shears

Scissors

Metre rule

Hook and eye

House has given permission for its designs to be seen, demonstrating the value of the antipodean relationship with Paris.

Worthing Museum and Art Gallery has one of these rare House of Youth pieces in its collection: it comprises a synthetic organdie strapless cocktail dress and short jacket. Synthetics were surprisingly popular with the Australian market because they didn't go out of shape or shrink and were easy to launder whether you wet- or dry-cleaned them. (Dry-cleaning, which arrived in Australia in 1913, had become big business: it was cheap and proven to be the best method of garment laundering, especially as it held colour fast and prevented sun bleaching.) The Dior fabric is a grey check and has a very bouncy handle. It is lined with taffeta but both layers have been tacked together and sewn as though they were one layer. I have produced a pattern for the dress but not the jacket. The jacket is very similar to the kimono blouse in Chapter 9. The pattern can easily be adapted just by cropping the length at the waist and making the button wrap at the CF wider and slightly curved. I cut this pattern over the longline bra and petticoat with the hip ruffle on.

Chapter 5 / The Strapless Cocktail Dress

Strapless Cocktail Dress

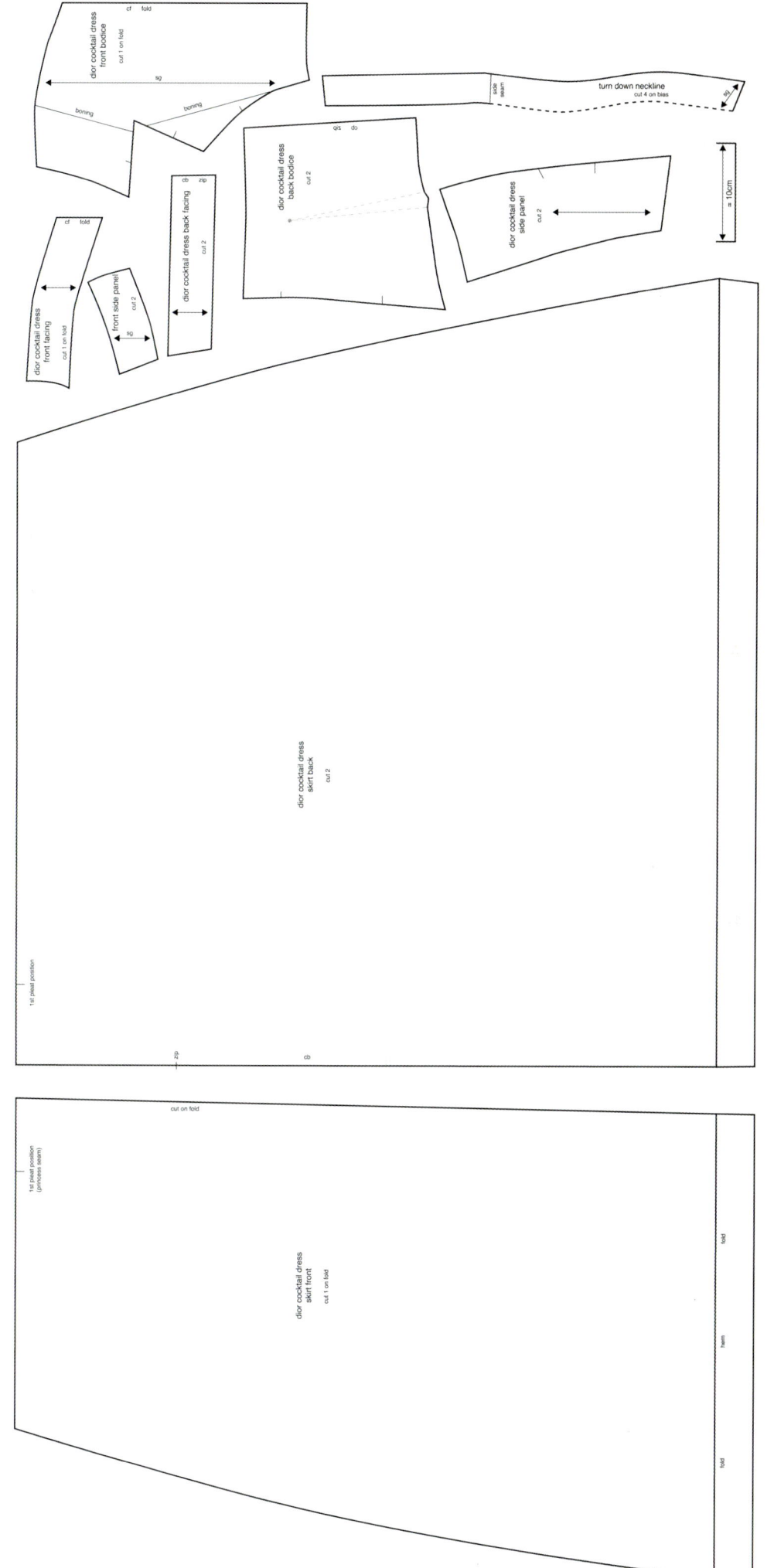

Cutting Out

As this is a check and the side seams are curved it is important to match up the checks as much as possible. The checks do not match exactly on the bodice because of the grain on the side front panelling and the curvature of the bustline. Instead it is best to match your checks horizontally starting from the CF and working outwards. Be aware that stripe or print matching also uses up a lot more fabric than normal, depending on the scale of the repeat. It is best to mark out each piece individually on the front of the fabric with chalk so you can see the motif placement, then transfer it to your pattern. Mark the position of your check on your paper pattern pieces – colour them in if you need to. The fabric can also move a little when you sew so it is best to leave 2cm/$^{25}/_{32}$ in seam allowance so that you can move the pattern pieces slightly to realign the check. As you are effectively creating double-backed cloth I would experiment with small swatches of different combinations first to see what works. I have used a synthetic check mounted onto a synthetic organza lining here because I wanted to retain the springiness of the original and a taffeta lining didn't do that. Then use the same pattern as the shell and cut the lining out separately. Snip all of your notches but don't cut beyond the sewing line. Mark off the position of the bone casing on the bodice before you sew.

Order of Construction

1. Mount the fabric pieces onto their corresponding lining pieces and tack together so the fabric layers effectively become one. (1)
2. Sew darts in the front and back bodice. Back-stitch at the dart points so that they do not undo. Press open over the ham and trim away the excess with the pinking shears.
3. Sew the front, side front and back pieces together and press the seams open. Pink the edges.
4. Pin the boning casing into position and stitch down, making sure it is next to and not on top of the bust point. (2,3)
5. Prepare the facing by stitching all the seams together and press them open, making one continuous piece. Pink the bottom edge and turn upwards. Press to get a crisp line then topstitch. (4)
6. Prepare the neckline detail. This is in two pieces so ensure you have a left and a right pair. Sew the side seams and the short edge only, leaving the top open. Trim the seam allowance down and snip into the curved bottom of each piece. Turn through and reshape. Use a scissor blade to gently push the corners out without going through. Press. (5)
7. Put the bodice flat on the table and line up the CF corner of the neck detail to the CF notch on the right side of the bodice. It should go round to the CB notch at the back of the bodice. The excess fabric at the back is for the zip so only tack from the CB notch round to the CF notch and round the other side to the other CB notch. (6)
8. Sandwich the neck detail between the bodice shell and the facing with right sides together. The facing will reach the full length of the shell. (7)
9. Snip into the CF seam allowance up to the stitch line to create a V or a notch. This will allow you to create the centre point of the sweetheart neckline.
10. Under-stitch the facing starting 2cm/$^{25}/_{32}$ in in from the end of the facing. (You will need this allowance to turn under for finishing after you have put the zip in.) Start by opening the facing flat away from the bodice and pushing the seam allowances up behind the facing. Topstitch on the right side of the facing close to the seam. Make sure the seam allowances remain even underneath, gently smoothing the fabric either side of the seam to keep it flat as you sew. This operation ensures the facing does not creep upwards and show

Tacking the shell and lining together.

Boning casing positioned next to but not on the bust point.

Bustline and boning casing of the original dress.

4. Preparing the facing.

5. Prepared neckline detail.

6. Positioning the neckline detail at CF.

7. Stitching on the facing with the neckline detail sandwiched between it and the bodice.

8. Under-stitching the facing to keep the neckline edge sharp.

9. Retrying the bodice on the stand over over the long line bra and petticoat with hip ruffle.

10 Lining up the checks at CB.

11 Lining up the checks at the side seam.

12 Lining up the pleats and the checks from the skirt to the bodice.

13 Joining and finishing the waist seam.

14 Finished waist seam on the original dress. (Worthing Museum and Art Gallery collection)

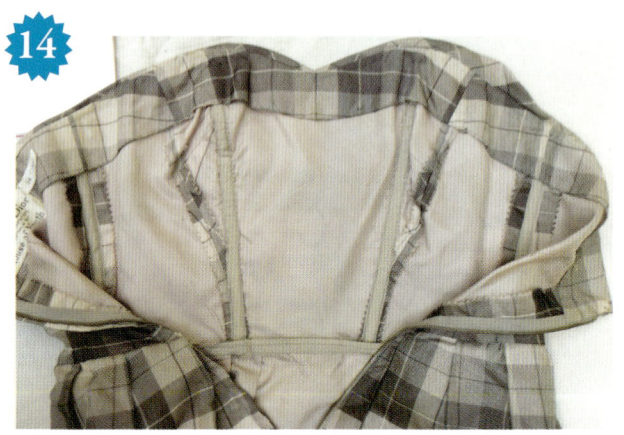

15 Laying the zip face down against the CB.

Chapter 5 / The Strapless Cocktail Dress

above the neckline. (8)
11. Roll the facing inwards and the neck detail outwards and retry on the mannequin to check the fit. If you are happy that everything sits correctly then give the bodice and neckline a press. (9)
12. Prepare your skirt back by checking the checks on the CB line up. Realign if you need to. Pin or tack together and machine-stitch together leaving an opening at the waist for the zip – this is marked with a notch on the pattern. Pink edges and press open. (10)
13. Repeat for the side seams, lining the checks up on the horizontal. Remember that the side seams are curved and will go off grain vertically; when you press the seams open it looks as if they are not aligned. Pink edges and press open. The tacking stitches holding the skirt fabric to its organza mount will be visible; when you are happy that the checks line up and that there is no unpicking to do, then they may be removed. (11)
14. The pleats all go in the same direction. Position them and pin or tack into position. There are three each side of the CF and the fourth is inverted, bringing the side seam back towards the front of the garment and creating that characteristic wide hemline. Initially I did this flat but had to move the pleats to realign the checks. It is better to work directly on to the stand and control where you put the pleats. Match the CF up to the CF of the bodice and pin the pleats equally on both sides. You can now make any adjustments to the depth or angle of your pleats whilst ensuring they line up to the bodice. Re-pin on the mannequin then tack to hold them in position before you machine-stitch. (12)
15. Machine-stitch the bodice to the skirt through the waist by pinning or tacking the right sides together. Press the seam open then press closed upwards into the bodice. Bind the seam with bias binding to finish. The bias will need to be the full waist length but stop stitching a couple of centimetres (an inch) short of the CB so that you can finish by hand once the zip is in: this technique has been used in the original. (13,14)
16. Now the dress is together you can put in the zip. The original has a centred metal zip. The top stop is $12mm/^5/_8$ in below the seam line, allowing for the extra turning down of the facing. You will also need a hook and eye to close the top of the dress just above the zip. Position the zip carefully face down along the opening edges of the CB on the right side of the dress and pin into place. Using a zipper foot put a tacking or holding stitch in at the edge of the zip tape furthest from the teeth. Now open out the left CB seam allowance and fold the dress out of the way to the right. Machine-tack the left side of the zip tape to the CB seam allowance. Turn the garment through to the right side and lay the CB as flat as possible. You can now see where the CB of the fabric will fold and close to conceal the zip teeth beneath. Starting from the bottom of the opening at the CB hand-tack the bottom of the zip and up one side to the neckline. Repeat on the other side. Tack $6mm/^3/_8$ in from the CB seam. Make sure you are going through the garment seam allowance as well as the zip tape. Start your machine stitching just outside the tacking at the bottom of the zip. Lift the machine foot with the needle still in the fabric and pivot the fabric when you change direction to stitch to the top. Make sure you are sewing through the shell, the zip tape and the seam allowance. Reverse-stitch a couple of stitches at the top. Repeat the process on the other side and remove any hand tacking. (15)
17. The original has a straight turned-up hem with a perfect check running round the circumference. Level the hem by putting the garment back on the mannequin and measuring up from the floor with a metre rule. Before turning up the hem, reduce the bulk in the seams by trimming the seam allowance to half the original width with pinking shears. With the wrong side facing upwards fold the hem upwards along the hemline and tack or lightly press. Make the hem allowance an even depth of $4cm/1^9/_{16}$ in and mark all round the circumference. Pin in position. If the hem ripples it is because the circumference of the raw edge is greater than the circumference of the skirt at the point you want to sew it. You will need to ease it in evenly by machine tacking $6mm/^3/_8$ in in from the edge and gently drawing up the fabric without creating large gathers. You should be able to shrink the excess away when you press the hem. Turn the raw edge over and over again and hand-stitch closed to the lining only with a slip stitch. Do not stitch through the shell.
18. Finish the bodice off by turning the facing back over the zip and hand-stitching down on both sides. Do the same with the binding at the waistband.

Suggested Adaptations

Using this method you will see the stitching on the shell of the bodice. If you do not want to see it then bone the lining first before tacking it to the shell. The stitching will be sandwiched between the two layers and effectively invisible. If you have extra fabric use it to make your own bias binding to match the shell of the dress for boning casings and through the waist. You could also add straps to the design if you want it to be more suitable for daywear.

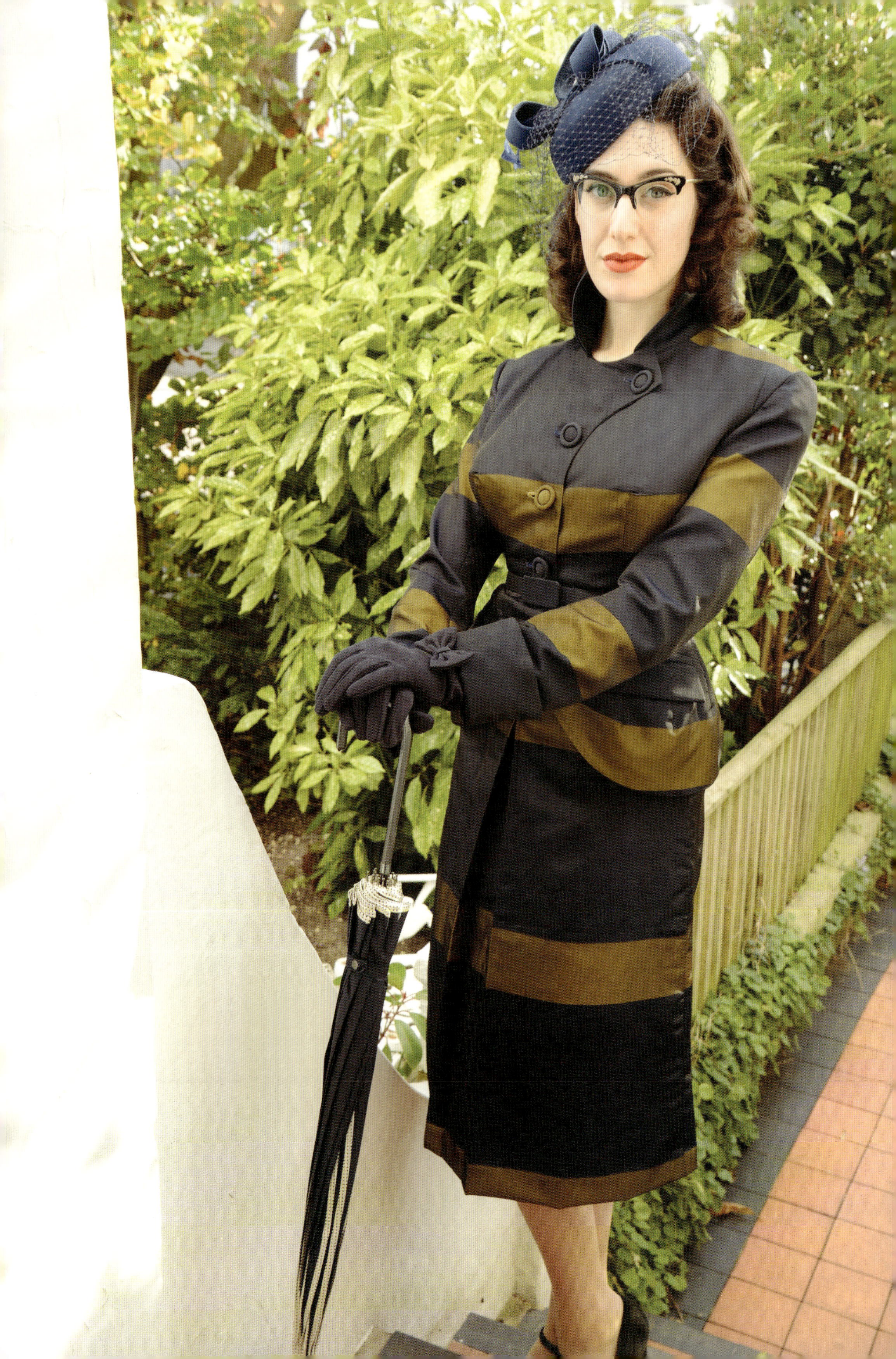

The Town Suit: The Soft Tailored Jacket

6

A well-tailored suit was a staple of the fifties wardrobe when women were expected to be impeccably groomed and dressed in public. Women found suits practical as they were appropriate for a wide variety of occasions, but note that these were skirt and jacket or coat suits and not trouser suits – the latter were not deemed socially acceptable until the 1960s. The 1950s continued the late 1940s style with very full skirts, cinched waists and sloping shoulders. Another popular silhouette was the narrow pencil-skirt look. Daywear consisted of skirts and jackets, which usually matched, or day dresses in tweeds and woollens. Rayon versions were promoted in magazines for summer.

Few designers chose to break from the New Look model for the rest of the decade, but a couple paved the way. Coco Chanel hated the New Look so much that she reopened her business after closing it at the start of the war. In 1954, she came back with the slim suit – the brand's signature look – in wools and tweeds. The jackets were boxy with no collar, and the skirts were straight and comfortable. Worth also offered a boxier cut, as seen in this cream silk day suit with pleated back. The silhouette feels ahead of its time and has more of a 1960s look.

Stylistically, for this project I have taken inspiration from a jacket designed by New York designer Hattie Carnegie to promote Celanese acetate ottoman fabric. Characteristically for the time, jacket suits were frequently photographed without a shirt or blouse being worn underneath. The result is a tighter fit and smoother silhouette. These soft tailored jackets are buttoned high at the neck and worn more like a modern day blouse. Depending on the cut of the neckline they would have been styled with scarves and complementary gloves to enhance the threequarter-length sleeve.

The Worthing Museum and Art Gallery has several soft tailored unlined jacket suits in their collection that were professionally manufactured. Analysis of the green floral suit featured provided me with an opportunity to identify the construction processes and method of assembly. The jacket has a slightly sloped shoulder line with a set-in sleeve. The two-piece sleeve is threequarter-length and cut narrow with no room for a blouse sleeve

Advertisement for Celanese acetate, US Vogue, September 1950. (Author's own collection)

The town suit. The soft tailored jacket front view.

The town suit. The soft tailored jacket back view.

The town suit, showing details of the soft tailored jacket.

Worth boxy jacket in cream silk. (Worthing Museum and Art Gallery collection)

Chapter 6 / The Town Suit: The Soft Tailored Jacket

Hollywood Model suit jacket, front. (Worthing Museum and Art Gallery)

Hollywood Model suit jacket, back. (Worthing Museum and Art Gallery)

The unlined Hollywood Model jacket with buggy. (Worthing Museum and Art Gallery collection)

MATERIALS AND EQUIPMENT

Fabric

Organza to stiffen

Thread for sewing machine and overlocker

Lining fabric

Shoulder pads and hip pads

Square of firm cotton or Silesia (sturdy twill-weave cotton) for pockets

Fabric belt

Cover buttons

Pins

Pinking shears

Fabric scissors

Overlocker

Cutting Out

This depends entirely on your cloth. As mine had a stripe in it I marked the position of the stripe onto the pattern pieces and cut them out individually on the right side of the fabric so that I could match up the left and right sides as I went. If you are using a stripe, decide where on the body you want to place it and line up the pattern accordingly before cutting out. I used the waist as the starting point. To line up the stripe on the sleeves I waited until the jacket body was constructed then pinned a calico sleeve on and marked the stripe's position on it. I transferred this to the pattern before cutting out. I used a 1cm seam allowance with 2cm at the sides and waist seam for adjustment; if you are using imperial then use $^5/_8$in seam allowance and $^{25}/_{32}$in at the side and waist. As fusible interfacings were not used in the fifties I have mounted my facings, collars and cuffs onto synthetic organza to stiffen them so that they could be cut out and the pieces tacked together before making up the

underneath. The shape is also enhanced by the sleeve pitch, which hangs forwards more than we would see in the more relaxed fit of today. The exaggerated shaping through the waist is created by two angled darts on each side with small functioning welt pockets. The jacket is faced but unlined except for the buggy – traditionally a buggy is a loosely attached lining at the back of a jacket that comes down about half way. It is used to reduce the weight and use of interlinings in summer jackets or for oddly shaped jackets. The jacket has a matching fabric belt. Initially I tried to source cloth close to either of the original sources but without success. Instead I have used the wrong side of a vintage acetate tie silk with a broad stripe because I liked the handle of it.

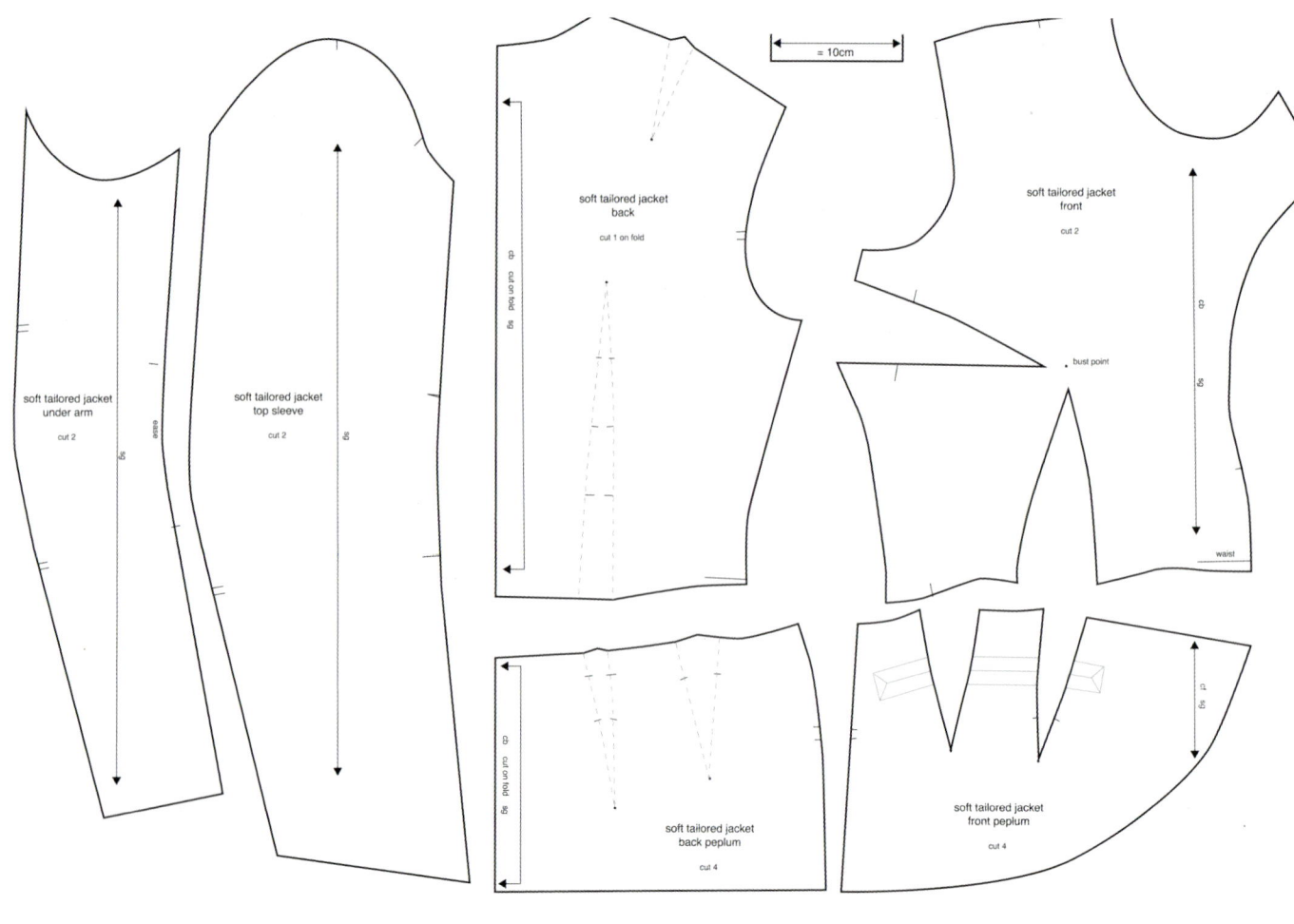

The Town Suit - Soft Tailored Jacket 1

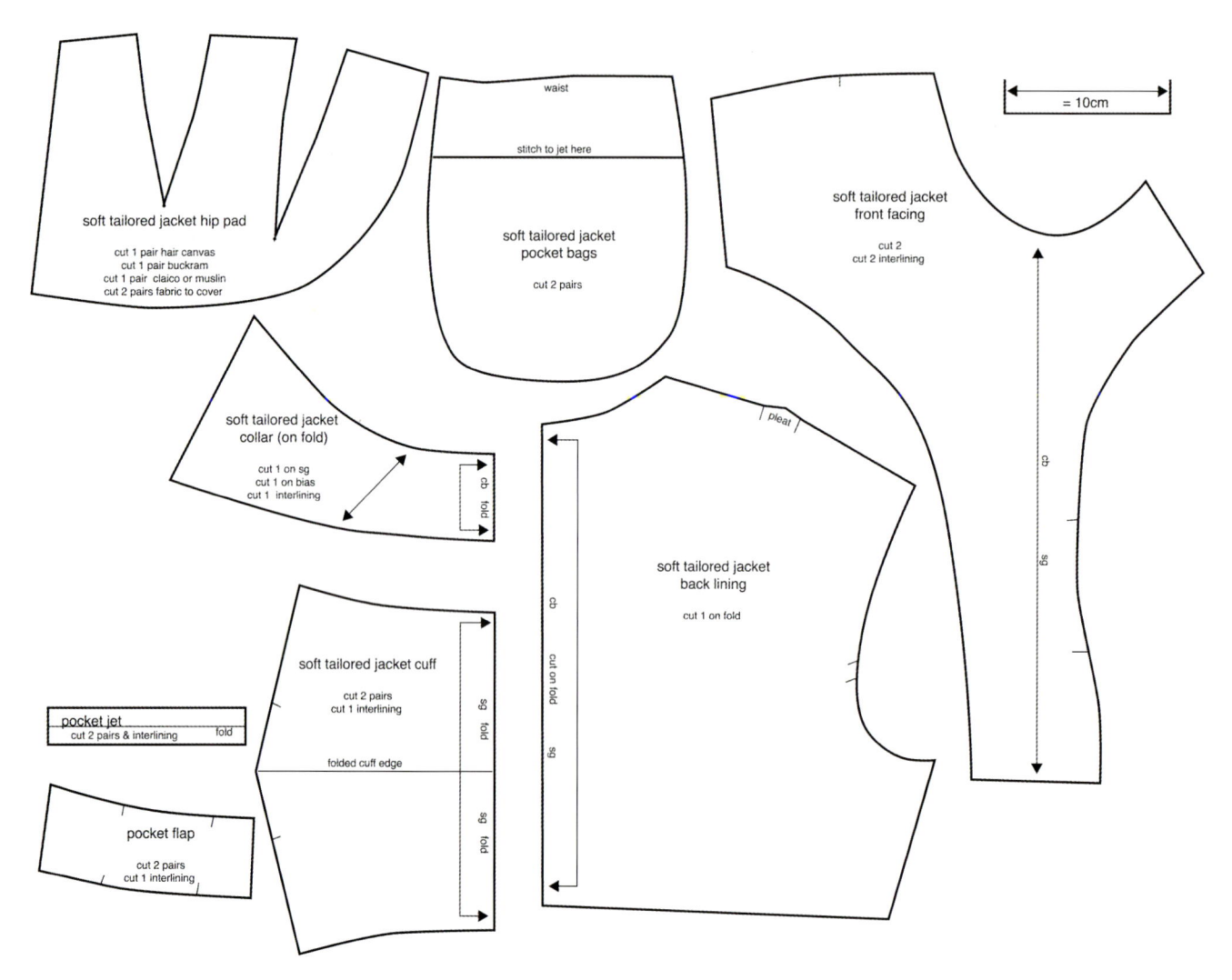

The Town Suit - Soft Tailored Jacket 2 Pattern

Marking the stripe on the pattern.

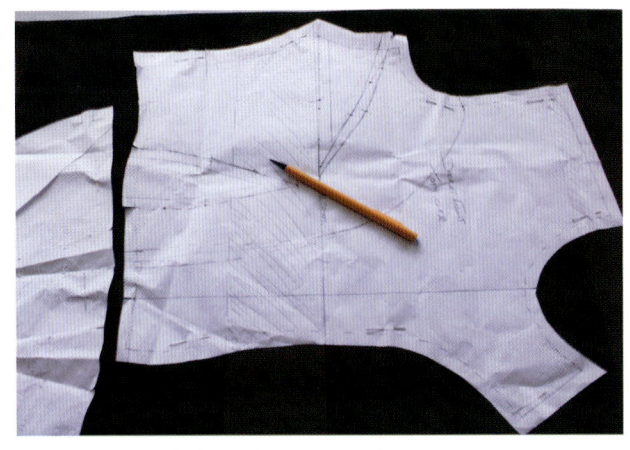

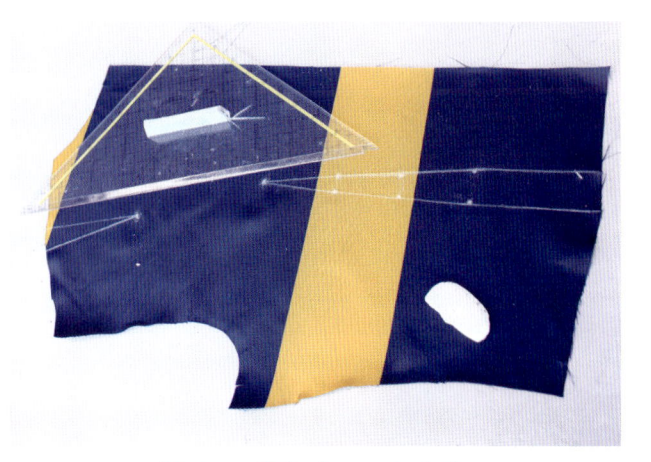

Marking off the darts with chalk.

garment. Overlock the side seams, shoulder seams, CB and inside edges of the facings before making up. Press these pieces and check them against the pattern to ensure there is no shrinkage. Pink the seams on the sleeves as per the original garment.

Order of Construction

1. Sew in the darts. Reverse-stitch the tips so they don't undo. It will be important to use the notches to line the seams up properly. Press the darts inwards towards the CF and CB. As the darts are so curved you will need to press on a ham or the edge of your sleeve board to achieve the shape of the bust point. (1)
2. Sew up the CB and side seams and press seams open. Sew the shoulder seams and press open. Pin the pleats in the lining and sew the front facings at the shoulder. Press the seams open.
3. Pin or tack the CF edges of the facing to the jacket and machine-stitch round to the collar notch. Trim off the corners before turning through, under-stitching and pressing. Start the under-stitching about 4cm/1$^9/_{16}$ in up from the waist. (2,3,4)
4. Prepare the collar by putting both pieces right sides together. Machine-stitch the outside edge. Please note that the shape of a 1950s collar has a shorter outside edge than you would expect for a contemporary collar so make sure you sew the correct sides. Trim the bulk from the corners and turn through. Before pressing, roll the seam edge between your fingers to position the seam just underneath the collar edge towards the under collar. (5,6)
5. On the wrong side sandwich the collar between the shell and the buggy lining at the neckline. The collar edge should line up to the collar notch on the jacket fronts and at the CB notch. Machine-stitch the neckline. Neaten any remaining visible raw edges by overlocking but leave the waist and armhole edges. (7,8)
6. Put the jacket on the mannequin and check the fit. It is also useful to run a line of tacking to mark the CF as this jacket has a double-breasted neckline. (9,10) 7. The jacket has jet pockets with a flap positioned at the top of the hip. (A jet pocket has a strip of fabric protecting the top and bottom of the pocket opening; the pocket bag is not visible from the

Pressing the darts.

2. Trimming the bulk from the corners.

3. Under-stitching the facing.

4. Pressing the lapel shape on a ham.

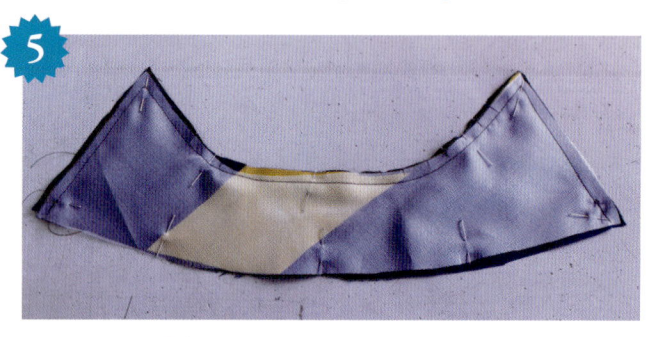

5. Collar machined on the short edges.

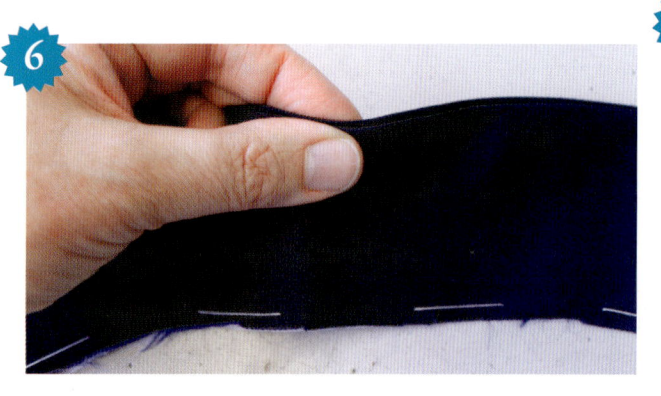

6. Rolling the collar edge.

7. Inserting the collar into the neckline on the wrong side. The collar is lined up at the CB.

8. Collar inserted viewed from the right side.

outside.) On the wrong side reinforce the placement of the pocket opening by tacking on a piece of firm cotton or Silesia. Make the pocket flaps by sewing wrong side to wrong side, trimming the corners, turning through and pressing. Chalk the pocket opening onto the right side. Place the top jet right side down on the opening line and tack. Sew the bottom jet to the bottom pocket bag and line up to the opening line. Mark the corners of the pockets and the ends of the

Fitting the bodice on the mannequin, front view.

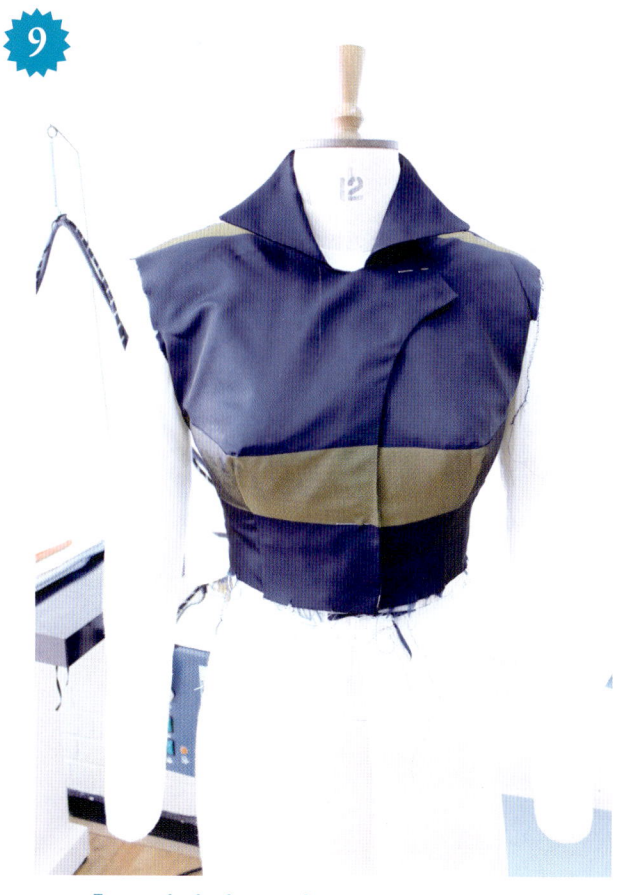

Fitting the bodice on the mannequin, back view.

openings with chalk or tailor tacks and machine-stitch the edges of the pockets from mark to mark. Cut along the pocket opening and snip diagonally from the ends of the opening into the corners of the pocket, forming a small triangle at each end. Don't cut through the stitching. Turn the jets and bottom pocket bag on the front through the opening to the back. Pull on the small triangles to square the corners of the opening and manipulate the jets to sit evenly in the opening and sew across the triangle onto the jets. Position the pocket flaps through the pocket opening and tack or pin into position, then machine-stitch through the ditch of the top jet to anchor in place. Turn over onto the wrong side and position the back of the pocket bag: it should go from the waist seam and cover the pocket opening and bottom pocket bag. Machine-stitch the bag to the jets and machine-tack at the waist. Pin the edges of the bag together – they are likely to have moved so trim and neaten them as evenly as possible before machining. The original jacket has pocket bags finished by overlocking but you could use bias binding to neaten. On the front lift the flaps and cross-stitch the jets closed until you want to use them. (11,12,13,14,15, 16,17,18)

8. To construct the peplum sew the side seams and centre back seams of both the shell and the facing. Press all the seams open but you do not need to overlock it as this would only create bulk. Attach the shell peplum to the shell of the jacket through the waist and press seams open then press down. With right sides together, sew round the hem and CF edges of the peplum facing and shell. Snip up to but not through the stitch line at the curved bottom to release the tension and let everything sit flat. Turn the jacket through and roll the hem edges of the facing and shell so that the shell rolls over the facing. Turn the seam allowance of the facing downwards and press. Hand-stitch to the waist seam to neaten, with all raw edges inside. I also used a hip pad made of a layer of buckram, a layer of canvas and a layer of cotton to hold the shape.

9. Line up the notches and machine-stitch the undersleeve to the oversleeve and press the seams open. Fold the cuffs vertically and machine the seam. Cut away the bulk at the corner, turn through and press. I put a seam through the outside edge of my cuff to ensure the stripes continued to line up. Put the cuff inside the sleeve and line the cuff seam up to the overarm seam. Sew the seam allowance on the right side of the fabric. Overlock the raw edge then

65

11. Tacking the back of the pocket opening.

12. Machining the pocket flaps on the wrong side.

13. Sewing along the pocket line on the wrong side.

14. Cutting along the pocket opening diagonally up to the corners.

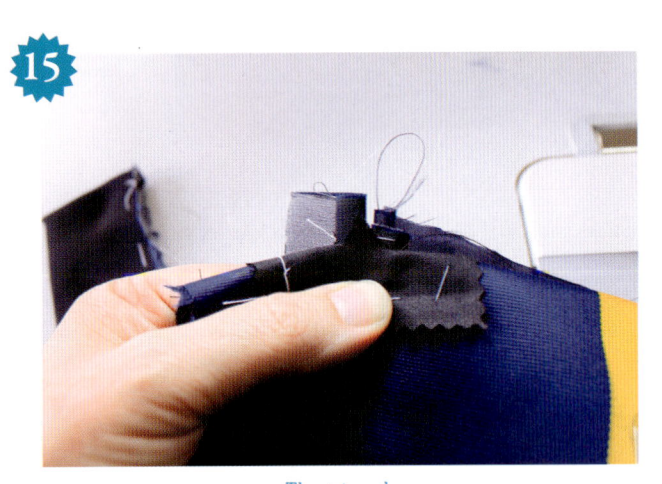

15. The triangles.

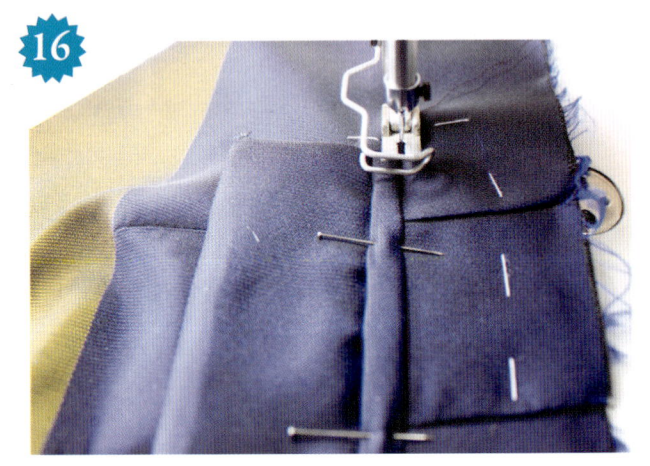

16. Machine-stitching through the ditch to anchor the pocket flap.

turn, pull the cuff through and turn upwards.(19,20,21,22)
10. Put the sleeve and the armhole right side to right side and line up the notches. There is very little ease but it is still better to pull in the ease at the sleeve head with a gathering stitch on the sewing line first before pinning into place. Tack in position and put back on the mannequin to check the pitch. Machine-stitch on the wrong side.
11. The original jacket had a shoulder pad covered with the lining and partially concealed with the buggy. I used pre-made shoulder pads and covered them. Position the pad into the jacket on a

Chapter 6 / The Town Suit: The Soft Tailored Jacket

Pocket from the wrong side.

Finished pocket.

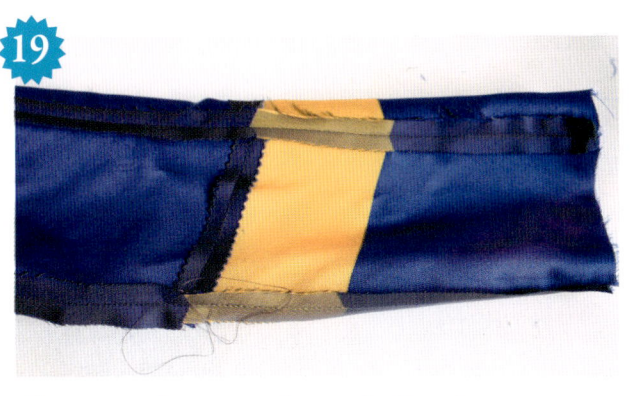

Sleeve seams being pressed open; the sleeve has an extra seam in it to ensure the stripes match up.

Machining the cuff.

Pressing the cuff seams after trimming away the corners.

Cuff attached to the sleeve.

Original shoulder pad covered by the buggy. (Worthing Museum and Art Gallery collection)

mannequin and catch down on the shoulder seam once you have sewn in the sleeve. The buggy is stitched down by hand to the side seam. (23)

12. The buttonholes are marked off on the right side. The ones here have been machine-stitched but you could use a jet to finish instead. The look is completed with cover buttons and a fabric belt.

67

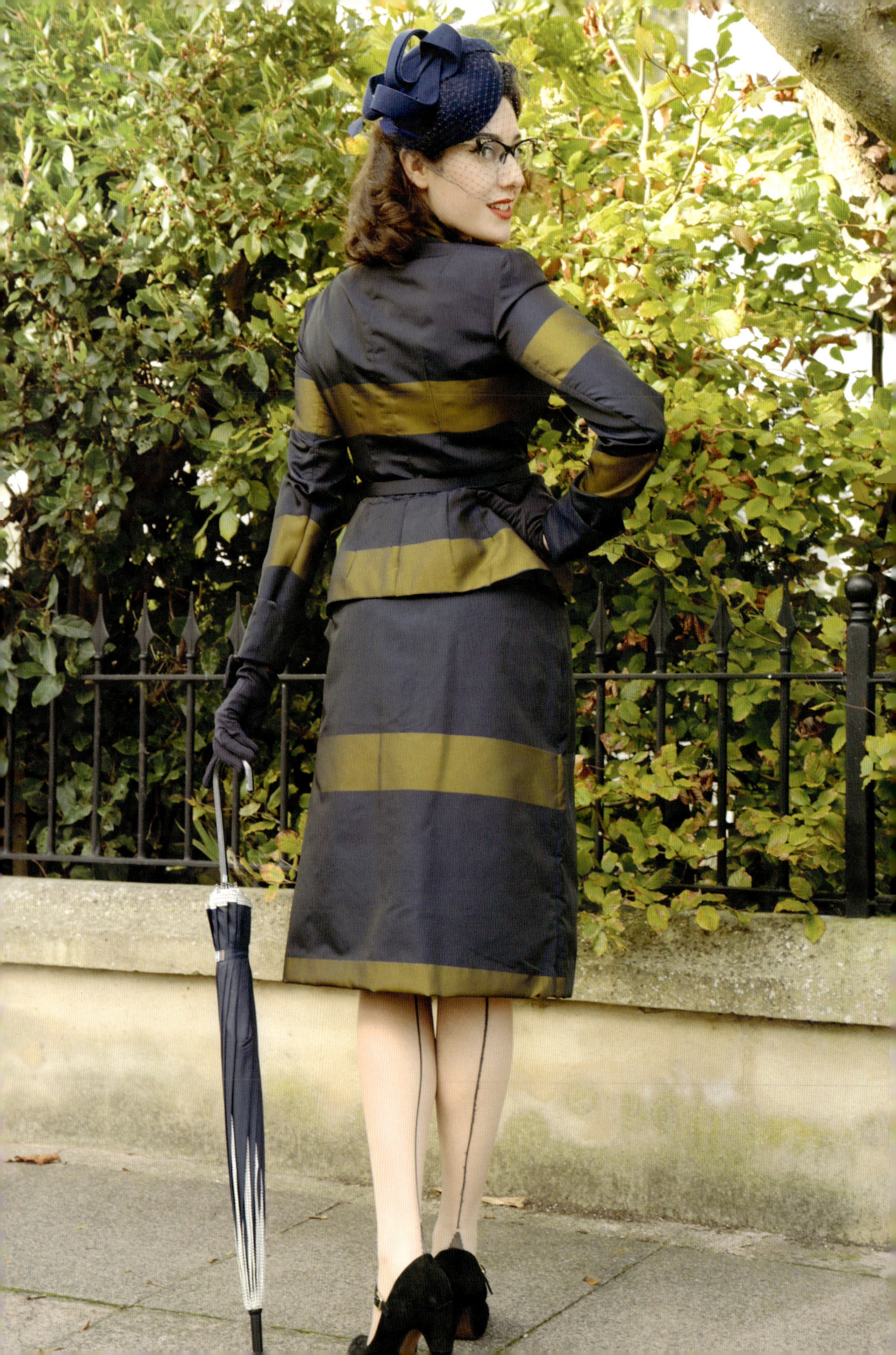

The Town Suit: The Chalk Line Skirt

In its September 1950 edition for the UK, under the headline 'American Ready to Wear Collections New Stars', *Vogue* declared the shape of the skirt to be 'the pivot of fashion' for that year. The article continued by stating that the 'peachskin fit and low flare' makes the skirt 'the' 1950s fashion figure in Britain, Paris and New York. 'The day skirt today is a slim skirt made mobile one way or another, made to walk, to sit, to climb in and out of American automobiles, to move about easily.'

In other words, the chalk line skirt had to allow women to function in their daily lives while still looking groomed and presentable and was a wardrobe staple for public duties like shopping, working, visiting and running errands outside the house.

The chalk line, with its characteristic slim fit through the hips, had a small amount of flare from the hipbone down. Obviously there were variants on this, like the 'half trumpet' popular in Paris, which was cut straight at the front and had a low flare at the back. Other styles included straight skirts with kick pleats and pleated godets inserted into side slits. In its various guises it stuck around for the whole decade with very little change to the fit, its iconic appearance frequently immortalized for fashion stills by fashion photographers such as Richard

The chalk line skirt worn with the bow tie blouse from Chapter 8.

A chalk line skirt with box pleat. (Worthing Museum and Art Gallery collection)

The same skirt turned inside out with the box of the pleat visible. (Worthing Museum and Art Gallery collection)

A chalk line skirt with three kick pleats. (Worthing Museum and Art Gallery collection)

Triple-pleat skirt turned inside out with pleat backs visible. (Worthing Museum and Art Gallery collection)

Chapter 7 / The Town Suit: The Chalk Line Skirt

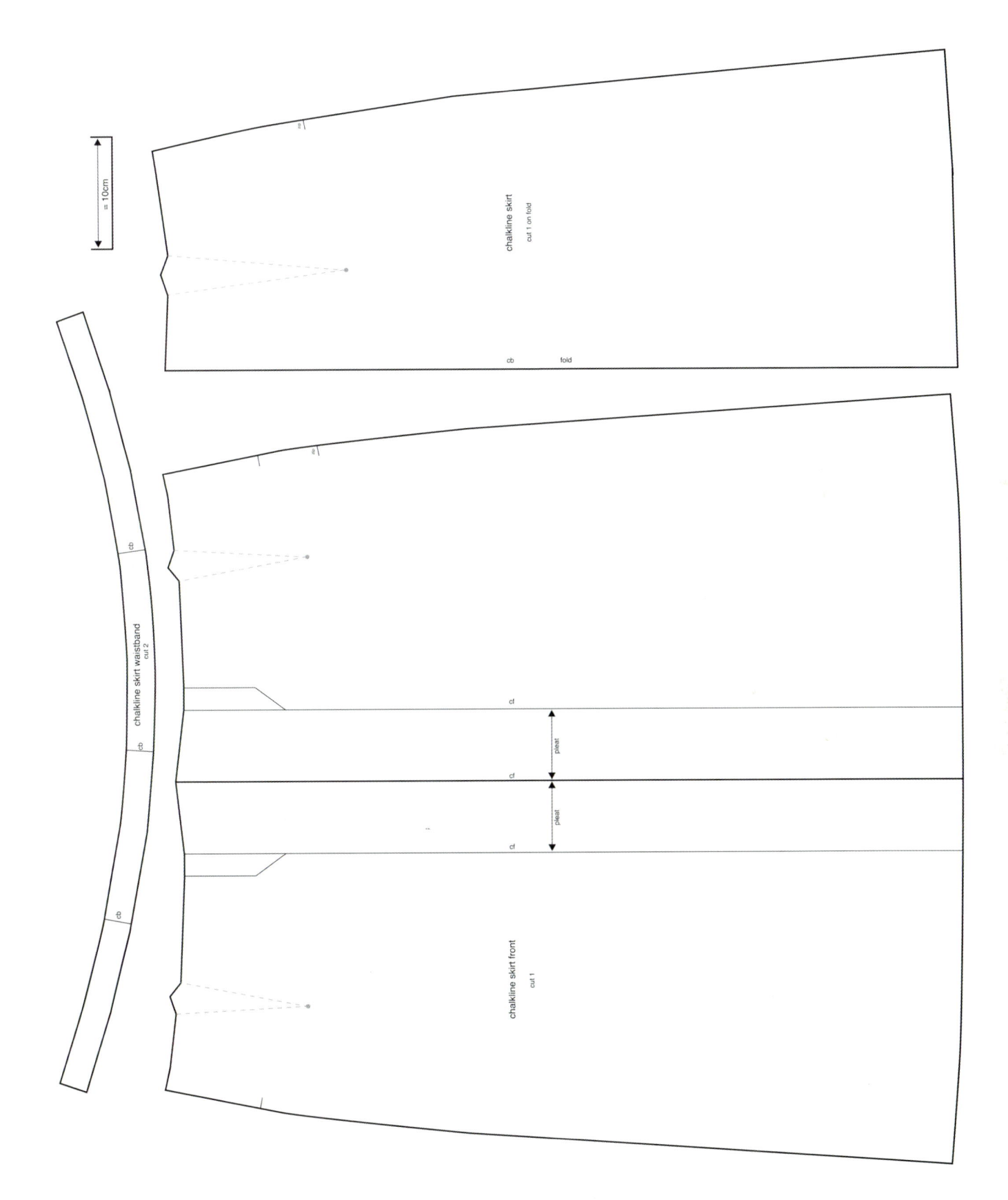

Chalkline Skirt Pattern

The stripe of the skirt lined up with that of the jacket.

Chapter 7 / The Town Suit: The Chalk Line Skirt

Avedon, Cecil Beaton and Irvine Penn. Their images – usually of beautiful young debutantes in designer clothing – over-accentuated the leanness of the style, suggesting that the skirt was significantly tighter than it really was. This fantasy was upheld by Hollywood starlets appearing in skirts so tight they had to be sewn into them and propped up on 'leaning boards' between takes because they could not sit down. This illusion gave rise to what we think of as the wiggle skirt – a significantly tighter version of the chalk line with daring side or front slits revealing a lot more leg than its original counterpart.

The leanness of the chalk line made it the perfect style for women with straighter, more athletic figures, as *Vogue* helpfully suggested back in 1950: 'To wear it well, you need a flat, taut hipline (perhaps a different girdle and some well-directed exercises …).'

The archives at Worthing Museum and Art Gallery have some wonderful examples of day suits with chalk line skirts demonstrating a variety of pleating techniques. The one shown here has a box pleat at the CF and straight-cut back. The original skirt this is based on matches the green floral rayon summer jacket in Chapter 6 and is unlined. Professionally made by a local company (Hollywood Model), it has used serging as a neatening and finishing technique. The second example, in a darker fabric, was made in a series of narrow panels – likely due to rationing – with the seams concealed in the middle of the pleat fold. The chalk line in this book has been cut over the girdle or belt from Chapter 3 to be worn either with the soft tailored jacket or with the bow tie shirt. It sits just above the natural waist and is very tight over the hip.

Cutting Out

As it matches the jacket, I have used the same vintage striped tie silk. The colour on the front was quite brash so I have again used the back as the right side. I wanted the stripes of the skirt to match up with the jacket so I matched the waist of the skirt to the waist of the jacket. The stripe aligned at the hip so I was able to mark its position on the skirt pattern pieces before cutting out. Mark the notches with a snip into the seam allowance. Mark the position of the darts and the box pleat. I have allowed 1cm seam allowance at the waist, 2cm at the side seam and 4cm at the hem but feel free to use imperial ($5/8$ in, $25/32$ in and $9/16$ in respectively) instead of metric. If you are using a plaid, stripe or motif and are trying to line it up, give yourself more seam allowance in case one layer stretches whilst you are machining and needs moving over a little to realign.

Order of Construction

1. Overlock all the edges of the pieces in matching coloured thread except the waist and waistband.
2. Pin or mark the darts in position on the front and back of the skirt and machine-stitch them. Run the stitch off the end of the dart and reverse back on to prevent it undoing. Try to keep the stripe aligned as the dart is closed
3. Fold the pleat into the CF of the skirt and pin both sides into position. This is a box pleat so make sure the 'box' is visible on the wrong side of the skirt front. On the wrong side, where the edges of the box meet at CF, tack them together and machine-stitch together 20cm/8in down; this will anchor the pleat in place. Turn the front skirt over and tack the pleat into position all the way to the hem to hold it whilst you press it. (1,2)
4. Press the darts inwards and lightly press the box pleat.
5. The zip can go in now as it is best if the skirt lies flat to do it. Sew the right side seam leaving an opening from the waist for the zip plus 5cm/2in or so for finishing. I used a 20cm/8in invisible zip and left an opening of 25cm/10in. On the right side press the seam lines so the skirt looks closed and you can also line up your stripes accurately. Position the zip wrong side up on the right side of the opening with the zipper open, then tack into position. You will need an invisible zip foot that unrolls the zip teeth as it sews. The stitch line is the pressed seam line and it should sit directly under the coil of the zip teeth. Repeat for the other side of the opening, closing the zip to check the tape position for any puckering before machining. The zip should be totally concealed on the right side and the stripes perfectly aligned. On the wrong side fold the seam allowance up with the zip sandwiched in between. Change your machine foot to a normal zip or single foot and sew down from just above the end of the zip to the side seam, closing the rest of the opening. It will be bulky next to the zip so get as close as possible. To finish the zip hand-stitch a small square of cloth underneath, turn the top edge and fold upwards. Hand-stitch the whole piece closed and anchor to the side seam. (3,4,5)

MATERIALS AND EQUIPMENT

Fabric

Threads (one for the sewing machine, three for the overlocker)

Pre-made waistband canvas

Invisible zip

Zip foot for sewing machine

Invisible zip foot for sewing machine

Hand-sewing needle for tacking

Pins

Button

1 Pleat being tacked on the right side of the skirt front; the darts are already positioned for machining on the wrong side.

2 Skirt front turned onto the wrong side with with darts machined and pleat tacked.

3 Machining the tacked right side of the zip with a concealed zipper foot.

4 Hand stitching a turned up square of cloth to the bottom of the zip.

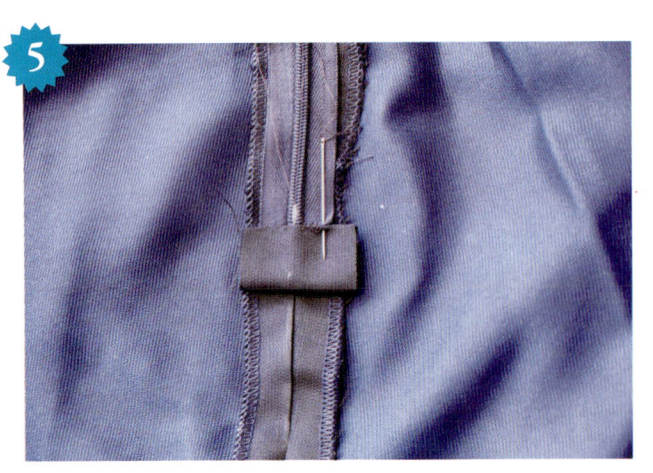

5 The finished zip end can now be anchored down to the overlocked edges of the side seams by hand.

6 Waistband being machined onto the waist.

Chapter 7 / The Town Suit: The Chalk Line Skirt

Waistband canvas is stitched to bias tape and the waistband folded downwards on the wrong side of the skirt.

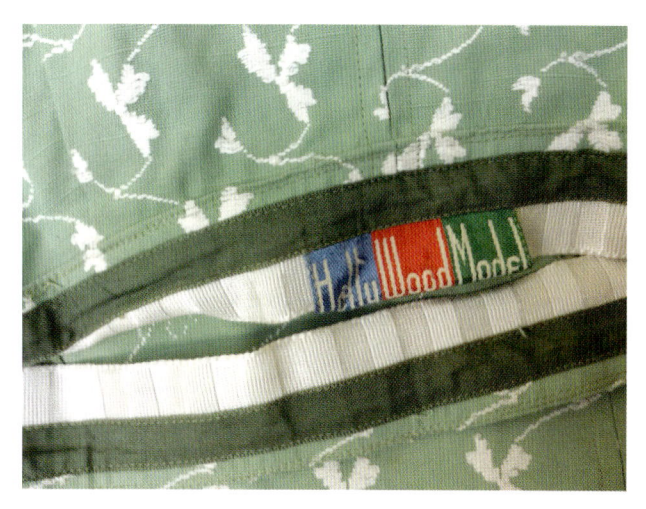

Original skirt waistband. (Worthing Museum and Art Gallery collection)

6. Sew the under seam of the waistband to the waist and press upwards. Sew a strip of bias binding to the top edge of the waistband and press flat. Stitch the waistband canvas to the bias tape and press downwards towards the waist seam. Turn the ends in and hand-stitch down. The waistband tape does not need to be stitched to the waist seam, as this is how the original is finished. (6,7)
7. Turn the hem up. Measure it to ensure it is level. Use a slip stitch to close the hem by catching the overlocking thread rather than the hem fabric and this will create less bulk at the fold of the pleat. Press and remove the tacking.

Suggested Adaptations

Change the position or number of pleats for a different look or remove it from the pattern altogether for more of a pencil skirt. There were no splits in chalk lines so you would need to add one if you want to be able to walk! Obviously a change in fabric (such as to a plain wool or a plaid for winter) will give the skirt a totally different look. You could also style it with the blouse in Chapter 8 and a small cardigan instead of the jacket.

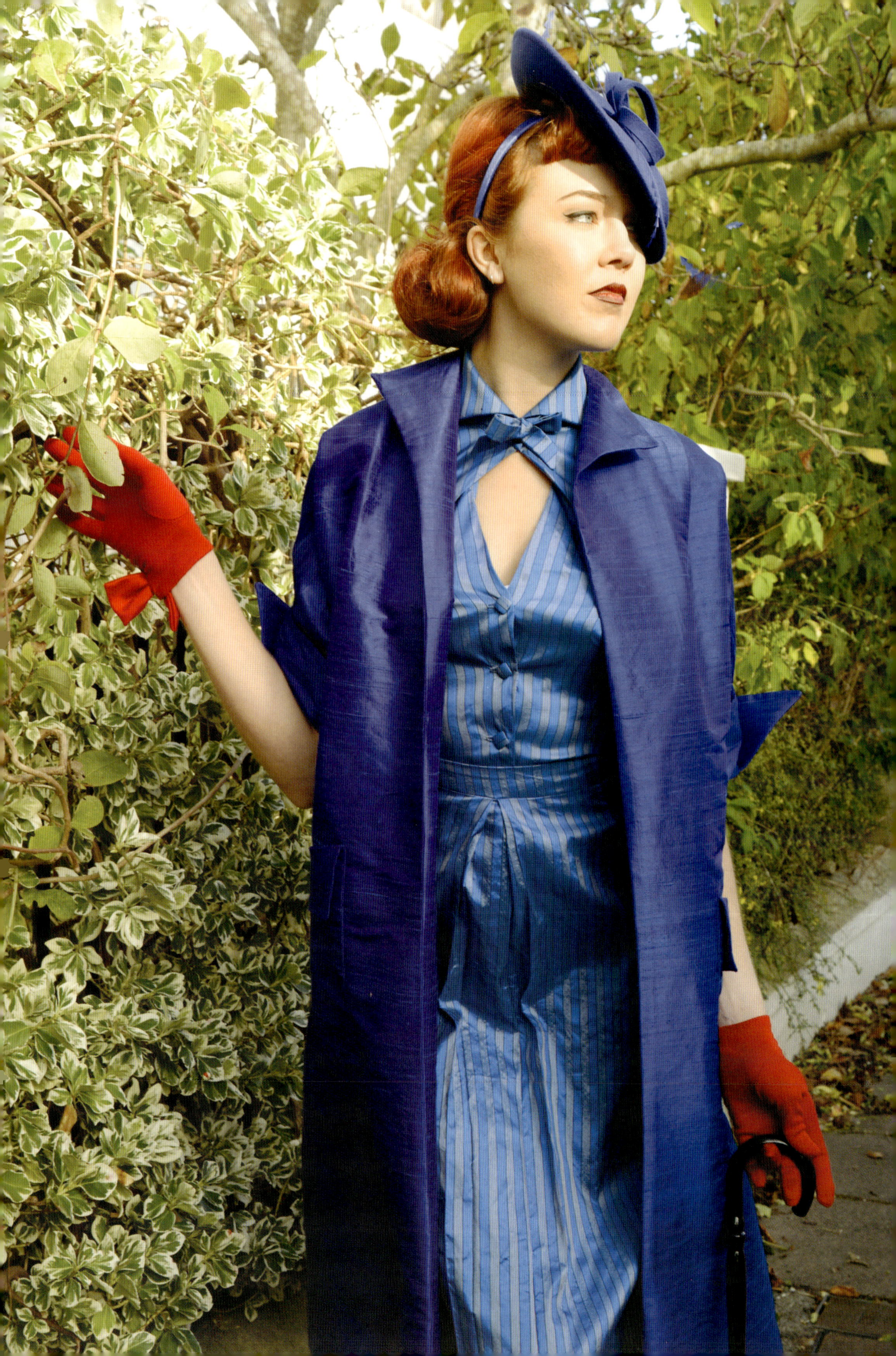

The Bow Tie Blouse

8

Throughout the thirties and forties, nylon had been exclusively owned and licensed by the DuPont company. As its applications were seemingly endless, by the late forties and early fifties the company was grappling with the tremendously high demand for its product for both domestic use (for example, for stockings) and its industrial use (for example, for parachutes, flak jackets, aircraft fuel tanks, shoelaces, etc. for the war effort). The company struggled to cope as everywhere nylon stockings appeared, and newspapers reported 'nylon riots', with hundreds of women lining up to compete for the limited supply of hosiery. Partly in order to meet demand and partly to avoid litigation based on the extravagant claims made by DuPont's marketing team, nylon was finally licensed to outside producers in 1951.

Nylon could now be used widely across a range of fashion products and not just exclusively for stockings and girdles. The variety of synthetic fibres was limited to rayon, acetates, polyesters and polyamides and manufacturers realized early on that the key to success in a highly competitive market would be to brand their products in a way that made them appear unique. This often involved creating a brand name for the fibre used in a specific range of textiles and in collaborations between nylon manufacturers and fashion designers who were supplied with free fabric and publicity. In 1955, DuPont was still the largest and had the deepest pockets and was able to heighten the glamour of its product ranges by recruiting the photographer Horst P. Horst to document the working processes of famous Paris couturiers like Coco Channel, Dior and Patou using nylon to create luxurious gowns. The glossy images were circulated widely to the international press across Europe and the US. This set a precedent for other campaigns and the sleeveless blouse in this chapter was part of a designer–manufacturer collaboration for the innovative Cumberland-based silk mill Sekers. The company was established in 1937 and originally produced high-quality silks and rayons for the fashion industry but switched almost exclusively to parachute nylon during the war. The company moved into innovative furnishing fabrics in the 1960s but not before it had been involved in collaborations with Christian Dior and Victor Steibel. Today the company focuses on interior design, creating luxury textiles and wallpapers for the hospitality and marine industries.

This blouse is based on my

Advertisement for Sekers nylon, UK *Vogue*, July 1955. (Author's own collection)

interpretation of an image and not on having seen an original garment. Interpretation is used widely in costume design for film and TV and works most believably when the design is manufactured using authentic methods for assembly and finishing. The detailing is also important, such as the right type of buttons. For reference I used the somewhat limited instructions from a vintage keyhole dress pattern and a vintage stitching and embroidery

The bow tie blouse (detail).

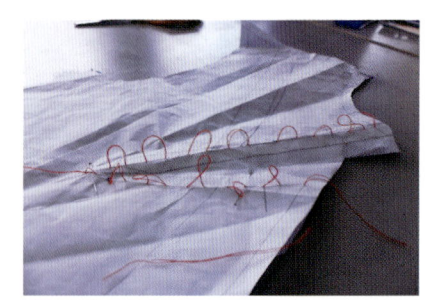

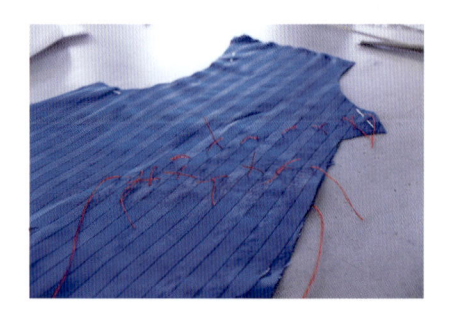

Thread marking and preparing the darts.

MATERIALS AND EQUIPMENT

Fabric

Collar canvas

Threads

Felling foot for sewing machine (optional)

Wadding for shoulder pads or pair of ready-made shoulder pads

Cover buttons

Organza to stiffen the facing

manual. The blouse has a collar and separate stand which creates the channel for the bow tie. The seams are felled and the armholes bound so the garment looks very neat inside. Small shoulder pads have been used as a counterbalance to the bustline and the pattern was draped over the bullet bra in Chapter 3. The blouse front has both a curved French dart and a folded dart at the neckline to create suppression through the chest and waist and fullness at the bust point. (A French dart comes up from low on the side seam or, as here, from the waistline and is usually larger than a simple dart; it may also be slightly curved.) I used bespoke square cover buttons and lined the stripes up to the stripes at the CF of the shirt. I have machined the buttonholes; you could do them by hand but they do not feel as robust.

Cutting Out

I used a fabric with a vertical stripe similar in width to the original image. Part of the success of the design lies in the direction of the stripe at the CF edge of the blouse so ensure that your stripes are aligned to your straight of grain. I used 1cm/$^5/_8$in seam allowance all round. This makes the flat felling fiddly so use a bigger seam allowance if you want but your finished seam width will also be wider. The angles of the darts have to be precise or the blouse doesn't fit properly at the bust point so it is best to tack these in using thread marking. Hand-tack the dart position loosely through the pattern paper then snip the loops open. Ease the pattern paper off the fabric, gently separate the fabric layers and snip through the middle of the threads.

There are a lot of small pieces to the collar. With this fabric it could not be cut on the fold because of the symmetry required for the direction of the stripes. Ensure your pieces all match up at the CB and note that the collar and canvas is cut on the bias.

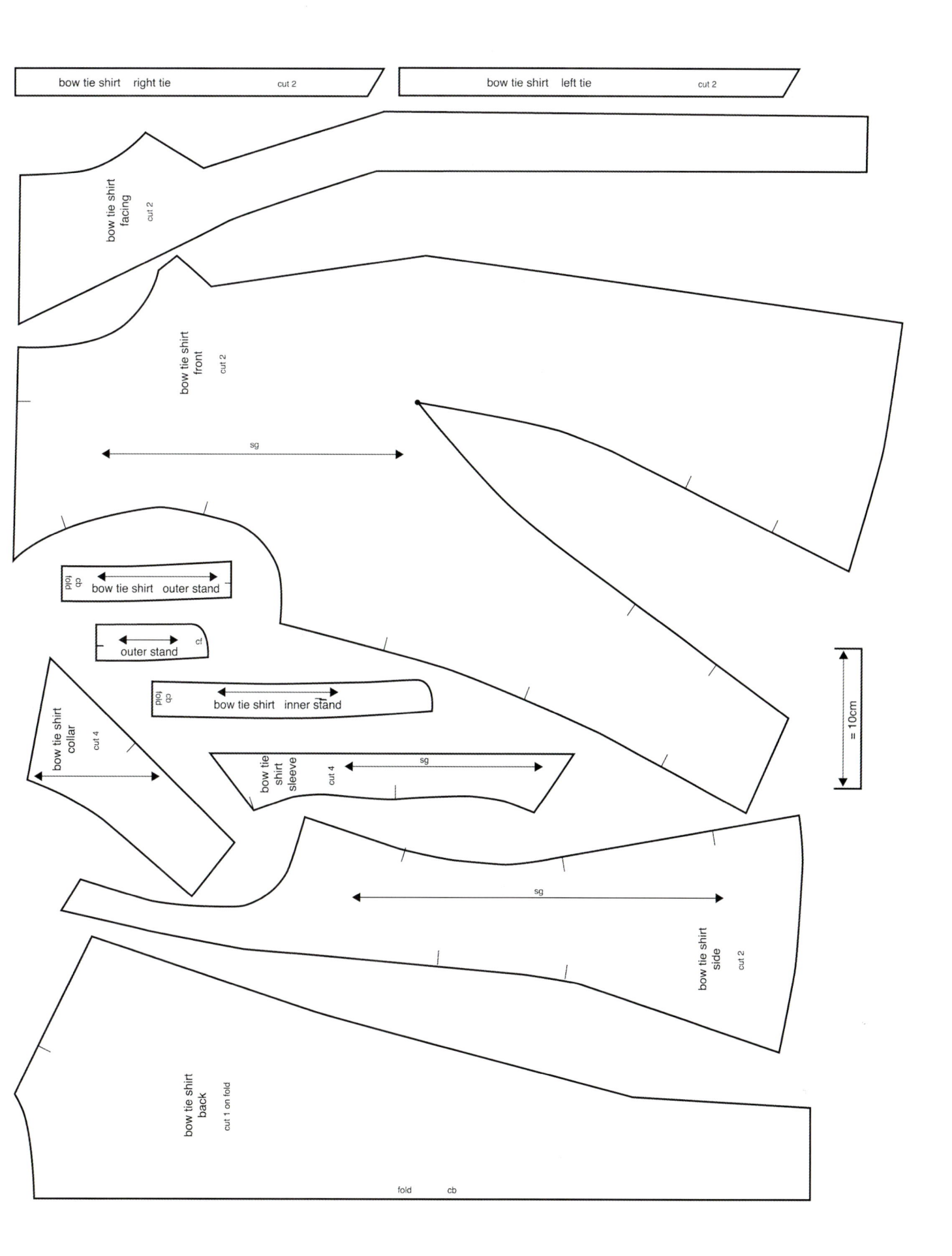

Bow Tie Blouse Pattern

Order of Construction

1. Construct the French darts from the waistline first. They are very wide so I have cut the bulk away from the middle and added seam allowance instead, so line up the notches to fit the curved edges together. Machine-stitch on the wrong side and press the seams open. Pink edges and press both seams in towards the CF. On the right side topstitch them down. (1)
2. The dart at the neck is really a fold anchored at the bust point. On the wrong side fold the dart into position and press the volume upwards and away from the CF. On the wrong side hand-stitch the underside of the dart from the bust point for approximately 3cm/$1^3/_{16}$ in to keep it sharp and in place: you should not be able see the stitching from the bust point on the right side. Press the bust point over a ham. Machine-tack or pin the top of the fold at the neckline to help anchor its position. (2,3)
3. Prepare the facings by turning the inside edge over and machine-stitching it down to finish. (4)
4. Attach the facing to the front of the blouse. At the CF make a notch the depth of (but not deeper than) your seam allowance at the apex of the keyhole. This is also the point where the neckline folds over itself. Machine-stitch up to the apex notch only and not beyond. Reverse-stitch to finish. Turn the facing through and roll the edges between your fingers, as with the jacket in Chapter 6, and press lightly. Open the facing out again and on the right side under-stitch the seam allowance to the facing along the CF. To finish the top of the facing, press the seam allowance from the notch inwards and see how it wants to lie naturally under the fold of the shell. Hand-finish closed on the inside. (5,6)
5. The side seams and shoulder seams are flat felled. This is a sturdy finish as well as decorative but as it is formed on the right side of the fabric the width has to be uniform. With the wrong sides of fabric together, stitch along the

1 Topstitching the French dart.

2 Hand-stitching the underside of the fold down at the bust point.

3 Pressing the bust point over a ham.

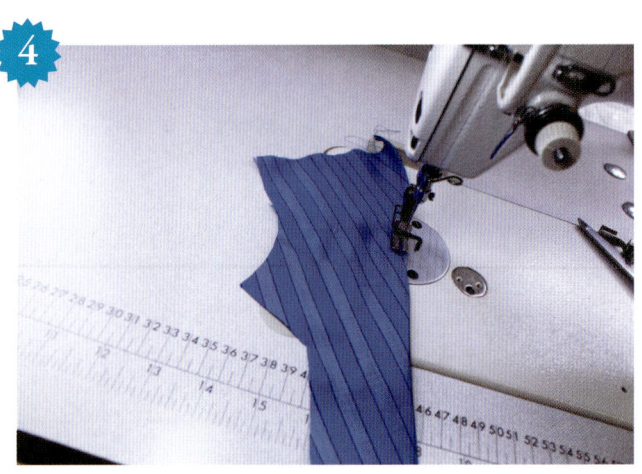

4 Topstitching the turned facing edge.

Chapter 8 / The Bow Tie Blouse

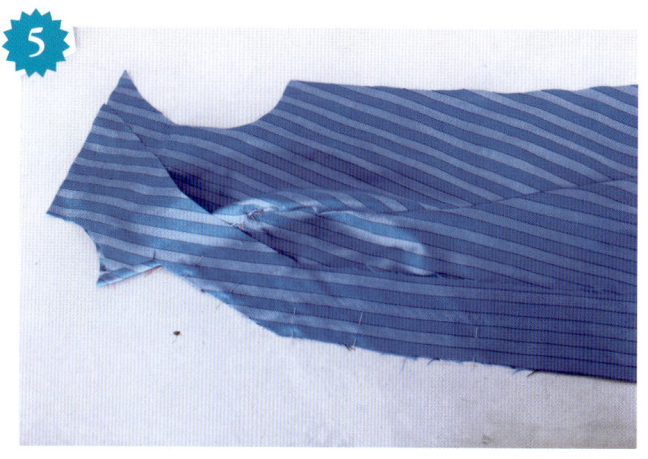

5 Facing pinned at the CF with a notch snipped at the keyhole apex. Please note the pins and the stitching do not extend beyond the notch.

6 Under-stitching the facing.

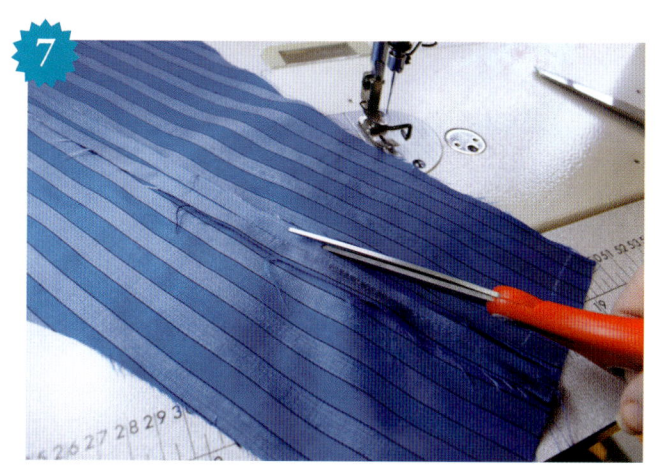

7 Trimming away one side of the seam allowance.

8 Machining the pressed edge down.

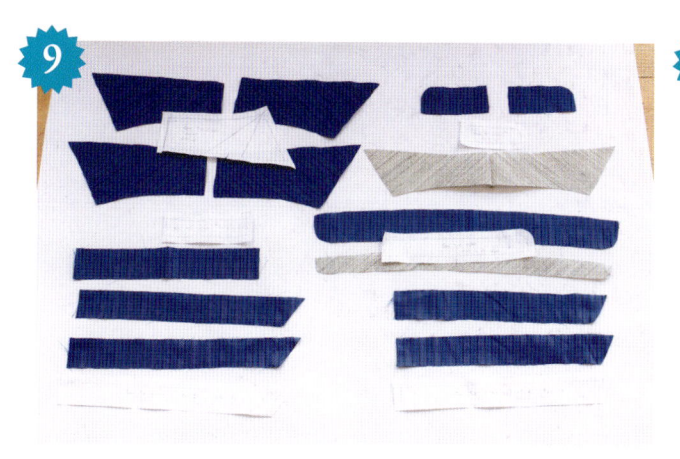

9 Lining up the stripes on the collar and ties.

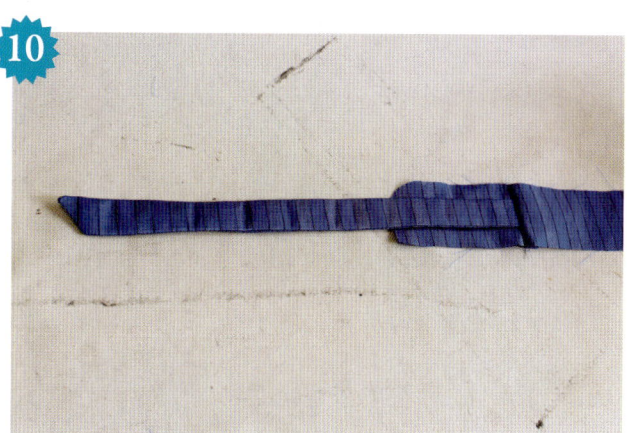

10 Tie sandwiched between the top collar stand seams seen from the right side.

11

Making the shoulder pad covers.

12

Finished shoulder pads.

13

Finishing the armhole with a loop of bias binding.

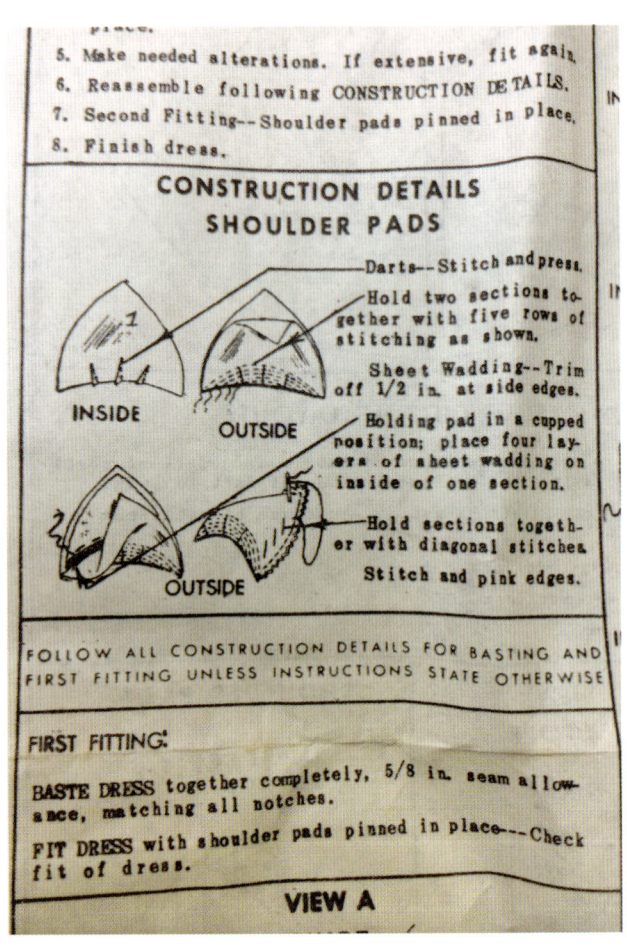

Butterick pattern 4538, instructions for shoulder pads. (Author's own collection)

seam line. Press open and then to one side. Trim the inner seam allowance to 3mm/$^1/_8$ in and press the outer edge of the other seam allowance under by 6mm/$^1/_4$ in. Stitch the folded edge down to the garment over the other seam allowance and make sure you stitch all of them down in the same direction. Make sure the shoulder seams go towards the front. Use a felling foot on your machine if you have one – it will roll the fabric and sew at the same time and you won't need to press first. (7,8)

6. Take time to align the stripes for the collar and ties before beginning the construction of the component parts. Pin the tie pieces right sides together and sew around the outside edges. Trim away any bulk at the corners and turn through. The channels are narrow so you might want to catch the closed end with a loop of thread on a needle and pull the end through; this is also a handy trick for pulling out corners to make them sharp. Press. Hand-tack the collar canvas to the continuous piece of the inner stand. Construct the top collar by sandwiching the finished ties between the back piece and the two front pieces either side. Machine-stitch together on the wrong side and turn back over. Make the collar next. Tack the canvas to the under

Chapter 8 / The Bow Tie Blouse

collar and machine-sew the halves of the top collar and bottom collar together. Press the CB seams open and put the top and bottom collars together right side to right side. Machine-stitch round, trim the corners, turn through and press. As with the jacket collar in Chapter 6 the collar tips are at the narrowest edge and not the widest so it will look like you have sewn the wrong pieces together at first. Sandwich the collar between the two pieces of the collar stand with the ties away from the edges, right sides to right sides. Make sure the bottom edge of the collar is aligned with the top edge of the collar stand. Machine-stitch round the length of the collar stand. Trim the corners away and snip in round the curve to release the tension in the fabric. Turn the whole piece through and press. The completed collar is ready to attach to the neckline. (9,10)

7. To attach the collar and stand, line up the notches of the top collar to the neckline at CF, CB and shoulder, right side to right side. Pin and tack. Before machine-stitching down, press the seam flat and trim and grade the seam allowances to reduce the bulk. Trim diagonally to remove any bulk at the ends. Carefully press the seam open then up into the collar. Bring the edge of the inside collar down to align with the seam line. Turn the seam allowance up into the collar and slip-stitch closed by hand.

8. You will need a pair of small blouse shoulder pads covered in the same fabric as the blouse. I have used shop-bought ones but included instructions from a Butterick pattern (no. 4538) if you want to make your own. Fold a small piece of your fabric in half. Place your shoulder pad on the fabric and trace round it in chalk leaving 2cm/$^{25}/_{32}$ in seam allowance. Cut out and pin with the shoulder pad sandwiched between the two layers of cloth. Machine-stitch as close to the edge of the pad as possible and trim the seam allowance down. Pink the edges to finish. Stiffen the cuff detail by tacking one layer of the fabric to a piece of organza. Fold the fabric in half, right side to right side, and stitch down the outside edges. On the wrong side, trim the bulk off diagonally at the corners and turn through and press. Line the notches up at the shoulder seam with seam allowances together. The cuff should be placed onto the shoulder of the shirt facing towards the collar. Pin or tack and machine-stitch on. (11,12)

9. To position the shoulder pads, put the blouse back on the mannequin and pin the CF closed. The edge of the pad should sit level with the blouse and cuff seam allowance and the centre of the pad should run along the shoulder seam. Adjust as necessary and pin into place. Hand-stitch the pad to the shoulder seam on the inside but make sure the stitching is not visible from the outside. Machine-tack the seam allowance of the pad to the stitch line for the cuff and shoulder. The armhole is then bound to finish it. Measure the circumference of your armhole first and cut a piece of bias binding to the right length plus seam allowance. Join the ends together to make a loop and press the seams open. Open one side of the binding and on the right side of the garment pin it to the seam line all the way round the armhole. Bias tape obviously has some stretch in it so if it is a little tight just ease it on. Trim the seam allowance of the blouse down to 3mm/$^{1}/_{8}$in and turn the tape through the armhole into the inside. The other edge of your bias tape should already be pre-pressed so pin flat to the armhole and either machine-stitch down or do it by hand with a slip stitch. (13)

10. Finish the bottom with a pin hem. Open out the facing first. Turn the edge up by 6mm/$^{3}/_{8}$ in and stitch a machine foot's width in from the bottom edge. Trim the raw edge down to the stitch line and roll over by 6mm/$^{3}/_{8}$ in again. Stitch again a machine foot's width from the fabric edge. Turn the facing back and catch by hand to the blouse hem inside. Press and mark off your buttonholes on the right side of the fabric along the CF. The cover buttons have a shank which is fine for the main body but I used a flat shirt button on the collar stand so that it didn't interfere with the bow.

Suggested Adaptations

Don't use stripes unless you feel really confident! The blouse is a really good shape and would work in plain cottons or silks and with floral print. If you are not trying to match anything up it will take less time to make. You could also make your own bias binding in a contrasting colour or print and use original vintage buttons instead of cover buttons.

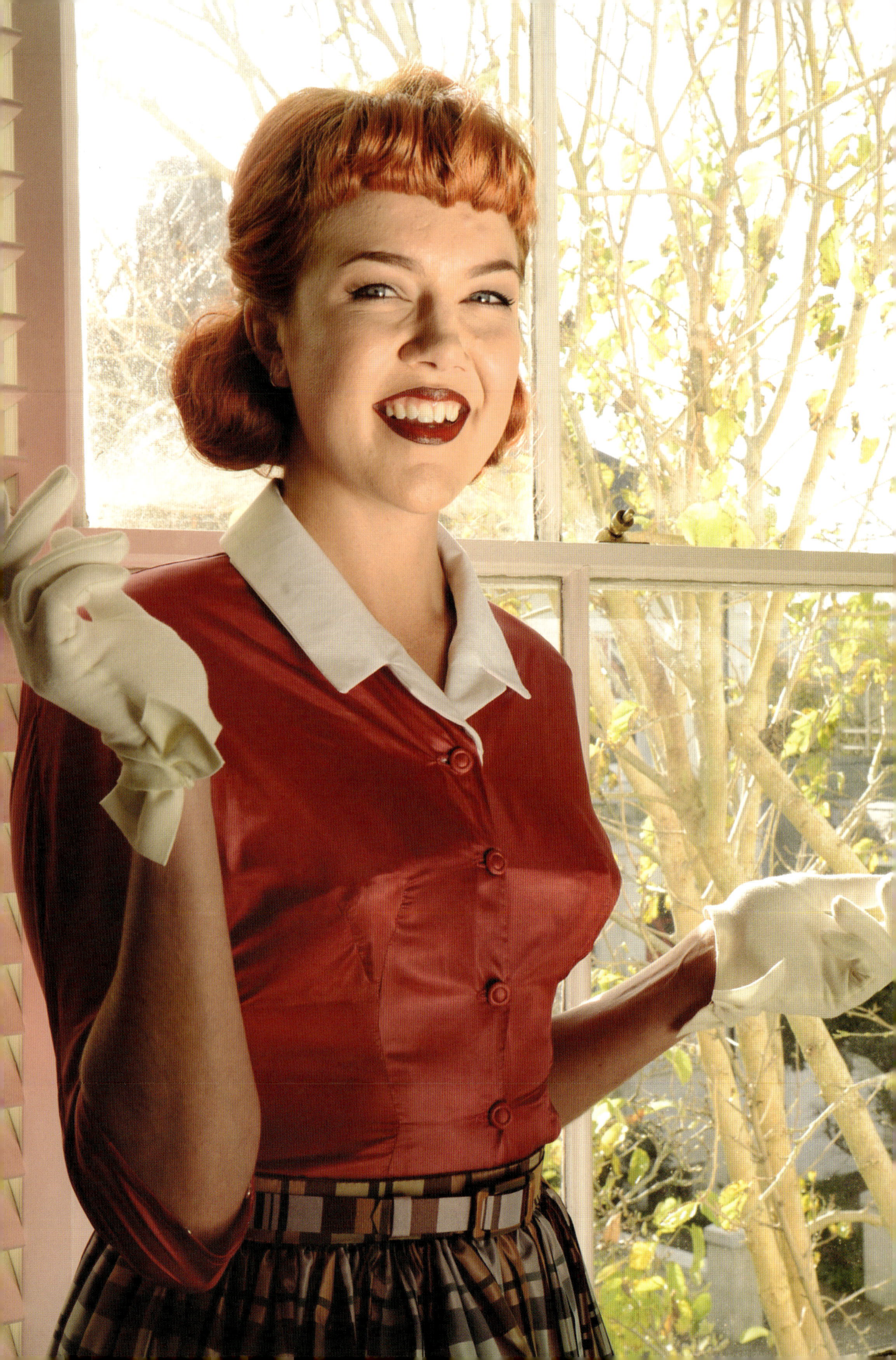

The Housewife's Kimono Shirt with Detachable Collar and Cuffs

The softer look of the idealized homemaker was frequently captured for film and TV in the selective wardrobes of actresses like Audrey Hepburn or Lucille Ball. Sheila Hardy offers an insightful foray into women's lives in the fifties in her book *A 1950s Housewife: Marriage and Homemaking in the 1950s*. She provides an anecdotal trip down memory lane challenging our preferred ideal of the 1950s woman as an effortlessly well-groomed homemaker hell-bent on finding, keeping and pleasing a husband. The daily routines she recounts highlight how physically demanding chores could be with no modern appliances. Her descriptions of fashions from the time also make it clear that you would not be scrubbing the cooker in a tailored and sculpted town suit or in a girdle you couldn't bend down in.

Aside from a housecoat to keep clothes cleaner, detachable collars and cuffs gave clothes more versatility and saved on time spent laundering. Worthing Museum and Art Gallery have a Wetherall nylon shirtwaister dress in their collection which provided an analysis for the way in which the detachable collar and cuffs were executed. The Wetherall company originated in Denby in Wales and moved to Bond Street, London in 1952.

Fitted kimono blouse worn with detachable collar and cuff with soft gathered skirt.

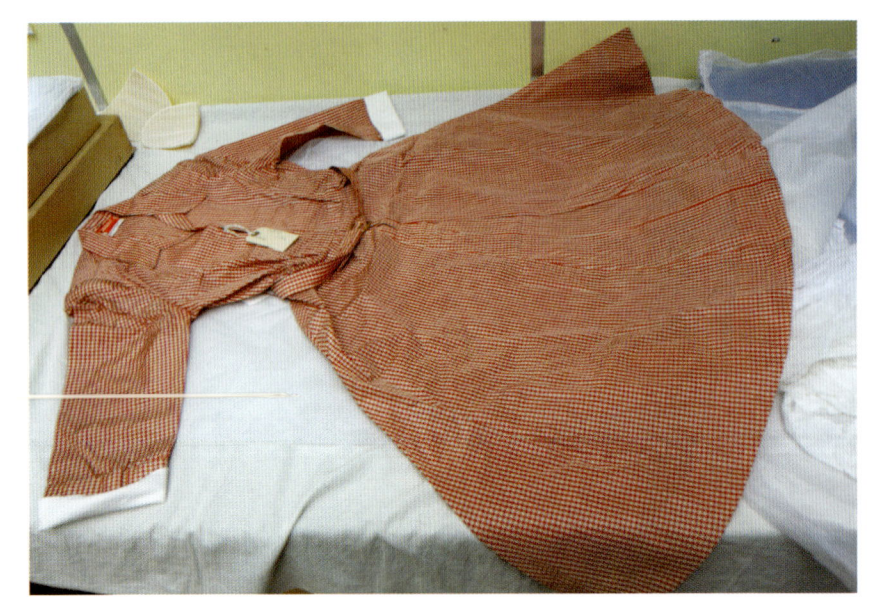

They specialized in smart sportswear and countrywear, often made in synthetic and cotton blends that could be worn in more than one way. This 'transformational' element was used as part of their advertising campaign as one of the company's unique selling points.

I looked at a large range of vintage patterns for this book and found consistent repeats for garments with kimono and dolman sleeves throughout the decade. The basic silhouette remained as standard with little deviation although the detailing changed. The shirts were all figure-skimming and shaped with either the

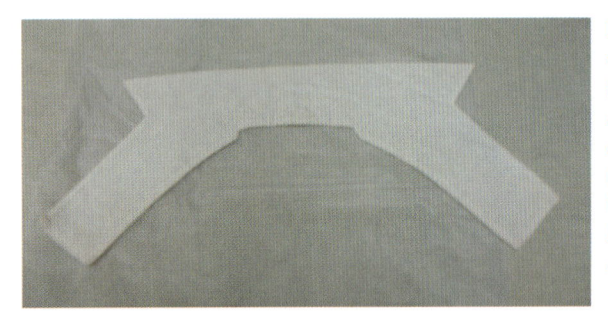

Wetherall shirtwaister dress without detachable collar. (Worthing Museum and Art Gallery collection)

Detachable collar piece for Wetherall shirtwaister dress. (Worthing Museum and Art Gallery collection)

Vintage Butterick pattern for kimono blouse. (Author's own collection)

Wetherall advertisement showing a coat worn four ways, *Vogue* September 1955. (Author's own collection)

Chapter 9 / The Housewife's Kimono Shirt with Detachable Collar and Cuffs

Fitted Kimono Shirt Pattern

MATERIALS AND EQUIPMENT

Fabric for the blouse

Fabric for the collar and cuffs

Threads

Pinking shears

Scissors

Pins

Cover buttons

Shoulder pads

Ham for pressing

Organza or net for facings and to reinforce the gusset

Canvas for collar and cuff stiffening

Press studs

Sewing needles

Sleeve board

Spray starch

forked dart used in this design or two separate waist darts. The kimono blouse has a characteristic overarm seam and a gusset inserted into the underarm: the gusset is usually a small piece of fabric inserted into a slash opening to provide ease for a comfortable fit. This one-piece gusset is harder to insert than a two-piece, particularly as it is embedded in a side panel, but it does eliminate the underarm seam entirely. Ideally you want the gusset length on the bias for maximum ease of movement. Preparing the gusset in the 1950s way is made slightly harder for not having access to a fusible interfacing, so feel free to cheat this fiddly technique! The method used here is from the *Odhams Encyclopaedia of Needlecraft* – also a car boot find – from 1952. The pattern was draped over the bullet bra from Chapter 3.

Cutting Out

This pink shirt is in a lightweight triacetate with cotton poplin collar and cuffs. You will need to mount the facings on organza to stiffen them slightly before construction. I have used 1cm seam allowance all round with 2cm at the side seams for adjustment: imperial equivalents would be $^5/_8$ in and $^{25}/_{32}$ in. The seams are pinked to finish. The pattern pieces are peculiar shapes so it is best to tack the CF when you are preparing the pieces for construction and use chalk to mark the gusset line. Do not cut into it at this point. I would also use tailor tacks or ordinary tacking to mark the dart points. It is also important to make sure the grain lines are right or the sleeve will twist. As the body and sleeve are effectively one piece, if your fabric is wide enough you can fold it in half and line the CB up to the fold before cutting out.

Order of Construction

1. Sew all the darts first. Please note there is an elbow dart for this design. My fabric is thin so I left the threads long at the top of my darts and tied a knot in them ending directly on the bust point but if you are using a cotton, silk or rayon then back-stitch to hold as usual. Press the large dart towards the CF and the smaller dart to the side to reduce the bulk. Sew the large curved dart on the back, matching up the notches first. Press towards the CB. (1,2)
2. Sew the side front panel to the front panel. Line up the notches and pin or tack together. It is easier to machine on the side where the darts are visible so that they don't roll backwards under the machine foot. Start machining from the point of the V where the two darts converge. Use a reverse stitch to anchor the end. Then, starting from the V again, sew the panel towards the side seam. This gives a sharper finish than trying to pivot the fabric around the needle to sew the seam in one go. (3)
3. Reinforce the gusset opening by tacking a strip of organza over the gusset line where the slit will be cut. To anchor the organza, stay-stitch with your machine no more than 3mm/$^1/_8$ in either side of the slit position. Press and cut the slit open. If you are working with a more stable fabric you may only need to reinforce the point of the slash opening (4,5).
4. To insert the gusset sew the underarm seam of the front and

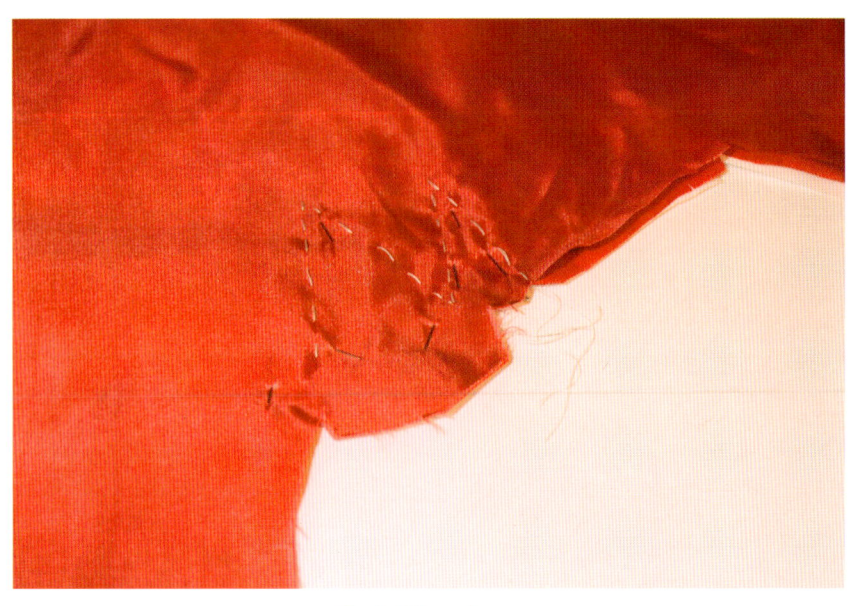

Tacked bust darts.

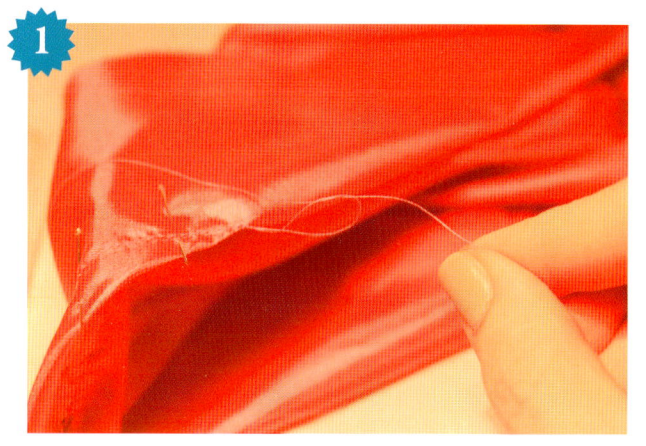

1. Knotting the threads at the bust point.

2. Pressed bust darts.

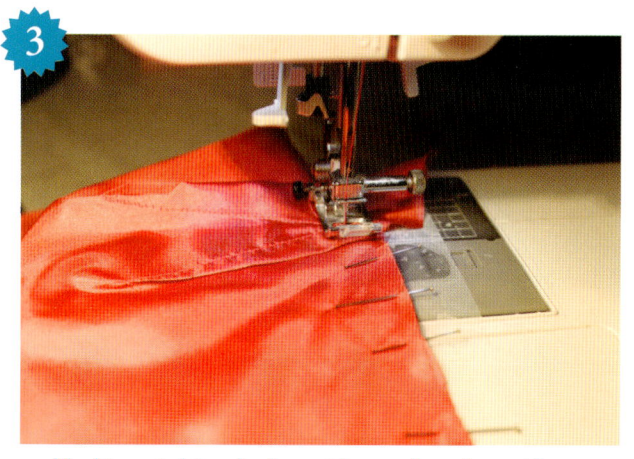

3. Machine-stitching the front side panel on, darts side up, starting where the bottom of the darts converge.

4. Preparing the gusset; note the finished side front panel seams.

5. Stay-stitching the reinforced gusset slit 0.5cm from the opening.

6. Slip-stitching the collar closed from the inside.

back of the blouse first. Put them right side to right side, line up the notches and sew up to the apex of the slash. Press the seam open. To position the gusset panel properly, lay the whole blouse piece right side up flat on the table. Now lay the gusset panel over the top, also right side up, lining up the corresponding corners of the gusset to the opening. Roughly pin into position and flip everything over so it is now all wrong side up. Carefully pin up the back side seam over the gusset and down the other side along the front side panel. Tack the seams together before machining round in one go.

You may be able to get the corners of the gusset sharp just by lifting the machine foot with the needle in and pivoting the fabric round. If you can't then fold the garment back along each side seam with the gusset behind the back or front pieces and overstitch each corner slowly, turning your machine

89

7

The finished raglan pad.

8

Blouse before pressing, without collar, cuffs and fastenings.

wheel by hand if necessary. If the apex of the gusset doesn't lie flat then snip up to the seam line on the blouse body only and press. The gusset should sit flat on top of the opening so your back side seams will be pressed towards the CB and the front side seams pressed towards the CF. Topstitching from the front is an attractive way to finish.

5. Turn the garment inside out so that you can line up the front and back overarms and machine-stitch them. Use a sleeve board to press the seams open.
6. Sew up the CB seam and press open if you did not cut your garment on the fold.
7. To prepare the neckline, tack your facings onto an organza or light canvas interlining on the wrong side. Finish the raw edge. You can overlock, turn and topstitch to anchor the interlining safely inside. Pin the facing to the front of the blouse along the CF. The blouse has a one-piece convertible collar with a revers so it won't button all the way up to the neck. Start machining from the revers notch. When you notch, snip down to but not beyond the stitch line. Reverse-stitch to anchor. Sew along the CF and trim the bulk out diagonally across the corners before turning through and pressing. Where the notch has been snipped, part of the seam allowance will be turned inside the facing and shell and the other part will be standing up ready for the collar to be attached to it. Under-stitch the seam allowance to the facing.
8. Prepare the one-piece convertible collar as per the soft tailored jacket in Chapter 6. Attach the under collar to the neckline. Position by matching up the CB notches first and pinning round until the end of the collar meets the facing notch at the front. Turn the facing inside out again and, starting just behind the notch where the facing seam is, begin machining all the way round the collar to just beyond the collar notch on the other side. You may need to snip down into the neckline seam allowance to, but not through, the stitch line to release the tension and get a better curve. Press with the seam allowance eased upwards into the collar. Turn the collar up and, working on the wrong side of the blouse, turn the collar seam allowance under and slip-stitch down onto the neckline. The hem of the blouse can be pin-hemmed as per the bow tie blouse in Chapter 8. The sleeves are bound using the same flat binding technique as the bras in Chapter 3. (6)
9. Prepare the shoulder pads as per the bow tie blouse in Chapter 8. Please note I have used a small pre-made raglan instead of a set-in pad this time. I eased the fabric cover on, pinned it into position and steamed the excess away but you could easily put a dart in it to

Chapter 9 / The Housewife's Kimono Shirt with Detachable Collar and Cuffs

9

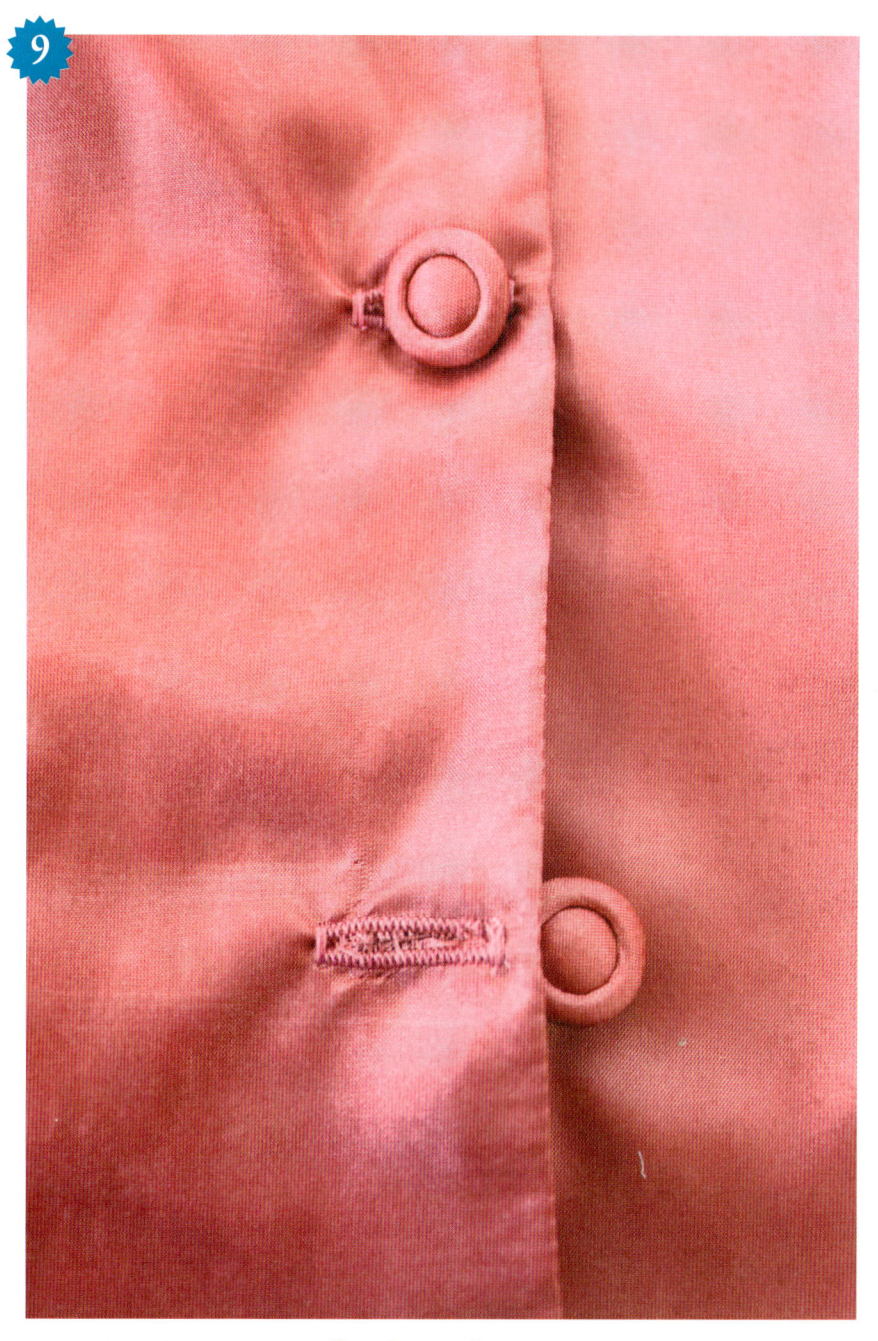

Bespoke cover buttons.

The Detachable Collar

The pattern for the detachable collar has a diagonal line running across it. Trace this off and cut out a pair in fabric along with the collar pieces. This part will create a flap where the collar and revers can be inserted: this is the method used by Wetherall. The tabs at the bottom of the collar roll over the break line of the shirt and sit against the facing on the inside. We have used a press stud for the left side and the button from the main blouse on the right. If you are putting a buttonhole in, line it up to the buttonhole on the blouse and make the shank of the button a little longer to accommodate both layers. (1,2)

1. Turn the edge of the revers flap and turn over onto the wrong side. Press and topstitch to neaten. Lay the flap over the corresponding ends of the under collar right sides up and tack together. Put the top collar and bottom collar together right side to right side and tack or pin. Leaving at least a 10cm/4in opening (5cm/2in either side of the CB) at the bottom of the collar, sew the two pieces together. There is a lot of shaping in such a small piece so snip into the seam allowance down to but not beyond the stitch line at the neck point where the seam curves steeply. Trim away excess seam allowance on any corners and trim down between the collar and revers. Snip into but not through the centre of the V or the collar notch on the outside edge: this will allow you to get a flat sharp finish when the collar is turned through. (3)
2. Pull the collar through the opening at the bottom so that it is right sides out. Press. (4)
3. The collar canvas is cut 3mm/$1/8$in smaller than the collar and inserted through the opening as a loose piece to reduce bulk. (5)
4. Press the seam allowance on the opening up into the collar and stitch closed by hand.

replicate the pad inside. To position the shoulder pads put the blouse back on the stand with the CF pinned closed. (7,8)

10. Mark the buttonholes on the right side of the fabric. Mine are machined (rather than finished by hand) and cut open: your sewing machine manual will have instructions for this. I have used bespoke cover buttons to finish. (9)

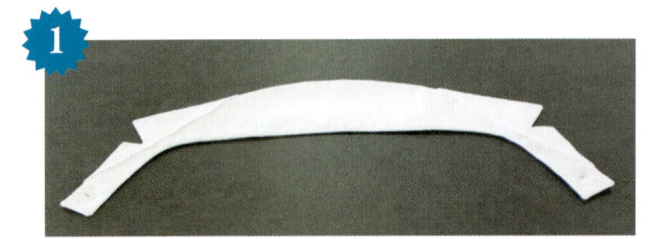

1. Detached collar.

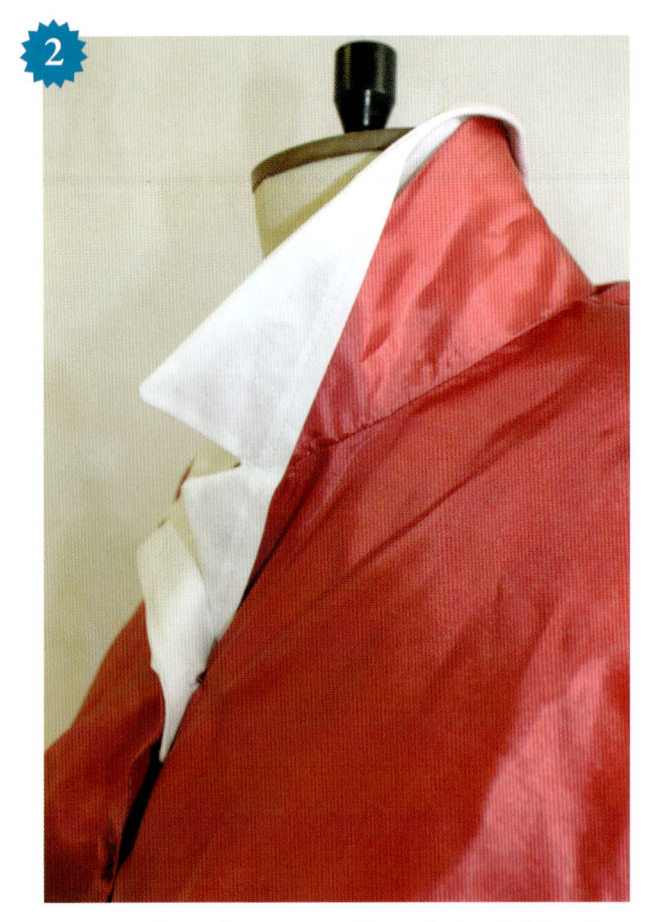

2. Blouse collar and revers inserted into the detachable collar.

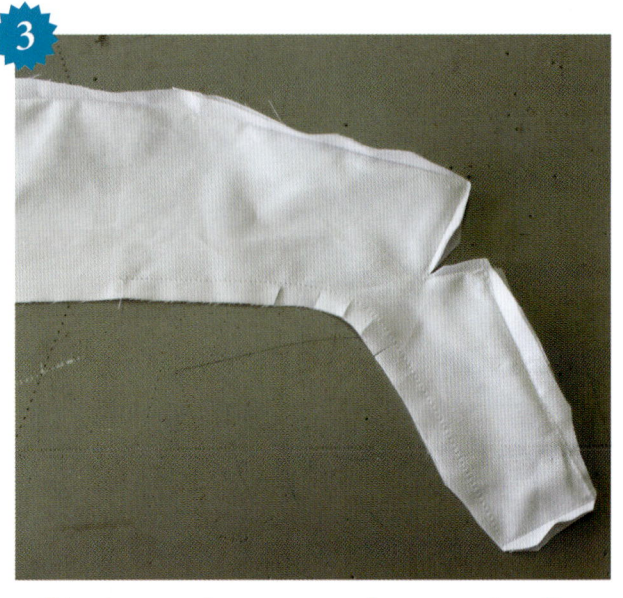

3. Trimming away the excess seam allowance on the collar.

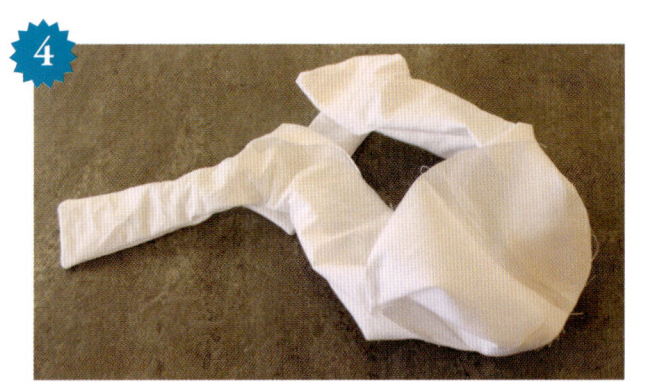

4. Turning the collar through.

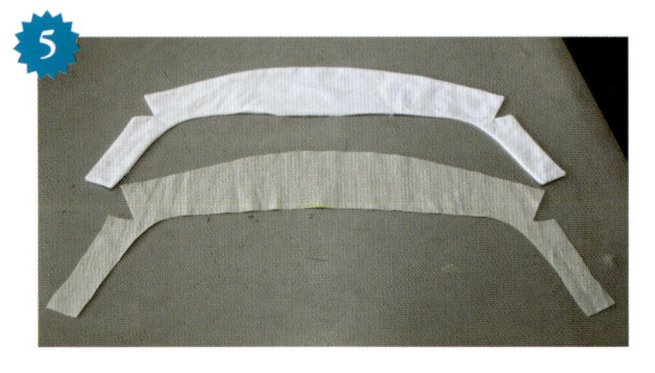

5. Collar and canvas; the canvas is 3mm/$\frac{1}{8}$ in smaller.

Chapter 9 / The Housewife's Kimono Shirt with Detachable Collar and Cuffs

The Detachable Cuffs

The cuffs are stiffened rectangles that are press-studded onto the inside of the cuff of the blouse. I have left the back seam open for the turn-up but you can also do them closed in one continuous loop as per the cuffs of the Wetherall dress shown near the start of this chapter. (1)

1. Tack the bottom half of the cuff to a piece of soft canvas. Fold the cuff in half with right sides together. Sew the sides up but leave the bottom open for now. Turn the seam allowances up and inwards to press. Trim the corners off on the diagonal and press the seams open on a narrow sleeve board. I used a thin piece of wood to get a sharp corner when pressing. (2)
2. Turn the cuff through and press on the right side. Topstitch around the whole edge, closing the opening at the bottom as you go. Press along the fold line. The fold line will become the bottom of the cuff once the press studs are sewn on. (3)
3. With the cuff opening placed against the overarm seam put the folded cuff over the bottom of the sleeve and mark off where you want your press studs. There should be enough to hold the cuff in place. (4)

Suggested Adaptations

The blouse is already versatile but you could play with the position of the buttons on the CF and group them in pairs rather than individually. You might also want to experiment with starching the collar and cuffs for extra sharpness. I used a spray starch before pressing for the final photos. You could also have a closed cuff as part of a set or put buttons on it so that you have more variants for the threequarter-length sleeve. You can also cut the sleeve short with or without the cuff: just make sure that the cuff circumference is the same as that of the sleeve.

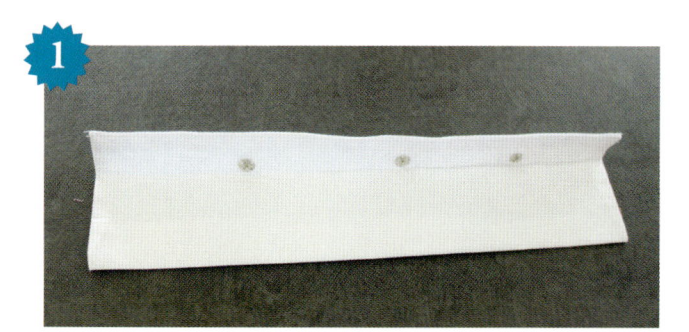

1 Detached cuff.

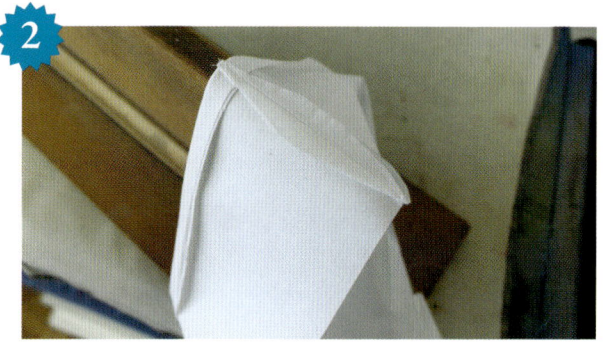

2 Pressing the cuff seam open; note that the seam allowance is pressed and stitched up inside the cuff.

3 Topstitching the cuff closed.

4 Finished cuff with corresponding pressstuds inside the cuff and inside the bottom of the sleeve.

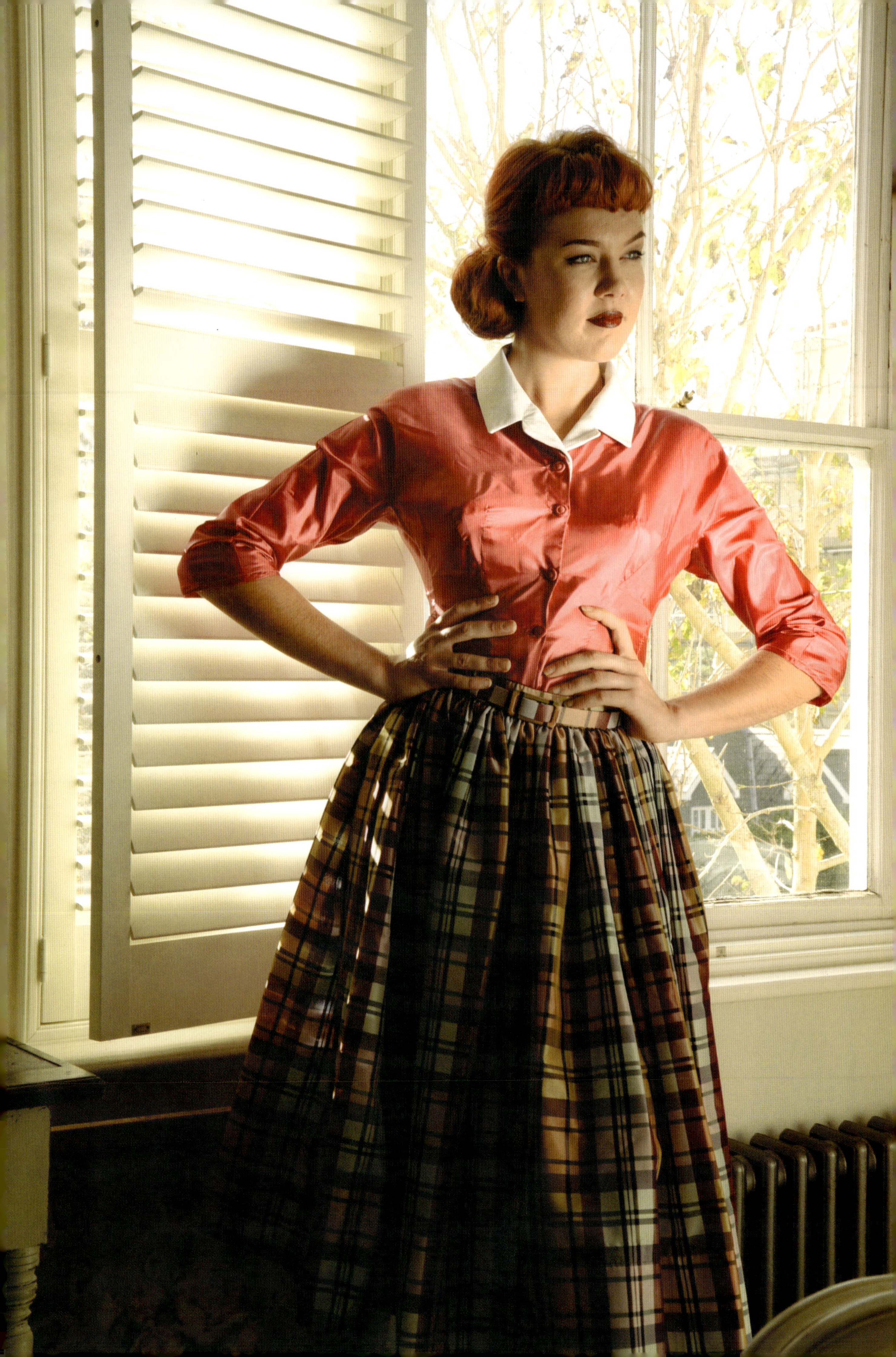

The Self-Neatening Gathered Skirt

10

The soft gathered skirt in this chapter and the fitted kimono shirt in Chapter 9 are inspired by a page in a scrapbook I bought at a car boot sale: a glamorous housewife has been cut from one magazine and glued next to the image of a brand new kitchen; on the other page are teenage girls (who look very much like the royal girls of the day) playing the piano; some children's fashions and a scenic view of Norfolk (according to the back of the postcard!) complete the page. Perhaps the images are not as random as they appear at first glance, but rather more suggestive of 'domestic bliss' from the scrapbook-maker's perspective. I was delighted when I tracked down the original image of the 'housewife' by chance and discovered that she was actually another example for the Sekers designer collaborations mentioned in Chapter 8: in this instance the collaboration was with the company Horrockses. Horrockses Fashions was one of most respected ready-to-wear labels of the late forties and fifties.

Founded in 1946, the company concentrated on the production of quality womenswear, beach clothes, housecoats and children's attire. Although produced in considerable quantities, the firm maintained an air of exclusivity with an emphasis on

The soft gathered skirt.

Scrapbook pages. (Author's own collection)

Sekers advertising campaign, UK *Vogue*, September 1955. (Author's own collection)

good-quality fabrics – especially cotton – with custom-designed patterns and couture styling. Horrockses designs had a distinctive look, celebrated for their lively floral prints and full-skirted summer dresses. The label is most famous today for its own collaborations with contemporary artists such as Eduardo Paolozzi, Alastair Morton and Graham Sutherland who created prints for their fabrics. Uncharacteristically for a Horrockses outfit this is quite restrained, with its plain shirt and striped skirt, but the cut of the skirt is synonymous with the brand.

This is actually a relatively simple

MATERIALS AND EQUIPMENT

Fabric

Scissors

Calico or cotton poplin for hem

Tape measure or metre rule

Pins

Hook and bar

Threads

Press studs

Organza to stiffen

Toile in calico.

Chapter 10 / The Self-Neatening Gathered Skirt

fold to self neaten

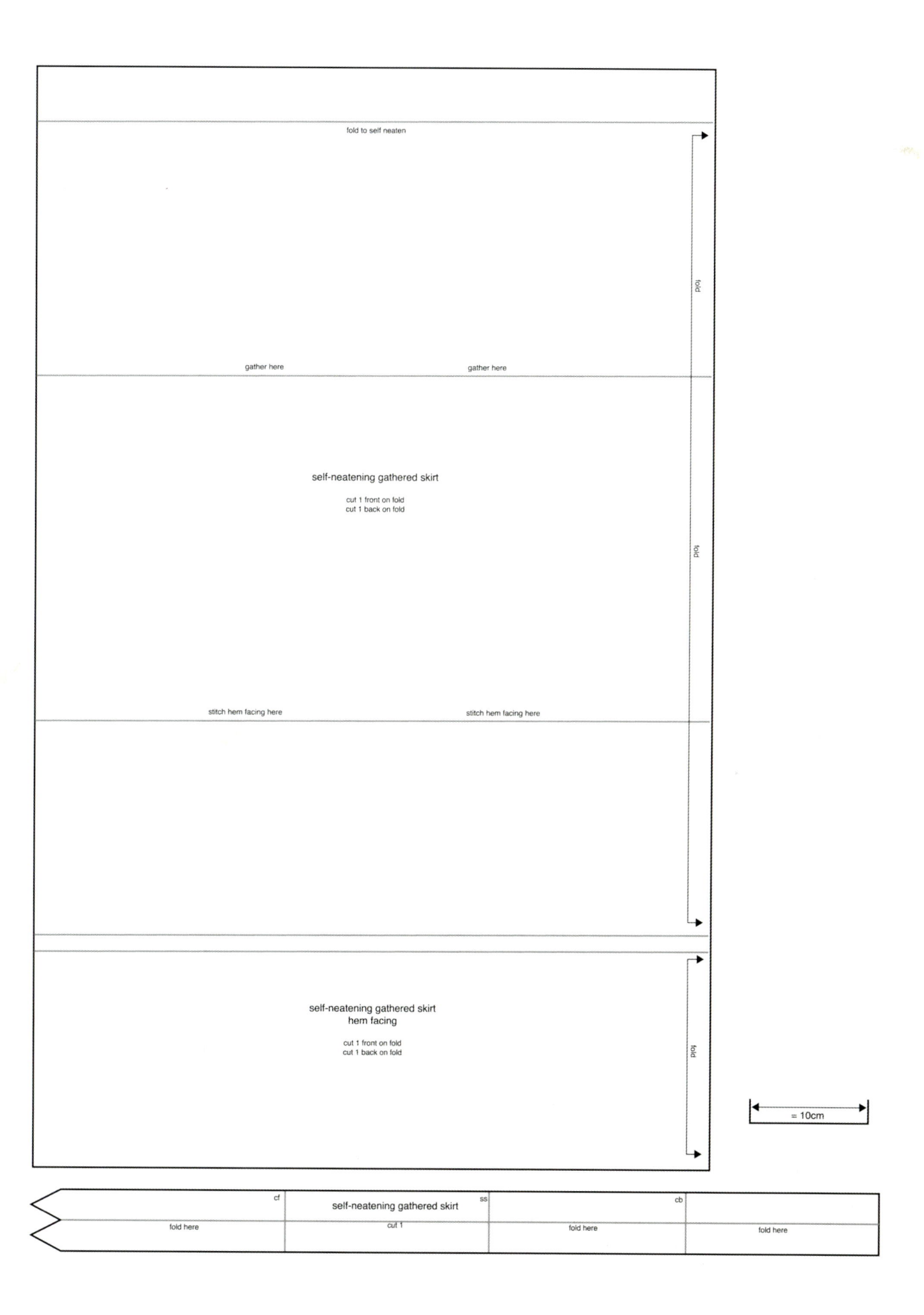

gather here · gather here

self-neatening gathered skirt

cut 1 front on fold
cut 1 back on fold

stitch hem facing here · stitch hem facing here

self-neatening gathered skirt
hem facing

cut 1 front on fold
cut 1 back on fold

fold

= 10cm

cf	self-neatening gathered skirt	ss	cb	
fold here	cut 1	fold here	fold here

The Self-Neatening Gathered Skirt Pattern

self-neatening skirt with an opening concealed in the gathers at the side. The selvedge creates a self-neatening placket and there is no zip and no lining. All in all it is effectively the same as many Victorian skirts from a century before. The silhouette is softer than the cocktail dress in Chapter 5 because it is not reliant on pads or ruffles underneath to give it shape. It was made to go over the petticoat in Chapter 4 and if you made one with a detachable ruffle you would most likely have taken it off when working around the house. The bottom has been reinforced with a calico strip: you will need to wash this to pre-shrink it before making the skirt. This pattern is ideal for fabrics with repeat prints and checks because it uses all the fabric from selvedge edge to selvedge edge and has a straight edge at the hem. There is no shaping at the sides so there is no matching up to do. The volume you create is dependent on the width of your cloth and there is no waste. The original instructions were in a UK edition of *Woman's Journal*, but unfortunately there are no pictures, so I had to create a calico toile first to see how the technique worked.

Cutting Out

I have included the pattern for this but you don't really need one. For the front, measure the finished length of your skirt. Add 1cm/$^5/_8$in seam allowance at the hem. At the waist add 21cm/$8^1/_4$in for the fold that will support the ruffle and an extra 4cm/$1^9/_{16}$in to fold under for self-neatening. Mark it out from selvedge edge to selvedge edge and repeat the whole process for the back: this will dictate the amount of cloth you need. If you are using a print it also gives you more control over the placement of the motif at the CF. In addition you only need to cut the waistband out. Whatever is left over can be used to cover buttons and press studs and get the matching belt made – you only need a strip 15cm/6in deep for this.

Order of Construction

1. Turn the top edge inwards 4cm/$1^9/_{16}$in and press the crease. This is the hem for the self-neatening section. (1)
2. Turn over inwards again 21cm/$8^1/_4$in and press the crease. The original fold should now be hidden. This new fold is going to create the self-neatening ruffle and will remain loose at the hip inside the skirt. (2)
3. Attach the calico or cotton strip to the hem of both the front and backs of the skirt, right side to right side. Machine-stitch on, turn through to the wrong side and press upwards. Roll the edges of the seam in your fingers as you

First fold for hem of skirt.

Fold to create self-neatening ruffle.

Overlapping opening being pressed; the front of the overlap is on the sleeve board. Note the self-neatened hem at the bottom of the ruffle.

Back seam allowance is not sitting flat but rolling forwards.

Chapter 10 / The Self-Neatening Gathered Skirt

5 Snipping diagonally from above the opening, but note that you may not be able to snip the whole piece on the diagonal. Snip to the very bottom of the opening.

6 Opening from the right side.

7 Machining down the neatened top edge of the calico.

8 Machining two rows of large stitches at the waist fold.

9 Pulling the gathering fabric gently along the two top threads.

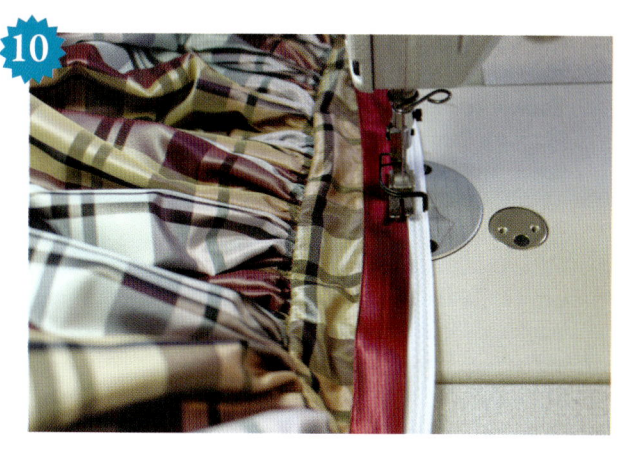

10 Machining the bias tape on at the waistband.

99

Closed waistband from the inside.

Waistband tape sitting behind the gathers.

press to ensure the calico or cotton remains on the inside of the hem. Don't stitch the top edge down yet.

4. Align the front and back of the left-hand side selvedges, right side to right side. Open out the calico hem at the bottom, align the hem seam and pin. Pin the selvedges together and sew up with a 2cm/$^{25}/_{32}$ in seam allowance. As the selvedge is woven there is no need to pink the edges. Press the seam open.

5. Hand-tack a strip of organza or cotton 4cm/1$^{9}/_{16}$ in wide and 25cm/10in long on the wrong sides of the right selvedge edges from the waist down. This side will be self-neatened to make a placket opening later and needs reinforcing. Sew 4cm/1$^{9}/_{16}$ in in from the edge. Leaving an opening of 20cm/8in from the waist, pin the front and back selvedge edges together, right side to right side. Repeat, opening up the calico and aligning the hem with the seams open. Machine-stitch with a seam allowance 4cm/1$^{9}/_{16}$ in deep. For the front opening, fold the seam allowance in half and press the crease. For the back seam allowance fold in half and press the crease. I pressed my seam fully open here so that I would have a crease as a guide for the placket depth on the right side. The front should now overlap the back. If you want to use buttons this is a good point to mark out their position on the back placket and their corresponding buttonholes on the inside of the front placket. The fastenings need to be concealed in the gathers so make sure the buttonholes do not go through to the shell of the skirt. (3)

6. The back seam allowance will be rolling forwards towards the CF at this point. To get it to lie flat, lift up the hem of the ruffle and snip across the back seam allowance only. Snip diagonally but note that you may not be able to snip the whole piece on the diagonal: snip to the very bottom of the skirt opening. This will release the tension and let the seam allowance roll open. Conceal the cut using the ruffle hem and hand-stitch to close. Make sure the stitching cannot be seen from the outside of the garment before pressing the seams open. (4,5,6)

7. Roll the calico hem back up and press a 1cm/$^{3}/_{8}$ in seam allowance under. Pin into position and topstitch into place no more than a machine foot's width from the edge. Make sure the shell fabric is not pleating from the front as you do so. Press the hem to finish. (7)

8. To gather the skirt use the technique described in Chapter 4. Sew two rows of thread along the waist edge of the fold and pull the top threads gently. Stop 2cm/$^{25}/_{32}$ in from the opening so that the placket remains flat. You are gathering a very large circumference onto a small waistband so the gathers need to be packed very tightly. The thread will snap if it is too long so split the skirt into sections and do a quarter or an eighth at a time. (8,9)

9. The waistband is finished very similarly to that of the chalk line skirt in Chapter 6. The gathering is fairly bulky so the waistband will be finished open with the gathering and seam allowance pressed upwards into the band. As it is on the fold it will look neat so it doesn't matter if it is exposed on the inside. Machine-stitch the waistband onto the gathers right side to right side. Topstitch the waistband tape to the seam allowance of the waistband along the seam edge. To conceal the join, topstitch bias binding over the top of the waistband and waist tape. The waistband should be the same length as the waist as the plackets are already incorporated. If you want you can shape the ends as a feature or keep them flat as I have done here. Fold the waistband in half outwards to machine down the

Chapter 10 / The Self-Neatening Gathered Skirt

ends of the waistband. Trim the bulk from the corners and turn back through to press. The edge of the bias binding should be at the edge of the fold on the inside. Hand-stitch the end of the waistband tape down and sit it neatly behind the gathering to finish. (10,11,12)

10. I used press studs for speed to finish and had a matching fabric belt made.

Suggested Adaptations

If you want a fuller skirt then join two lengths of fabric together at the selvedge edge for both the front and back before you gather. If you want a garment that really looks like a Horrockses skirt, change your fabric for an all-over floral print in cotton.

Horrockses have recently relaunched some of their prints as bedding, giving you plenty of fabric to work with if you buy a sheet! I would also suggest putting in a simple side pocket or a patch pocket on the front if you are using a plainer fabric.

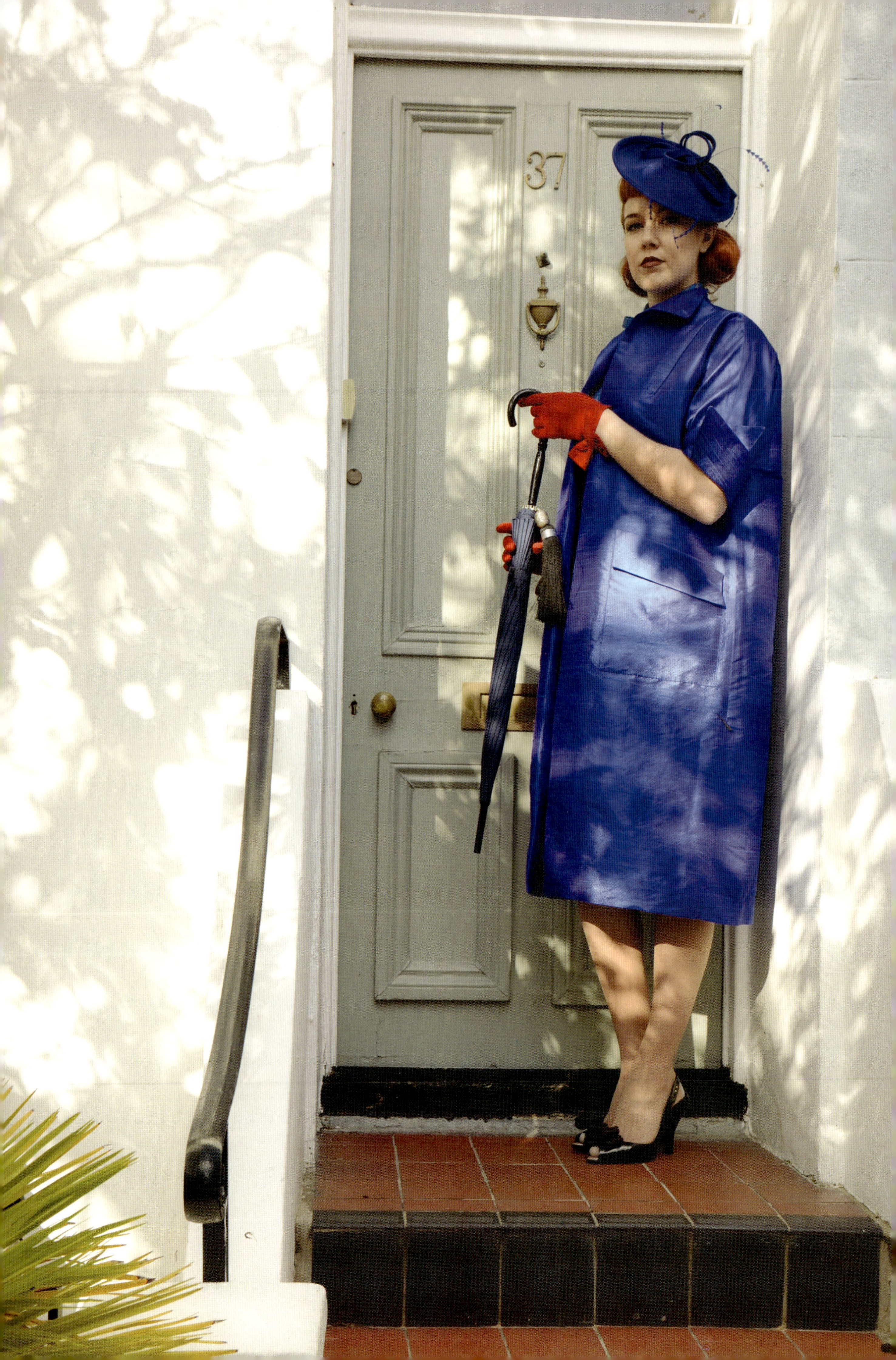
37

The Manteau

11

The French word *manteau*, meaning coat, was originally used as a term to describe a loose gown or cloak worn by women in the seventeenth and eighteenth centuries. In fifties Britain the coat was mainly referred to as a topper or top coat. More colloquial names included a noun that referenced the shape or purpose of the coat first; for example, duster coat, swing coat, pyramid coat, housecoat, and so on.

With regard to silhouette, coats of this decade fell into very distinctive style categories dictated by designers of manteaus on Paris catwalks, and whilst these styles weren't copied verbatim the essence of the design obviously was. Coat lengths were either to the hip (a half coat) or long and to the mid-calf or floor. The full coat was the most common style and was defined by its volume. Fullness of the coat was usually at the bottom and designed to go over big skirts and petticoats. It came in a range of wools and camel hairs or fur and cashmere, if you could afford it, for winter. The same style lines were made in lighter-weight wools, cotton blends and new synthetics for spring and autumn, and most likely coordinated in colour or pattern with the outfit worn underneath. The swing coat had the most volume, with the fullness beginning from the shoulder instead of

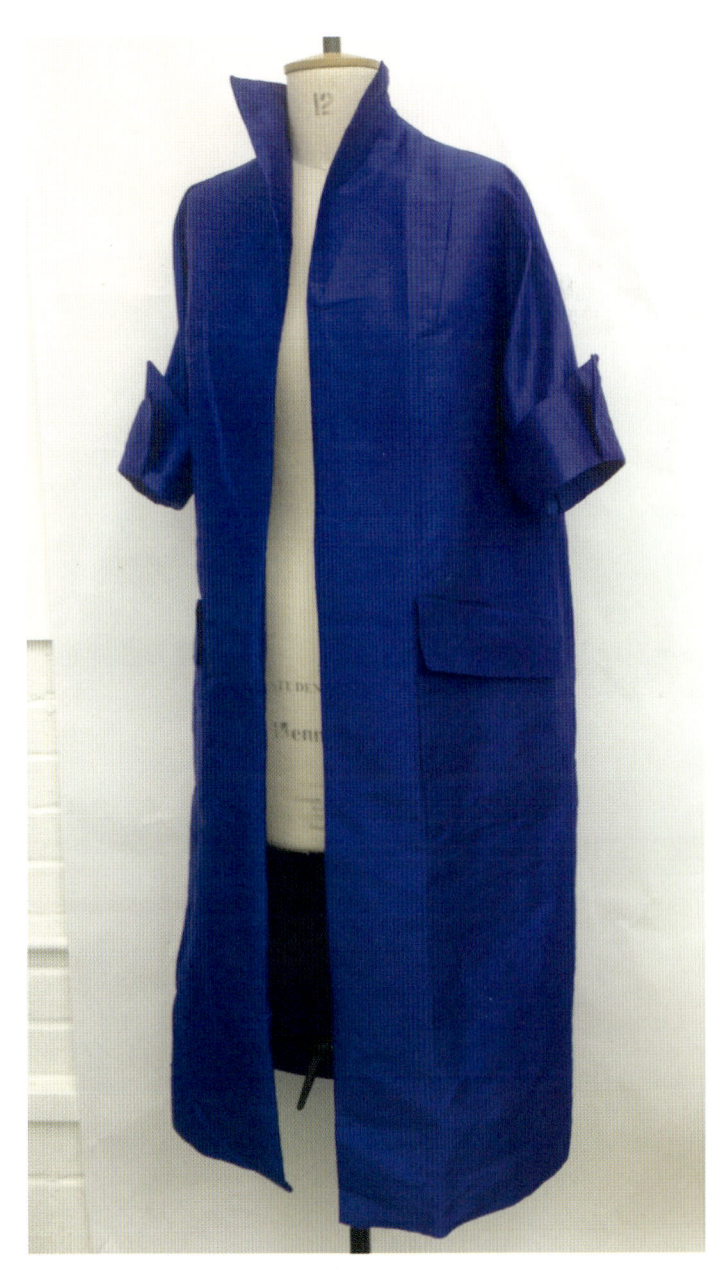

The manteau or edge-to-edge coat.

key features like the collars, revers and buttons were slightly larger, the shoulders were slightly more padded and the sleeves cut longer, all to mimic the proportions of a coat.

Spring coats were frequently left open without any fastenings to reveal the coordinated dress or skirt and blouse underneath. This 'edge-to-edge' finish gave it its name, the clutch coat, as wearers frequently had to hold the front closed. Another common design feature was to match the lining to the dress if the coat shell was a coordinating or contrasting solid colour. Unlike the oversized collar of a winter coat they were characterized by a shawl collar and a wide bracelet- or elbow-length sleeve. From a pattern-cutting perspective, for this era, most of the coat styles I have seen either in pattern books or archive pieces are based on the kimono, with the body of the coat and top sleeve cut in one, with or without an underarm panel and gusset. The sleeves are characteristically wide with large cuffs and collars. There is very little in the way of detail – usually just a large button or two. The coat itself was less roomy but could still be worn with either a full skirt or a chalk line. It also gave rise to the evening coat where the style was maintained but made in more luxurious fabrics. I have selected it because it is more easily adaptable than a winter coat and, depending on your fabric choice, could easily be repurposed as a housecoat worn over the housewife skirt and blouse or as a beach coat over swimwear.

The source of inspiration for this manteau is a selection of spring coats from the Worthing Museum and Art Gallery collection and a vintage pattern for a summer-weight coordinating dress and coat set. As with other projects in the book I have compared the museum pieces with photos and fashion spreads from the period and have cross-referenced with existing patterns. The first coat I analysed is a mid-length, mushroom-coloured edge-to-edge coat. It has no buttons or fastenings so both sides meet at the CF. It is made in a synthetic

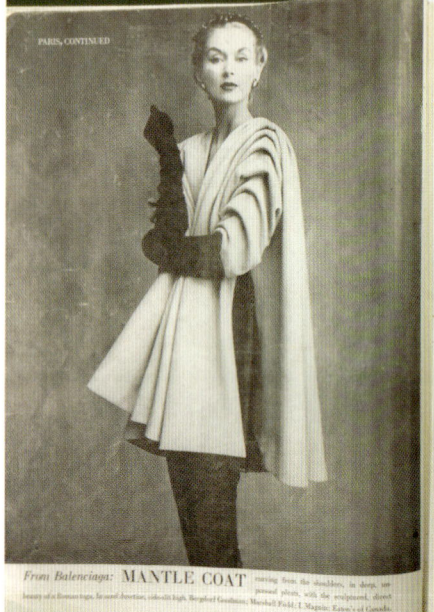

Fashion spreads featuring the new season's volume silhouettes from *Vogue* for autumn/winter 1954/5. (Author's own collection)

the waist, and was a popular choice in post-war Britain. A cause for its popularity was actually very practical as the early fifties saw a boom in births and with more pregnancies came a need for more roomy but stylish garments. This style allowed women to maintain active lives when out in public and was actually quite radical at the time. An alternative style was the swagger coat, which fitted closer to the body but had pleats at the back for volume and movement. Worn with or without a belt it was intended to mimic the hourglass shape of the dress underneath. As with other aspects of 1950s dress it was a style borrowed from the Victorians and later inspired the coat-dress – a double-breasted dress mostly worn in winter. There was no back zipper because the buttons at the front were fully functional and the

Chapter 11 / The Manteau

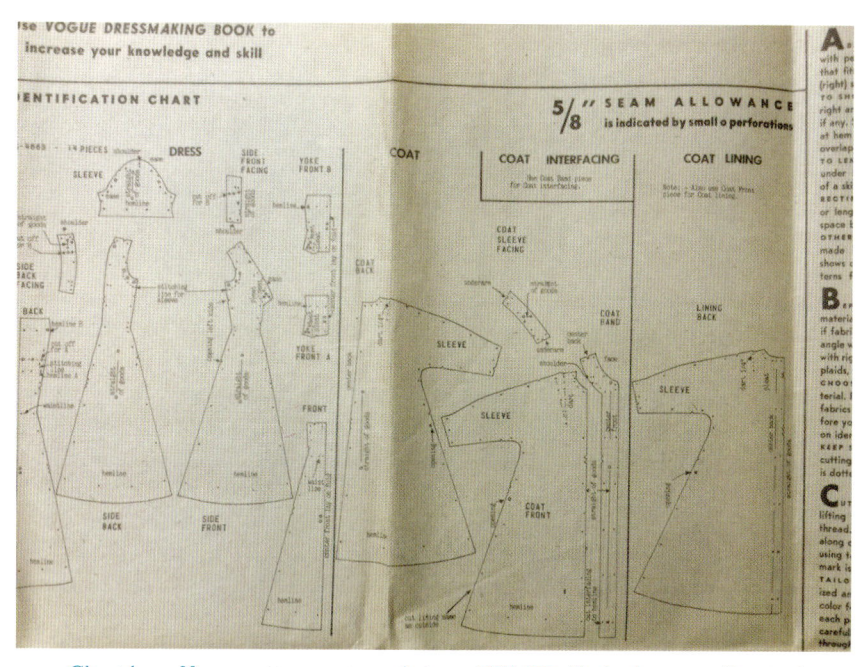

Chart from *Vogue* pattern, autumn/winter 1954/55. (Author's own collection)

Vogue Special Design pattern for kimono-style coat. (Author's own collection)

silk with a slubby texture reminiscent of a more expensive silk dupion. It is dry-cleanable and was made by Russell Stuart of London in the 1950s. The collar has the look of a set-in collar but is in fact like a shawl collar where the front is grown on and shaped to create the revers. The collar is then sewn into the neck opening and up at the centre back. Shaping has been created over the shoulder by using darts at both the front and back neck to keep the silhouette lean at the top and accentuate the volume at the bottom. The plain appearance of the coat is offset by the pocket flap extended from a princess seam panel and fastened closed with a cover button. The

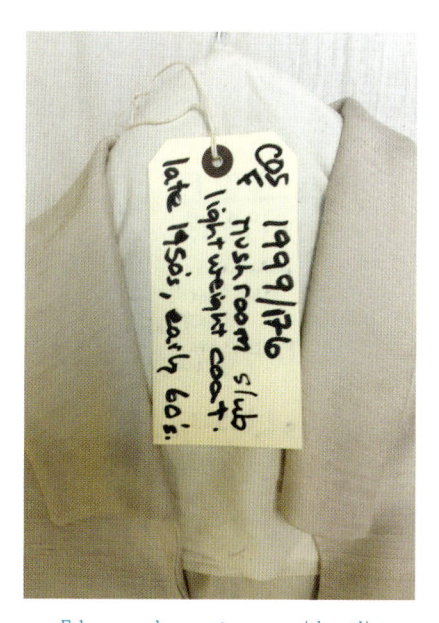

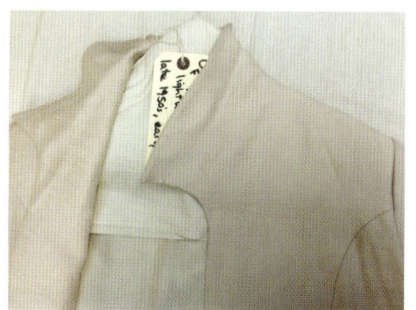

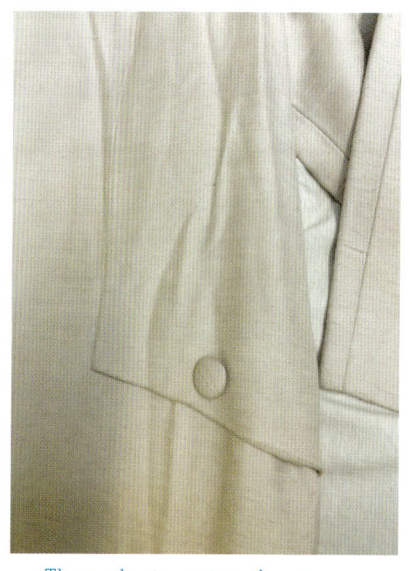

Edge-to-edge spring coat (detail).

Russell Stuart coat showing collar grown on and cut in one piece.

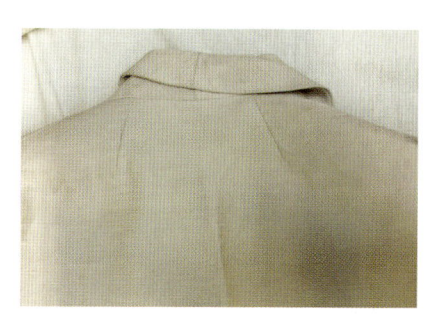

Russell Stuart label and cleaning instructions.

Russell Stuart coat, back neck darts.

The pocket is cut into the princess princess seam at the front and closed with a cover button.

armhole is wide and boxy with a two-piece set-in sleeve that has been seamed directly onto the overarm, creating a more rounded shoulder line. The coat is fully lined and machine-stitched closed at the hem.

The second archive piece is similar and made around the same time but by a different company, N. Dingle and Co. based in Plymouth. I did investigate the origin of the coat as possibly having been an in-house line from the Dingle's department store. House of Fraser bought the chain in 1971, so I used the House of Fraser archive to investigate the store history, including the lines it would have carried, but to no avail so its provenance remains a mystery. The coat is made of a synthetic and cotton blend tweed in pink and grey. Like the

Narrow vertical jet pocket set into the front of the coat.

N. Dingle & Co. Ltd label.

N. Dingle & Co. Ltd clutch coat, circa late 1950s.

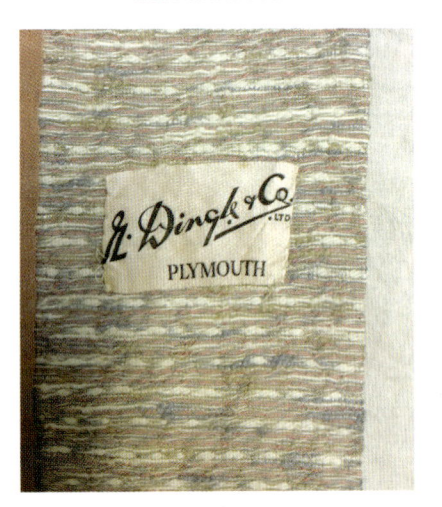

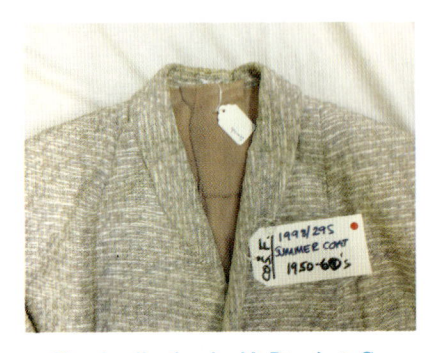

Shawl collar for the N. Dingle & Co. coat.

Underarm panel and grown-on half cuff.

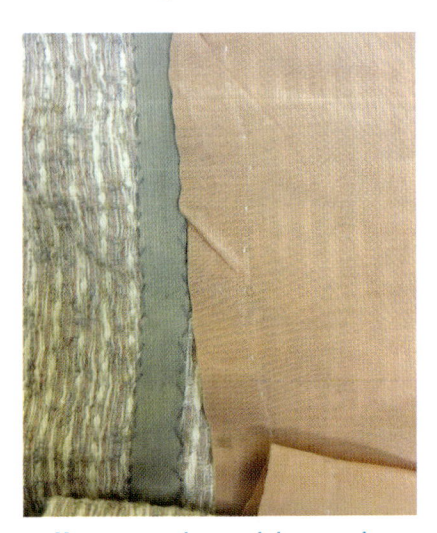

Hem is turned up and the raw edge bound with cotton tape. The lining is finished hemmed separately and hangs loose.

Chapter 11 / The Manteau

Russell Stuart version, it is edge-to-edge at the front with no buttons to fasten. This version also has a shawl collar. It also has darts to shape the coat close to the neck and over the shoulder. This coat more closely resembles a kimono, with the body and overarm cut in one piece and the gusset being embedded into the underarm sleeve. The bracelet-length sleeve has a turn-up cuff to finish. The pocket is a simple vertical jet pocket with no fastening. This coat is also fully lined but the lining is loose and the raw hem finished with a bias tape. Once upon a time both of these coats may have come with a matching dress or skirt.

The Butterick pattern is one from my collection and, although it is a size 16, it is actually quite small across the back and chest so I only had to make a few adjustments to the length and fit before using it. It was bought from Bentall's department store in Kingston upon Thames in 1956: this store was originally opened in 1867 by Frank Bentall as a drapery and haberdashery shop and, surprisingly, was retained by the family until 2001 when it was bought out by their former business rivals, the Fenwick family. One aspect of the design that I particularly like is the large deep pockets. These are probably more of a nod to Chanel than Dior in terms of seeking inspiration from the Paris catwalks. It is widely known that Chanel did not approve of her male couturier counterparts' vision of womanhood in the fifties and instead championed her own simpler less constricted clothing designed to marry style with function. She designed in response to the tasks undertaken by busy post-war working women. For example, her pared-back tailored jackets much loved by Jackie Kennedy became available in 1954 in direct response to the impracticalities and constraints of running errands in town in clothes with wasp waists and corsets. It stood to reason, then, that Chanel was also a fan of a more masculine deep functioning patch pocket that allowed women to actually fit their hands inside. These deep and well-shaped pockets became

Pattern envelope for Butterick clutch coat and matching dress.

synonymous with Chanel coats and jackets as the decade progressed; as time ran on into the sixties this easier style of dressing was more readily embraced. Chanel's 'little French jacket' of 1954 had four patch pockets – two hip pockets and two smaller breast pockets. Visible pockets had almost exclusively been the domain of menswear until this point and although she had been designing sportswear with visible pockets for women since the 1930s they did not catch on. Chanel experimented with wearing both menswear and womenswear herself and had them put into her own clothes to hold lipsticks, coins and cigarettes. Unlike Chanel, the pocket on this pattern does have a pocket flap cut at an angle, reflecting the angle of the cuff. Stylistically this makes this clutch coat an interesting hybrid between the two couture sensibilities, allowing the average woman to be conformist and rebellious all at the same time.

Typically the pattern tissue has no markings, only stamped holes to indicate dart and pocket positions, seam allowance, notches, and so on. It has clearly been used and is rather fragile. The envelope does, however, include instructions which I have used and a lovely small paper advice

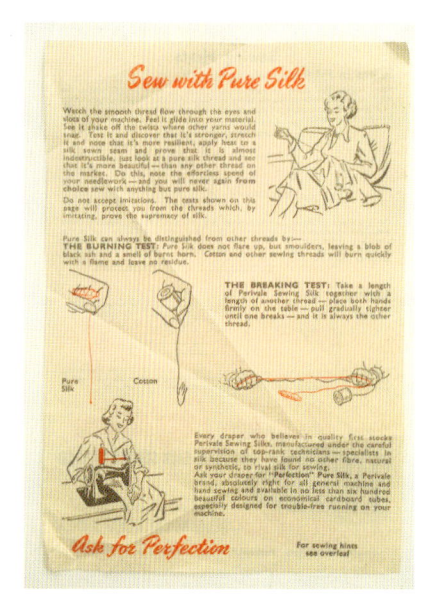

Advice slip from inside the pattern envelope, front.

supplement giving the home dressmaker hints and tips for finishes to encourage them to use pure silk thread. The inclusion of advertising or additional instructions had been around since the 1920s and became standard for all shop-bought patterns in the 1950s. Normally they related either to the store that supplied the pattern or to a haberdasher's or draper's. In the early fifties they also included housekeeping and dressmaking tips.

Cutting Out

As the main coat pieces are quite large they will need to be chalked out on the right side of the fabric and cut out singly unless your fabric is very wide. In that case fold it in half before pinning the pattern to it. Mark all the notches. The Butterick pattern this is inspired by also advises to tack down the CF and CB and only remove the tacking after the garment is finished. This version is unlined but if you are lining yours then cut the lining the same as the shell minus the width of the facing. The interlining needs to be 3mm/$^1/_8$ in smaller than the collar and facing so trim this away before tacking on. Mark the pocket position on both front pieces with tailor tacks or chalk. I

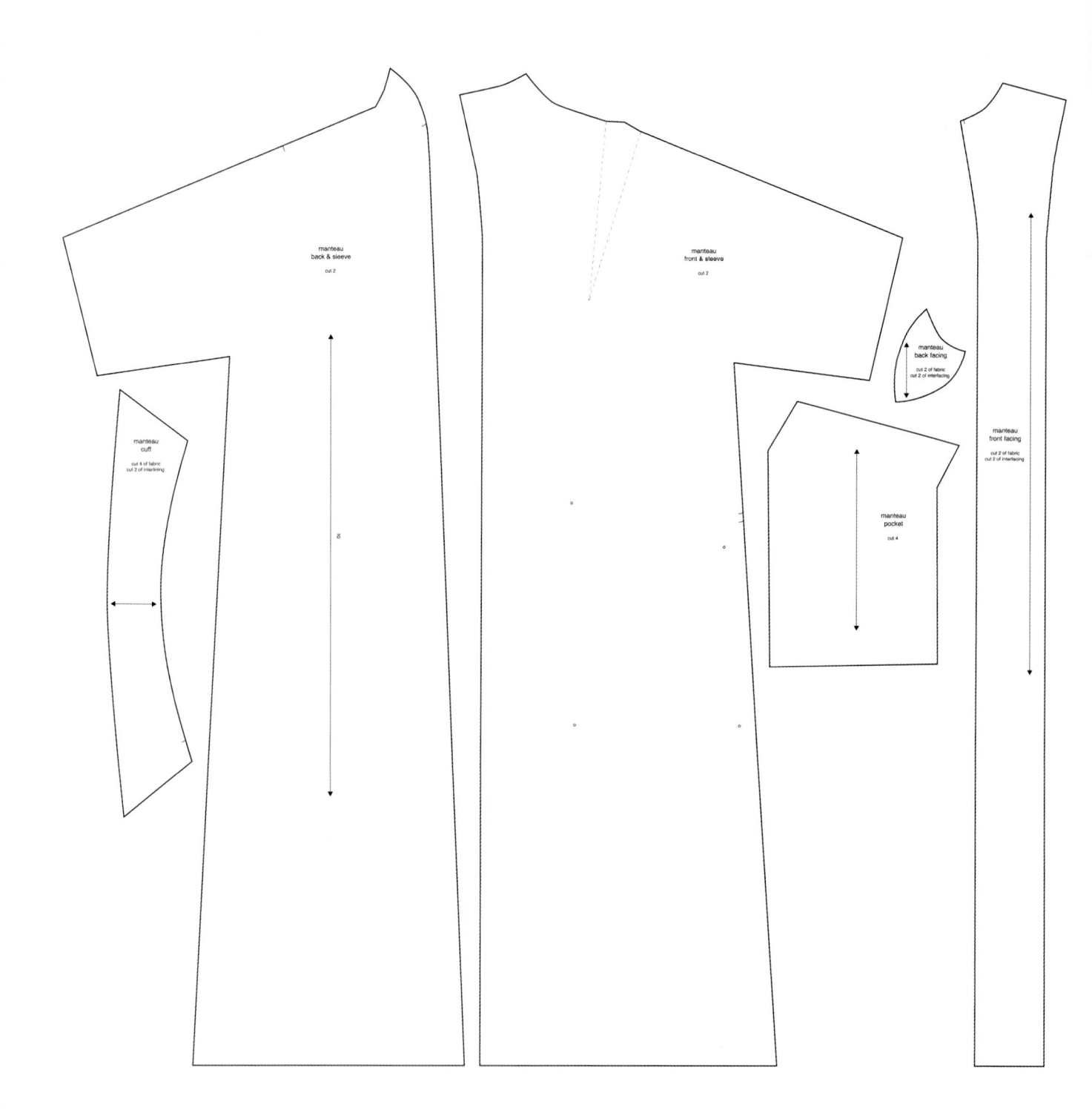

The Manteau Coat Pattern

Chapter 11 / The Manteau

MATERIALS AND EQUIPMENT

Fabric for shell

Fabric for lining (optional)

Interlining/organza

Thread

Hand sewing needles

Cover buttons (optional for decorative pocket)

Bias binding

Overlocker and threads

used a non-fusible Vilene for my interlinings as I didn't have any black organza for my facings but you can use either for the same effect. You may find the organza will give a bouncier, rounder-looking finish.

Order of Construction

1. Tack the interlining to the inside of the back neck and sleeve, then machine-stitch the CB seam from the neck notch down. Press the back seam open and bind the edges to finish or turn under and topstitch down to neaten. (1)
2. Tack the interlining to the inside of the coat front and sleeve. Sew the neck dart and reverse-stitch to hold the dart ends. Press towards the CF. (2,3,4)
3. Prepare the pockets next. These will be bagged out separately before being positioned on the coat: they are effectively a double layer put right sides together and stitched around the outer edge. Leave an opening at the bottom to turn back through. Trim the corners and turn right sides out. Press the pockets and slip-stitch the opening closed at the bottom. Line the pocket up to your tailor tacks or chalk marks and tack into position on the coat fronts. The top flap rolls back down on itself so only tack downwards from this point, marked with pins in the picture. Topstitch the pockets on by machine and roll the flap down. Press lightly. (5,6,7,8)
4. Stitch the shoulder seams together. Overlock or bind the raw edges of the seams to finish if you are not lining the coat. You will be sewing up and round the neck, which is curved: to get this to sit flat snip into the curve up to but not through the sewing line to release the tension. Press open. (9)
5. Prepare the front and back neck facing. Stitch the curved CB seam and then stitch the back neck to the front facing at the shoulders. Press the seams open. If you are not lining the coat then turn the inner edge of the facing inwards and topstitch to finish or bind. (10)
6. Pin or tack the facing to the coat shell making sure the CB seams and shoulders match up. The revers has a slight curve to it so snip into it up to but not through the seam allowance to release the tension and get the shape to sit flat. Trim the interfacing close to the stitch line and trim the seam at the collar points. Turn the facing inside and press. Under-stitch if you wish, then hand-stitch the seams of the facing to the seams of the coat shell. Press. (11,12,13)
7. Stitch the underarm seams. Snip the curve and press open. Overlock or bind to finish the raw edges.
8. To make the cuff, tack the interfacing to the inside of one cuff section, right sides together, Stitch the two cuff pieces together along the sides and top, leaving an opening at the bottom to turn back through as per the pockets. Trim the seams, turn through and press. Slip-stitch the opening closed. Repeat for the other cuff. Tack or pin the cuff into position on the sleeve with the raw seam sandwiched between the cuff and the outside of the sleeve. You can leave the edges raw or finish them with bias binding. Catch the cuff upwards into position with a hand stitch. The seam should sit just inside the sleeve and not on the edge. Press gently. I have used a shop-bought raglan shoulder pad which I covered in the same fabric as the coat, then hand-stitched into position on the shoulder seam, as with the soft tailored jacket in Chapter 6. (14)
9. Gently press the hem upwards and machine-sew a flat bias binding to the edge if you want the finish to look like the Dingwall original. For ease I have overlocked my hem on this occasion. Pin or tack into position and slip-stitch closed by hand. Roll the facing over the hem and slip-stitch the lower edge of the facing in place. (15)

Suggested Adaptations

For a stylistic adaptation you could consider a lining that matches the dress or lining the pockets. The pockets could also have a decorative cover button in the same fabric. The coat and either a blouse and skirt or the cocktail dress from Chapter 5 could all be made in the same fabric. Fabric should be selected depending on purpose – wool or cotton for daywear, silks and taffetas for evening wear. Alternatively it could be made in a cotton print and worn as a housecoat. You could also shorten the sleeves to sit above the elbow before attaching the cuff for high summer and wear it over a bathing suit. For the photos I remade the chalk line skirt in a fabric that matched the bow tie blouse but this combination could easily be replaced with a dress, and I chose a silk dupion that would colour coordinate.

1. Tacking the interlining to the back neck. 
2. Neck dart marked out on the wrong side. 
3. Sewing the neck darts. 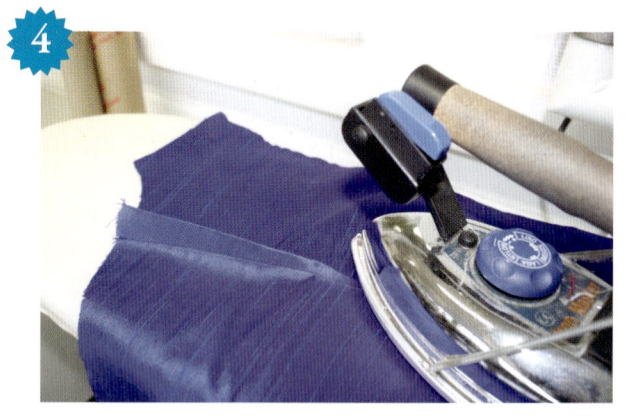
4. Pressing the neck darts towards the CF. 
5. Bagging out the pockets. 
6. Opening left at the bottom of the pocket bag. 
7. Pair of bagged and pressed pockets with the opening closed. 
8. Positioning a pocket on the coat front.

Chapter 11 / The Manteau

9 Stitching the shoulder seams together.

10 Stitching the back neck to the front facing.

11 Trimming away excess seam allowance and interlining to reduce bulk at the collar seams.

12 Snipped seam allowance inside the revers.

13 Attaching the facing to the seam with a hand stitch.

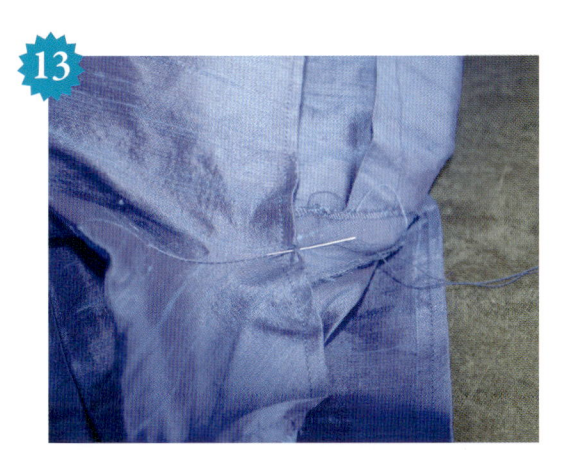

14 Attaching the cuff to the sleeve on the right right side; the opening of the cuff sits over the back seam or hind of the sleeve.

15 Hem and facing slip-stitched closed.

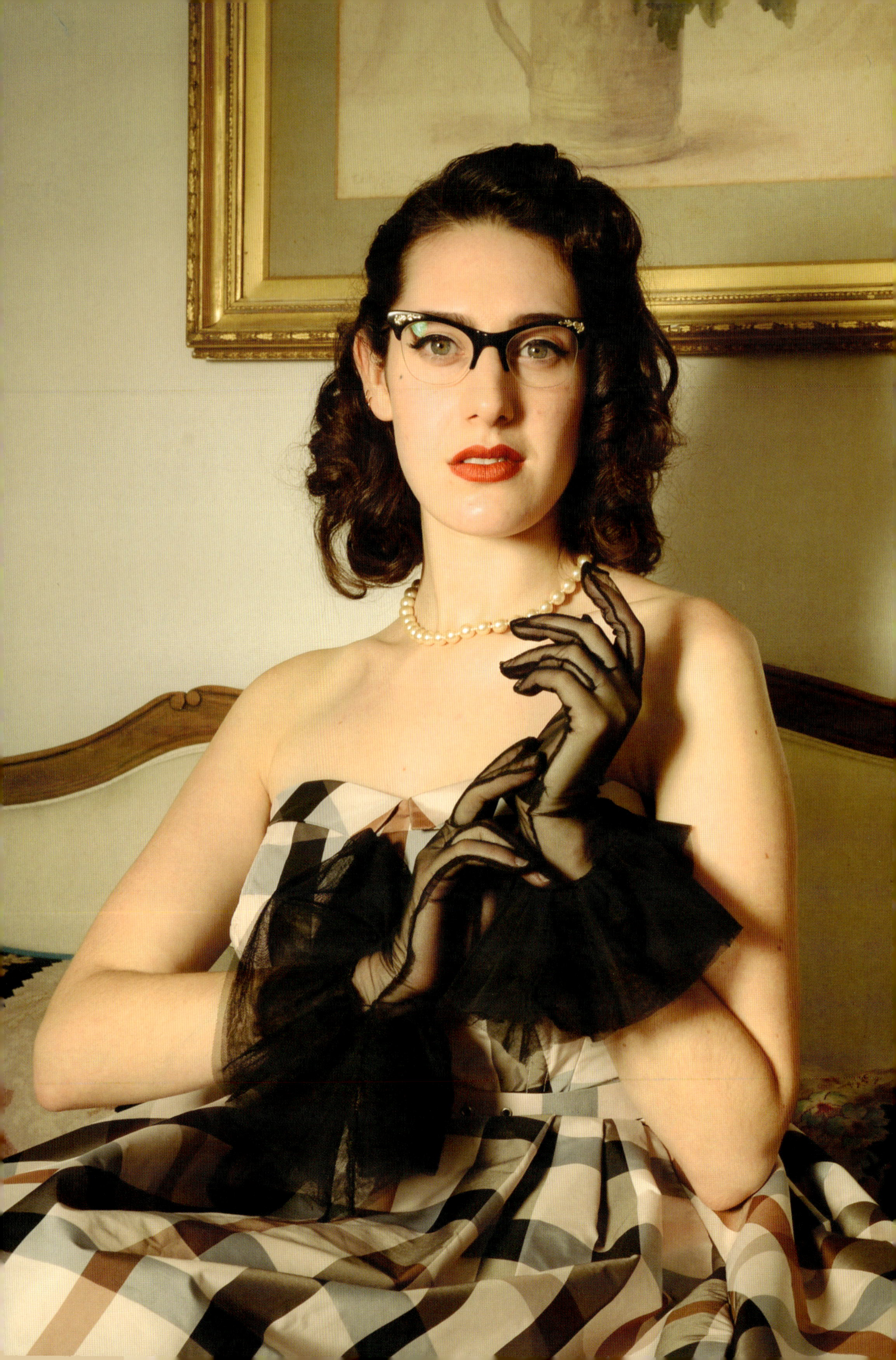

Creating the Look

12

What do I need to know to select a design that is good within itself, is becoming to me, is suited to a specified occasion and is modish?

Jessie Lambert Fielding,
Elements of Clothing Construction Manual, 1955

Our personal identity is important and how we dress is one aspect of our lives that we can make choices about. One of the best parts of working as a costume designer for film and TV is that all clothes and accessories are carefully and purposefully chosen before they appear on screen. This chapter is all about bringing the projects in the book to life in a way that feels as believable but also as accessible as possible. There are key accessories that have helped to do that and are synonymous with a bygone era; for example, hats. As a result I have focused more on those, particularly as they are more specialized and you may need more help with sourcing and fitting them. I have mentioned bags and shoes but in a lot less depth as I have assumed that the modern woman has more experience in sourcing and fitting those than she would a pair of gloves or stockings. In the pursuit of a believable look I would also like to add that the photos from the shoot in this book have not been altered in any way in post-production. The models' silhouettes are as they have been created by wearing the foundation garments using the patterns in the book. We have shot everything using natural light to keep what you see as natural and attainable as possible.

In *Style Surfing*, author Ted Polhemus says that human beings have always used their appearance as personal advertising – a calling card signalling who we are and where we are at – and in the 1950s, a totally coordinated look was considered the epitome of style and good taste. The Paris catwalks took a very dominant approach to fashion with the male couturiers expressing their opinions very strongly about working a complete and uncompromising look. The expectation was that you bought into one look, along with all the appropriate accessories from one designer. For example, if you had a Chanel suit you would also have to have the bag, shoes, gloves and pillbox hat. The more eclectic approach we take today of, say, wearing a designer jacket with a pair of ripped jeans would have been unheard of. The reality of couture is that only 1 per cent of the world's population can

Accessorizing chart in the colours of the season, *Harper's Bazaar*, September 1955. (Author's own collection)

Gloves should be worn on the streets of cities and large towns, when going to church, to a luncheon, dinner or reception; a dance, a wedding or an official function ... Smart women usually wear gloves while travelling on a train or plane ... or in any public conveyance. On formal occasions, gloves are worn by the guests and by the hostess, while she is receiving.

Jessie Lambert Fielding, *Elements of Clothing Construction Manual*, 1955

and have ever been able to afford a full couture wardrobe and the rest of society has always used focused research to find images from magazines, films and now the internet as inspiration to recreate our own version of that look. In so doing we also get to dress to suit our own budget, body type, colouring and lifestyle.

There are excellent websites like www.vintagedancer.com where they offer a social history or commentary on a specific item from a particular era (for example on hats) and follow it up with photographs of faux vintage pieces with links to the online stores of their suppliers. Prices are always included. It is fascinating to read around your subject matter in more depth. If you want a broader look at the clothing and styling from the period I recommend reading Mike Brown's *The 1950s Look: Recreating the Fashions of the Fifties* and Paula Reed's *Fifties Fashion Looks that Changed the 1950s*. Both show a broad range of styles and show the decade in context by including world events and developments in design for the home, like furniture, appliances and food, as well as cars, film and lifestyle. There is a plethora of visual referencing on the internet so curatorial websites like Pinterest are really useful.

I suggest heavy and selective editing and ultimately a range of focused boards by item rather than hundreds of boards with a generic look. For example, your initial board about hats could later be broken down further by hat type. If you are less digital, then using a physical mood board where images you have cut out or copied can be organized and collated also works and you can make note of stockists as you go. Based on my research I have opted for a very specific ladylike look for 1950s dressing based almost exclusively on images from glossy magazines like *Vogue* and *Harper's Bazaar*. I have not, for example, included younger teen styles like that of the Teddy boy or girl even though I understand their importance in that era. The garments in this book are, however, easily adaptable to your personal tastes by making fabric changes and by being styled in a different way so these looks can still be achieved.

I used a great many fashion editorials and advertising from original 1950s magazines to determine what looks I wanted for this book; at the same time I identified what accessories I needed to make the look complete. I then did a specific internet search to find either replica accessories or something close to the originals that I could use as a base to build on or embellish. Obviously I could have looked for original accessories and lucky finds from vintage fairs but I didn't want to leave anything to chance for the shoot. Instead I wanted to demonstrate that with a bit of research it is relatively easy to achieve a vintage look by using modern products in the right way. It is worth keeping your own contacts and suppliers list for future reference. If you become a repeat customer, then over time you can build up a rapport and maybe be offered discounts and previews of new stock. If you are buying online or are unsure of your choice until you try it on with your outfit, then only use suppliers who have a good returns policy.

Gloves

Images of gloves being worn date back as far as manuscripts from the tenth century and have formed part of costume worn by royalty, bishops and high-ranking members of society. Obviously they have a practical use as protection from the weather, particularly the cold, as there was little in the way of heating in many buildings in bygone days. Even in the fifties the environment was not as heavily sanitized as it is today – think of smog, whooping cough, diphtheria – and germs were very easily spread by touch, so gloves were also used for hygiene. Obviously the aesthetics were to be considered and, with a few exceptions such as on the beach, women wore gloves of some kind all year round. As you can see from the extract above, gloves came with a plethora of social rules and etiquette. These particular rules are from an original fashion atelier manual for fashion tutors at the Florida State University from 1955. Although its main purpose was as a technical guide for delivering a pattern-cutting and garment construction curriculum, the first third is given over to making suggestions to help young ladies in their understanding of how to dress and behave in polite society. For example, it was obligatory that a lady only removed her gloves to eat, drink, smoke or play cards! Her glove fingers were to be tucked into the wrist opening of her blouse or jacket for these activities and taken off altogether to eat but only once seated at the table. It was suggested that the prudent young lady might want to accommodate this extra bulk in the cut of her sleeve or instead use a handy device known as a glove clip. (For reference, vintage glove clips are more attractive than new ones so source these on eBay or at vintage fairs.) Other glove etiquette stipulated how they could be worn indoors, outdoors, shopping, driving, walking, holding hands, and so on. It was also acceptable to shake hands with gloves on unless meeting someone of high social standing like the prime minister.

Chapter 12 / Creating the Look

Nearly all women and girls owned one or more pairs of gloves before a radical shift in attitudes to womenswear in the sixties.

Gloves are notoriously difficult to make because the gussets are so small. Traditionally they are also made in fabrics that are difficult or highly specialized to work in such as goatskin and silk jersey. The University of Creative Arts (Rochester, UK) has these beautiful kid leather gloves with a tiny manipulation detail. The leather has been gathered and stitched around small buttons with shirring elastic; the buttons have then been removed whilst a puffy circle of leather remains. The technique is similar to a stitching technique used to prepare pre-dyed fabric for shibori (where it is tied around a button or bead to create a soft decorative cushion or puff). The gloves were made by Lorna Elizabeth Drury as a passion project; she was a highly skilled embroiderer and dressmaker and worked for the House of Worth until 1968 when it closed. There are a series of samplers and tester pieces so it is likely that she was making them for herself as there is an original template where she has drawn around her own hand to start. They are tiny – a size 6 – and extremely delicate. I have included images of her bespoke pattern pieces, but not a pattern. If you want to make your own I recommend the tutorial on www.glove.org as a starting point, but be prepared to remake several times.

For the shoot I used gloves supplied by Cornelia James. After World War II, Cornelia James was famous for creating and supplying gloves in a huge range of colours and tones. She worked with couturiers and leading department stores all over Europe and was nicknamed 'the Colour Queen of England' by *Vogue* magazine. She has been dressing Queen Elizabeth's hands since 1979 and now also dresses the hands of another famous royal person, the former Kate Middleton, now the Duchess of Cambridge. The gloves are hand-made and the range includes evening, opera and wedding gloves, as well as 'shorties' for daywear.

As with clothing, some glove fabrics hold up better than others; for example, undamaged vintage silk gloves are fairly hard to find these days for that very reason. Sheer and extra delicate fabrics are prone to runs and rips. Pale leathers and suedes stain easily, and synthetics often absorb dirt and stains and aren't quick to release them upon laundering. Try and think about where you'll be wearing your gloves and what you'll be doing in them while they're on before you pick a pair. Traditionally (and still to this day if you think about the way Queen Elizabeth dresses), gloves were available in relatively few standard lengths, but you can expect to

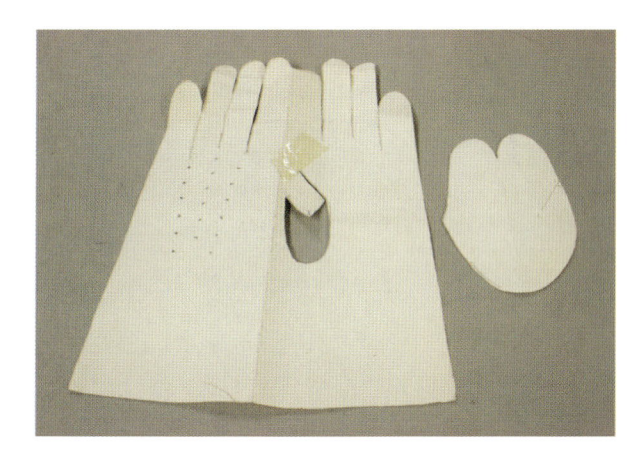

Prototype glove pattern by Lorna Drury. (University of the Creative Arts archive)

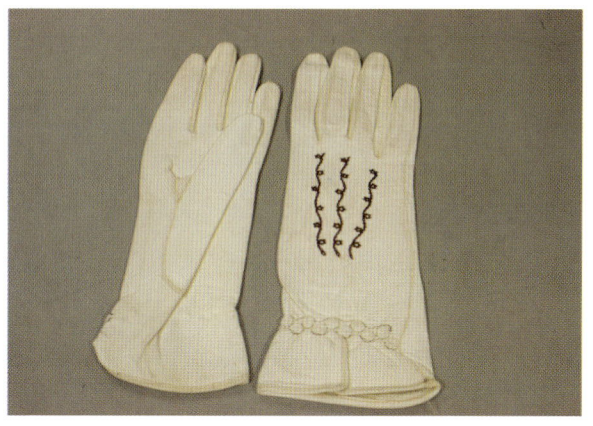

Finished bespoke gloves by Lorna Drury. (University of the Creative Arts archive)

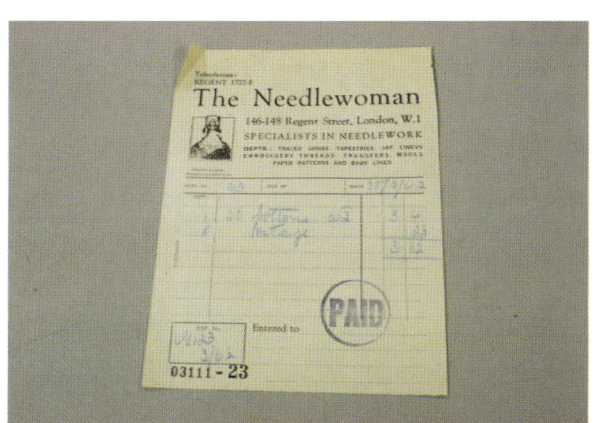

Receipt for the tiny buttons used to create the shibori embellishments on the finished gloves by Lorna Drury. (University of the Creative Arts archive)

Cornelia James opera and evening gloves.

Glove sizes	In Inches	In CM
XS	6	15
S	6 1/2	16 1/2
M	7	18
M/L	7 1/2	19
L	8	20
XL	8 1/2	23

Glove size chart.

Rules for Wearing Gloves

- The shorter the sleeve, the longer the length of the glove can be. For example, an elegant sleeveless summer dress could be worn with gloves up to the elbow or with shorties if desired.
- Opera gloves (especially those with buttons) are not usually worn during the daytime.
- Fabrics need to work in tandem to ensure that your gloves and your clothes look their best together. Generally speaking, similar fabrics and fabric weights go well, but a subtle degree of contrast (say, nylon gloves with a silk dress or crochet gloves with a cotton blouse) can be absolutely beautiful.
- Sheer gloves are beautiful, especially if they have frills, ruffles, pleats or ruching on them; they tend to suit the warmer half of the year because their daintiness complements spring and summer fashions and fabrics better than the sturdier winter styles.
- Consider your other garments, accessories, shoes and handbags when selecting your gloves. You want them to complement or tastefully stand out from these items, but not to look comically out of place.
- If you're wearing a jacket, blazer or coat, let the hem of your sleeve overlap with your gloves at least a little, or vice versa, so we don't see a flash of bare skin. When in doubt, opt for longer rather than shorter glove lengths. Please note that I deliberately broke this rule because I thought the red shorties would work really well with the blue manteau so this is only a guideline in modern society!
- To build up a basic glove wardrobe include at least one dark- and one light-coloured pair of wrist- and elbow-length gloves. These four or so pairs, especially if they're in various fabrics, sheens, weights and so on, will provide you with a surprising number of stylish options especially if, like me, you are prepared to be a little flexible with the rules.

buy the following:

Wrist-length gloves (also known as 'shorties'): the shortest style of glove, these hit at or slightly above the wrist bone and are very versatile.

Gauntlet gloves: characterized by a turn-up or cuff (be it subtle or dramatic) that often points outward (much like the sleeve styles on some 1950s dresses), gauntlet gloves often came part-way up the forearm, though they could be wrist-length as well. They were a popular style and remain a dramatic, beautiful way to add a stylish dose of mid-century pizzazz to any ensemble.

Classic, bracelet- or coat-length gloves: different names for the glove length that commonly measures 33–36cm/13–14in long and hits at the mid-way point, or a little above it, on the forearm. A very flattering and versatile length, this style commonly involved ruching, which offered the wearer the ability to length or shorten her gloves by stretching or bunching the fabric (to a degree) to suit her sleeve length.

Elbow-length gloves: as their name suggests, this length of glove hits at, just below, or slightly above the wearer's elbow. They are usually the most dramatic length of glove seen during daytime wear in the mid-twentieth century and were often sported in the evening, especially in settings where opera-length gloves might have been a touch too formal or impractical.

Evening or opera gloves: generally a more formal style of glove that hits above the elbow (and in extreme cases can reach all the way up to the armpit). During the Victorian era and early twentieth century, in particular, they often featured rows of small buttons (as did many gloves of all lengths in general), which could be fastened by hand or with the use of a specialized tool called a glove hook.

Mousquetaire gloves: an old-fashioned style of formal evening glove dating back to at least the sixteenth century; they have a small number (often three) buttons at the wrist so that a lady can slide her hand out of them when needed (such as for eating) but have the rest of the glove remain in place (she then slides her hand back in, without needing to take her gloves on and off entirely to do so, once she's finished eating, smoking, etc.).

To find out your glove size, measure around your hand just below your knuckles. Use your dominant hand (that is, the one you write with) as it will be a little bigger than the other. Glove sizes come in numeric or letter sizes depending on the manufacturer and I have included a chart for you to work it out.

Chapter 12 / Creating the Look

Hats and Hair

Dior proclaimed that the hat was to be the focal point of any fashion statement, setting the tenor for the overall picture and placing emphasis on the face and the individuality of the wearer. Traditionally, hat shopping used to begin with a trip to a milliner: from the 1800s right through the 1950s every major European city had a large number of hat shops with different specialisms. As they do today, some milliners worked collaboratively with fashion designers to create hats that often offset the volume of the garments and making them either very small or very large. Hats were held on the head using elastic linings and long hatpins. They were made from straw, wool felt or satin for evening, and were often decorated with feathers, beads, ribbons, flowers and netting (which would have been made of nylon in the 1950s). They were worn in a variety of colours to match every outfit. Popular large hat styles in the fifties were the flying saucer, bucket and lampshade. Flying saucer hats, also called coolie hats, were shaped like, well, flying saucers. The hat is virtually flat with dressed curls of millinery wool and feathers and is held on with a band – a modern spin on the old-fashioned elastic. They were wide at the bottom and came to a rounded point at the top. They were fairly flat – the slope of the sides wasn't steep, and the brims were wide – and they could even be 30cm/12in or more in diameter. The bucket hat was smaller, fitted to the head: it was shaped like an upside-down bucket, flat on the top and slightly wider at the bottom. These hats sometimes had small brims on the bottom as well. Lampshade hats were a little bit larger than bucket hats, fitted to the head but worn pulled down a little farther. They had a rounded top and a second, wider tier that curved downward and functioned as a wide brim. Pillbox hats continued to be a popular small hat style. They were circular in shape and not very deep, covering just the top of the head. One is being worn by model Ruth with the town suit (*see* Chapters 6 and 7); this one uses elastic to hold it in place and it is dressed with Russian veiling. The stockists are listed in the Stockists and Suppliers section.

The post-war years of the 1940s and 1950s saw many women choosing for the first time not to wear hats on a regular basis for a variety of practical and lifestyle-led reasons. Generally speaking though, the average woman in the fifties would have had a collection of hats in a variety of types and weights, frequently choosing hats that were small and close to the head. Hairstyles had a part to play in what women chose and generally hair was long and not cropped and put up in a variety of different ways so I would suggest deciding on your hairstyle and hat in tandem. Hairdresser Belinda Hay has a brilliant book called *Style Me Vintage* which has easy step-by-step instructions for a variety of different styles from the era. Curls were very desirable at the time and considered to be very sophisticated. The 'poodle' was a style that swept the hair up at the back and sides and gripped it onto the top of the head: the hair on top was then tightly curled. The most popular adopter of this style was Lucille Ball. Chemical perms were much safer and more reliable in the post-war era. Many women would go to their hairdresser at least every six weeks to get their hair permed and set. For those who couldn't afford frequent visits to the hairdresser, home perm kits were now on the market for the first time. Other women opted for a softer-looking curl or wave, a look epitomized by Marilyn Monroe or Elizabeth Taylor. The look was achieved with a weekly wash and 'set' at the hairdresser's. Not all homes had access to hot and cold running water and in the post-war years many still

Faux vintage embellished flying saucer hat.

Faux vintage pillbox hat with embellishment and Russian veil.

Advertisement for a home perm kit, UK *Vogue*, June 1956. (Author's own collection)

Advertisement for home perm kit, *Woman's Weekly*, August 1955. (Author's own collection)

shared standpipes at the end of the street, making this level of frequent grooming difficult to achieve consistently at home.

Model Ruth (*see* opening images for Chapters 4, 5, 6, 7 and 12) achieved this look using rollers, backcombing and some kirby grips. Most women would have had a set of hair curlers and learned to roll up and pin curls at home as readily as they had learnt to sew. The iconic vision of women from the forties and fifties with their hair under a scarf was a direct result of lean times when they were unable to go to the hairdresser's or find and buy hair products. Our other model Edie (*see* opening images for Chapters 1, 3, 4, 8, 9, 10 and 11) took her inspiration from pin-up girl Bettie Page, with a short curled fringe. The same look can be achieved with longer hair by wrapping it around a hair pad (a small foam sausage) at the front and curling and pinning the rest up. Hair dye was also significantly more sophisticated and safer in the 1950s, with platinum blonde, red and gold being popular choices. Chemical hair relaxants were also introduced during this decade but the lye-based products were infamous for causing scalp burns and for being unsafe. Many of these products were not withdrawn from sale until as late as 2011 even though no-lye relaxers have been available since the 1990s. As hairstyles grew in size in the early 1960s, hat styles had to adapt and they became tiny poufs of veil or pillboxes that perched on the back of the head. The hair usurped the hat in terms of being key to defining the look of the decade.

For ladies who wanted to make soft hats in the same or a complementary fabric to their outfits there were paper patterns available. Millinery manuals, like the 1953 edition by Mrs Gladys L. Old, were also very popular. Mrs Old actually self-published her manual. As with other manuals of the day written by women, it would have been regarded as a vanity project and not have been considered worthy of a proper publishing deal. This explains its somewhat shabby appearance, with its soft cover and spiral (this one has been replaced for conservation purposes) and contents printed on cheap paper. It is likely that it would have been written as a teaching tool to accompany millinery classes taught by Mrs Old and allowing her skills to be passed on to other women. The book content covers historical hat shapes, terms and equipment, but does not include paper patterns. It does provide the instructions to draft hats, particularly brim and beret hats, and allowed ladies more artistic self-expression. The preface is accompanied by a diagram that makes it all look so easy and reads:

> A woman loves to be an individual, especially in her selection of a hat. She loves to put her own personal touch to its creation ... The aim of the following lessons is to present the methods of making basic hat patterns. By thoroughly mastering the principles involved, the student should be able to vary these patterns to her own need.

To find out your hat size use a soft tape measure and place it around your head, positioned mid-forehead and just above the ears. If your hat is to be worn at an angle measure round where you want the hat to go. Measure in centimetres or inches and find your size on the hat size chart, which has been adapted for women from one used by famous hatmakers Lock & Co. Traditional hatmakers by royal appointment, their hat shop is the oldest in the world and its doors have been open since 1676: it is also the oldest surviving family-run business. The accompanying illustrations are by the wonderful Gladys L. Old.

Rules for Wearing Hats

- Your hat should complement your entire look so ensure you choose your outfit first. Your milliner will be able to help you choose a hat that is the right colour, size and proportion for your outfit; alternatively, if you are shopping for your hat on the high street, take your outfit with you. If you are shopping online try it on all together then decide whether to keep or return it.

EU size in cm	53	54	55	56	57	58	59	60	61	62
UK size	6 1/2	6 5/8	6 3/4	6 7/8	7	7 1/8	7 1/4	7 3/8	7 1/2	7 5/8
US Size	6 5/8	6 3/4	6 7/8	7	7 1/8	7 1/4	7 3/8	7 1/2	7 5/8	7 3/4
Inches	20 7/8	21 1/4	21 5/8	22	22 1/2	22 7/8	23 1/4	23 5/8	24	24 1/2
	SMALL S	SMALL S	SMALL S	SMALL S/M	MED M	MED M	LARGE L	LARGE L	X LARGE XL	X LARGE XL

Hat size chart.

- Choose the right hat to complement your face shape. If your face is round, opt for an angular hat that cuts across the face; or you can soften a more angular face with a rounded hat with soft trim.
- Your hat does not need to match the colour of your outfit exactly but you should choose a colour that tones well to pull your look together.
- To ensure your hat is being shown to its full potential, you should wear your hair neatly up or away from your face. Never wear sunglasses with your hat.

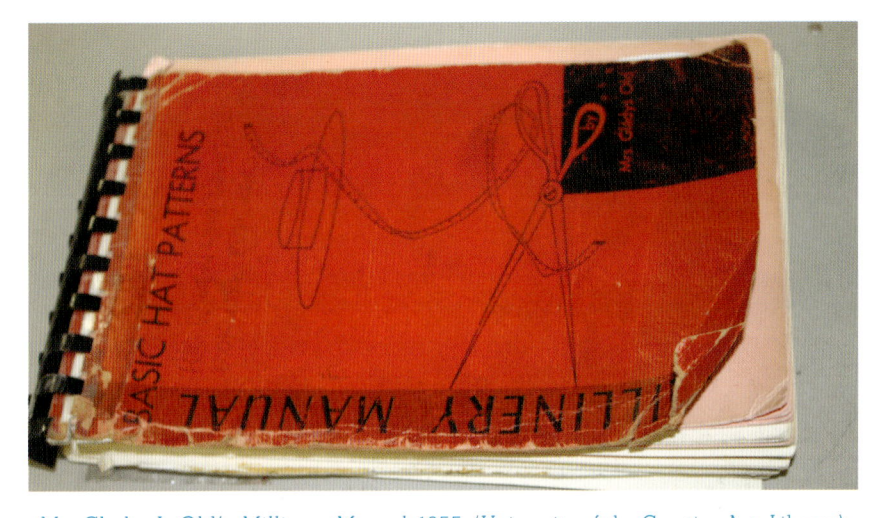

Mrs Gladys L. Old's *Millinery Manual*, 1955. (University of the Creative Arts Library)

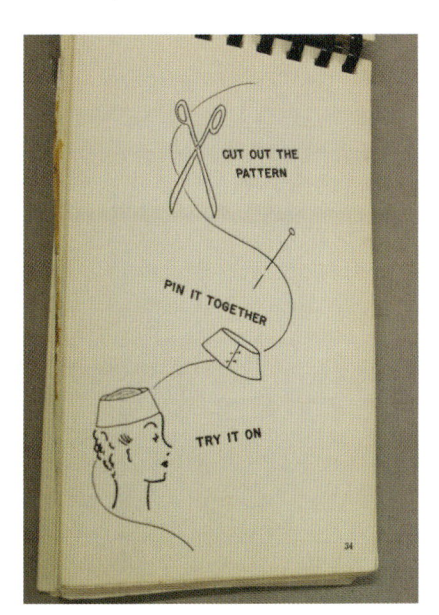

Illustrated overview of the hat-making process, Mrs Gladys L. Old's *Millinery Manual*, 1955. (University of the Creative Arts Library)

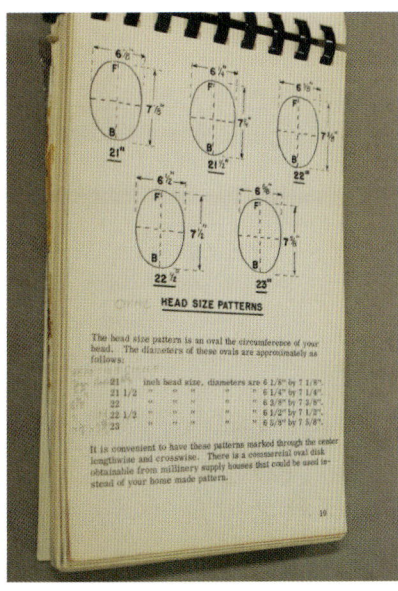

Diagrams and notes for calculating head sizes, Mrs Gladys L. Old's *Millinery Manual*, 1955. (University of the Creative Arts Library)

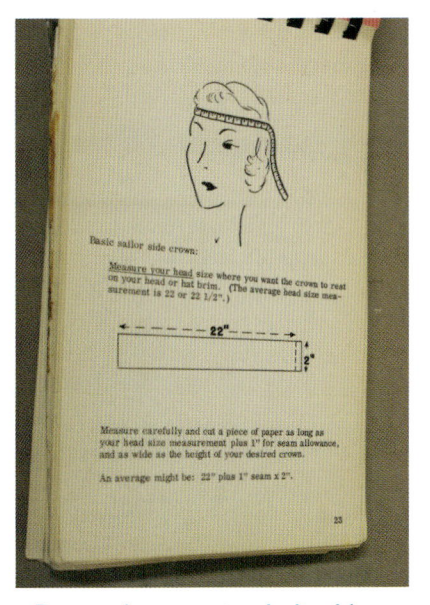

Diagram for measuring the head for a sailor cap, Mrs Gladys L. Old's *Millinery Manual*, 1955. (University of the Creative Arts Library)

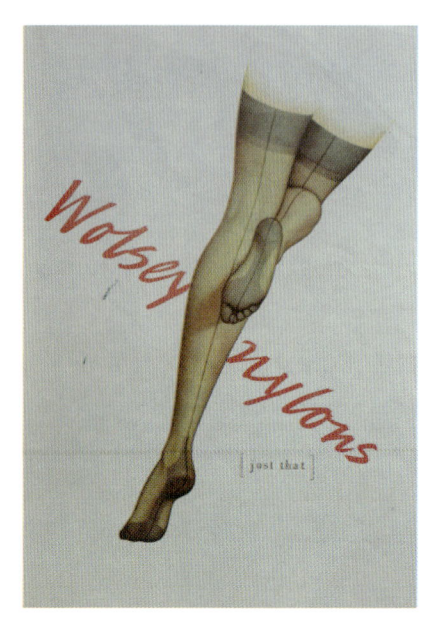

Advertisement for fully-fashioned, seamed stockings, *Vogue*, June 1956. (Author's own collection)

Circular knitted seamless stockings, *Woman's Weekly*, August 1955. (Author's own collection)

- Ensure you are visible underneath the brim of your hat. Opt for side-sweep hats or a perching or disk hat.
- Do not get a straw hat wet! Store it in a cool dry place, preferably in a hatbox, where it can remain dust-free until you want to wear it.
- Handle a hat by the brim and not the crown or you will distort it.
- To clean a hat, gently brush it with a pure bristle hat brush over the steam of a kettle. You can also gently reshape the crown in the same way if you have squashed it.

Stockings

Seamed stockings are an easy way to add a bit of vintage glamour to your look. Most 1950s stockings were fully fashioned, meaning they were knitted into the shape of a leg rather than the stretchy tubes they are today. Held up by garter belts or girdles, nylons were sized to fit by the size of the foot. They didn't always fit the shape of the leg, and girls had to constantly run to the ladies' room and fix nylons that had sagged at the ankles or twisted at the seam. By the end of the decade, circular knit seamless stockings were also available but less widely adopted.

'Stretch' nylons, containing up to 10 per cent Elastane, were also introduced. Aggressive marketing campaigns ensued to educate retailers and consumers on the better quality of fit created with circular knit and seamless stockings, but it took a while for them to catch on. Unlike 1940s stockings, 1950s seams were very visible and often black, regardless of body tone. Stockings worn during the day were usually the colour of skin or a couple shades darker for a tanned look and had names like 'Nude', 'Beige', 'Taupe' and 'Bronze'.

Visually, apart from the seams, the heels were the most exciting part of wearing 1950s stockings. Practically speaking, they were often reinforced to help prevent runs and holes. Sometimes called 'personality heels', they were detailed and sexy and added a little personality to the outfit, depending on what you chose. A plain heel stocking was a simple Cuban heel where the design was a squared-off block just above the shoe line. Fancier heel types extended the design up the back of the lower calf. Designs might be stitched in with black thread or 'flocked' with a velvet-like dust pressed into the nylon. Most designs were geometric (squares, points, arrows, checks and so on) but there were also dots, lace effects and double stripes – these were known by the general name of 'harlequin' heels. It was also possible to order nylons with one or more monogrammed initials. To ensure the durability of 1950s nylons and stockings, women would be wary of the length of their nails and sometimes even wore gloves while dressing in sheer stockings to make sure they didn't snag them.

You will need to know two specific measurements to buy your stockings: your foot length and your leg length. Stocking manufacturers originally all adhered to strict guidelines to create a universal size chart using a number to denote the shoe size or foot length followed by a letter denoting the length; for example, 10.5M. (Here we briefly have to resort to imperial measurements to explain the process.) Each size is measured from the toe to the 'middle' or 'centre' of the heel. As most of us can only guess where this 'centre of heel' is, the process can be inaccurate so it is more common to measure to the 'end' of the heel (the far right edge of it) in inches. You can subtract $^3/_4$ in/2cm from this 'overall length measurement' to get the true stocking size, in other words a size 10 stocking will measure $10^3/_4$ in/27.3cm. The second measurement will determine the length of the stocking to the top of the welt so factor in how long or short you want to wear your suspenders first. To see if you need a stocking that is a short, medium, long or extra long, measure from the bottom of the heel to the very top of the welt position and check on the measurement chart included. Please note that this measurement is not the same as your inside leg measurement. You can apply these measurements if you are trying to measure existing stockings flat on a table or on your leg before you buy. I have also included a column for modern-sized stockings, but these are likely to include stretch of some kind and may not be fully fashioned – it depends on how authentic you want to be. I used the Glamour range of stockings from What

UK shoe size	Vintage stocking size (foot)	Vintage stocking size S (Heel to top Welt in inches)	Vintage Stocking size M (Heel to top Welt in inches)	Vintage Stocking size L (Heel to top Welt in inches)	Vintage Stocking size XL (Heel to top Welt in inches)	Modern sizing
3	8 1/2	26 - 27	28 - 29	30 - 31	32 - 33	S
4	9	28 1/2	30 1/2	32 1/2	34 1/2	S/M
5	9 1/2	29–29 1/2	31-31 1/2	33-33 1/2	35-35 1/2	S/M
6	10	30	32	34	36	M/L
7	10 1/2	31	33	35	37	M/L
8	11	31 - 32	33 - 34	35 - 36	37 - 38	L

Stockings size chart.

New stockings from What Katie Did, selected for coloured heels, seams and welts.

Katie Did for the shoot. As they are modern hosiery and not fully-fashioned vintage stockings, they come in 15 denier and contain stretch nylon with Elastane. They come in two sizes covering UK dress sizes 10 to 18 and heights 152cm/60in to 180cm/71in. The retro-style stocking tops, or welts, also stretch, unlike their vintage counterparts, making them more comfortable for bigger thighs. I selected them because I particularly liked the colour range of the heel and seam, such as Edie's stockings with baby-blue welts worn with the bullet bra and girdle for Chapter 3.

With different size systems and measuring units in different countries, it can be difficult to establish what the right size is to buy. As a precaution, I have also included measurements in inches and then converted them into centimetres on the stockings chart. I have included women's international shoe size comparisons for the UK, US, Europe and Japan. If you want to do your own conversions there are 2.54cm to an inch.

Rules for Wearing Stockings

- Roll the stocking up and gather it in your hands before sliding the foot in. Begin with the toes and unroll the stocking upward, making sure to centre the foot and leg seams.
- If you don't get the seam straight first time, don't try to adjust on your leg. Take the stocking off and start again.
- Your stockings should be the correct length to meet the garter belt. Back garters should be fastened first and then the front at the reinforced hem to help avoid runs.
- When wearing stockings, avoid objects and furniture with sharp edges. Take your rings off before you put on or take off stockings and before washing them.
- Keep stockings in a separate laundry bag and hand-wash them with gentle soap flakes. Hang them up to dry by their toes.
- If it is your first time wearing real nylons, double-check the size is correct before opening the packet as hosiery is not returnable.

The Handbag

By the mid-1950s, the 'match everything' aesthetic ruled. Many design houses offered to make matching fabric bags out of the same cloth used for a lady's outfit. Clothing catalogues paired dresses with matching handbags and accessories to encourage women to buy an entire wardrobe. Leather was the most sought-after status material but cloth handbags remained a good option for a tighter budget. Synthetic materials made cloth bags even more affordable. By

Vintage article about models from Paris Paris with accessories from London stockists, *Woman's Weekly*, August 1955. (Author's own collection)

Mid-decade stilettoes and wedgies, *Woman's Weekly*, August 1955. (Author's own collection)

comparison, for well-off women, 1950s day bags might be made of expensive leather from unusual animal skins – antelope, calfskin, ostrich, gazelle or pigskin. In a decade where social standing was so important, expensive handbags were also often finished with the logo or label of the favoured fashion house. This denoted the wearer's ability to visually convey their knowledge of fashion and their personal wealth. Economies were recovering from the effects of World War II and with this trajectory came the need for domestic life to portray the image of ultimate perfection and homely harmony frequently expressed through the vehicle of women's clothing.

Perhaps the first 'status handbag' was the now famous Chanel 2.55. After being in retirement for over a decade, in 1954 Chanel reopened her fashion house. In keeping with her stylish yet comfortable aesthetic, the label produced classic designs with a boxy silhouette. The 2.55 handbag was created in February 1955 (hence the 2.55 title). The bag was made of padded and quilted leather or jersey in a handful of neutral tones. Chanel chose to incorporate her logo on the inside of the bag within the lining, although the bag was instantly recognizable as a Chanel by its design alone. In the 1950s, there was an abundance of glamorous celebrities gracing the covers of magazines, newspapers and movie theatres. In 1956, Grace Kelly was pictured holding aloft her classic Hermès bag (promoting speculation that she utilized it to conceal her pregnancy). Thereafter, the Hermès travel bag became known as the Kelly Bag.

Proponents of the New Look often favoured a bulkier bag reminiscent of a Victorian carpet-bag with ornate handles and feet on the square base to protect the leather. This style of bag signalled the re-emergence of the folding bag frame and was combined with new inventions in fastenings. The twist lock, briefcase lock and slide lock all contributed to a sophisticated but modern aesthetic in direct contrast to the functional utilitarian bags of the 1940s. Often now referred to as 'granny bags', these cumbersome bags may have been practical because of their size, but very rarely featured in fashion editorials for fear of disrupting the silhouette of the skirts.

Chapter 12 / Creating the Look

Retro-look stilettoes and high-heeled pumps for the shoot.

Shoes

With so much new emphasis on the rest of women's fashion, 1950s shoe styles became understated accessories. Instead of bold patterns and fancy adornments, shoes were simple, classy single-colour pumps, flats, wedgies and loafers. Black and brown were the main choices for daywear, while brighter colours were acceptable for summer sportswear or house slippers. Shoes also coordinated perfectly with an outfit's accessories, matching bags, gloves, belts and even jewellery perfectly. In the early 1950s the stiletto court and pump shoes were all the rage. At an extreme, the former were very tall, with 10cm/4in spiked ultra-thin heels. Early on, the heels ended in a small metal cap that left dents in soft wood floors and women were frequently banned from wearing them in various public spaces like libraries and expensive restaurants. They were very impractical and mostly only worn for very special occasions, for short durations, and by fashion models.

TV actress Lucille Ball wore tall chunky ankle strap shoes through most of the early 1950s. These were a carry-over style from the 1940s as worn by many pin-up girls. While many shoes retained the thicker heels of the war years, especially for working women, most fashion followers preferred the smaller narrow-heeled shoes or kitten-heels as they were more modern and more practical. For evening wear, jewel colours and metallics, especially glittery gold and dark silver, were fashionable. For everyday wear, around the house or running errands, a thicker low- to mid-heeled pump was the best choice. Black was the colour that went with the most outfits, so every woman had at least one pair. Teenagers and housewives also wore saddle shoes: these were flat oxford shoes with black soles, heels and central upper panel and white toe and upper heel panels. They were usually worn with a pair of bobby socks – white socks rolled or folded down two or three times at the ankle – but never with stockings. White shoe sections had to be kept in pristine condition, so girls would clean and shine their shoes nightly and buy new ones as soon as they began to show signs of wear.

Stockists and Suppliers

Corsetry (Fabric, Boning, Trims, etc.)
Vena Cava Design, at www.venacavadesign.co.uk
Farthingales Corset Making Supplies at www.farthingalescorsetmakingsupplies.com

Fabrics and Haberdashery
MacCulloch and Wallis, at www.macculloch-wallis.co.uk
Borovicks Fabrics Ltd, at www.borovickfabricsltd.co.uk
Whaleys (Bradford) Ltd (UK), at www.whaleys-bradford.ltd.uk
Harlequin (bespoke cover buttons and belts), at www.harlequin-uk.com

Pattern-Cutting Supplies
Eastman Staples Ltd (UK), at www.eastman.co.uk
Morplan, at www.morplan.com
Kennett & Lindsell Ltd (UK) (mannequins), at www.kennetlindsell.com

Re-Digitized Vintage Patterns
My Vintage Wish, at https://www.etsy.com/shop/MyVintageWish

Pre-Made Petticoats, Bras and 1950s Accessories
Vivien of Holloway, at https://www.vivienofholloway.com
What Katie Did, at https://www.whatkatiedid.com
Cornelia James Gloves (by Royal Appointment), at https://www.corneliajames.com
www.glove.org

Suggested Reading and Information Sources

Books

Barnfield, J., *The Vintage Pattern Selector: The Sewer's Guide to Choosing and Using Retro Styles* (Bloomsbury, London, 2013).

Brown, M., *The 1950s Look: Recreating the Fashions of the Fifties* (Sabrestorm, Devizes, 2006).

Demarchelier, P., *Dior Couture by Demarchelier* (Rizzoli International, London, 2011).

Dior, C., *Dior by Dior: The Autobiography of Christian Dior by Christian Dior, De Luxe Edition* (V&A Publishing, London, 2015).

Dressmaking Made Easy with Le Roy (Associated British Paper Patterns Ltd, Bletchley, 1953).

Emery, J. Spanabel, 'Dreams on Paper: A Story of the Commercial Pattern Industry', in *The Culture of Sewing; Gender, Consumption and Home Dressmaking*, 235–253 (Berg, Oxford, 1999).

Fernault, H., *Haute Couture Ateliers: The Artisans of Fashion* (Vendome Press, New York, 2014).

Fischer, A., *Basics Fashion Design 03: Construction,* 2nd edition (Fairchild Books, London, 2015).

Haslam, G. A., *The Haslam System of Dress Cutting: Illustrated Book of Drafting,* Books 33–40, 1st editions (n.p., Bolton, Lancashire, 1953–55).

Haslam, G. A., *The Haslam System of Dress Cutting: Vintage Pattern-Making for 1950s Fashions* (Bramcost, n.p., 2010).

Hay, B., *Style Me Vintage* (Anova Books, London, 2010).

Howlett, D., et al., *Encyclopaedia of Needlecraft* (Odhams, London, 1953).

Johnson, P., *New Complete Guide to Sewing; Step-by-Step Techniques for Making Clothes and Home Accessories* (Readers Digest Association Canada, Montreal, 2002).

Lambert Fielding, J., *Elements of Clothing Construction: Laboratory Manual* (Florida State University, Gainesville, FA, 1955).

Old, G. L., *Millinery Manual: Basic Hat Patterns* (Columbia, US (1953).

Polhemus, T., *Style Surfing: What to Wear in the Third Millennium* (Thames & Hudson, London, 1996).

Reed, P., *Fifties Fashion Looks that Changed the 1950s* (Conran Octopus, London, 2012).

Teunissen, J., et al., *Fashion Accessories,* 2nd edition (ArtEZ Press, Arnhem, 2008).

Periodicals

UK Woman's Journal, 1952–55.
Vogue, 1952–57 (both UK and US editions).
Harper's Bazaar, 1949–56.

Websites

My main recommendation is the V&A Museum's digitized costume collection at https://www.vam.ac.uk/collections/fashion

https://www.chemheritage.org/distillations/magazine/nylon-a-revolution-in-textiles

http://www.collectorsweekly.com/sewing/patterns

http://www.corneliajames.com

http://www.craftsy.com

http://www.fashion-era.com/1950s/1950s_3_fashion_dressmaking.htm

http://www.glove.org/Modern/myfirstgloves.php

http://www.lockhatters.co.uk

http://www.oldpatterns.com/

http://www.paintedladylondon.com

http://www.sekersfabrics.co.uk/about-sekers/

http://www.vintagedancer.com

http://www.whatkatiedid.com

Museums

Brighton Pavilion & Museums, Brighton and Hove, East Sussex
Victoria & Albert Museum (V&A), London
Worthing Museum and Art Gallery, Worthing, West Sussex

Acknowledgements

This book would not have been possible without the support of a lot of people. Thank you to Gerry Connelly, Senior Curator at Worthing Museum and Art Gallery, for allowing me access to such a wonderful collection and for your expertise and knowledge. Thank you also to John Bright at Cosprop for allowing me access to the wonderful Madonna/Dior gown and the Liberty bodice and petticoat.

I am also extremely grateful to Sarah Hobbs at Vena Cava Design for her generous sponsorship of materials and notions for all of the bras and girdle; this has really helped me to create something believable. Thank you to My Vintage Wish for permission to use images from their digitized vintage patterns.

Thank you to Chip Harris from the BA Hons Fashion Atelier at UCA for allowing me to use the workshop to produce the projects and to Michelle Mills in particular for tackling the girdle and blouse patterns and for turning her hand to some vintage millinery. Her technical know-how, enthusiasm and passion for all things vintage made it a pleasure to work with her. Many thanks to Leah Murphy for being an excellent intern, and especially for making and covering various versions of shoulder, hip and bust pads. Thank you too to Suzanne Rowland for her excellent advice and for cheering me on to the end.

A big thank you to the brilliant Carol Seatory for her knowledge and advice and for digitizing and scaling the patterns.

Thank you also to Ruth and Edie for modelling, Maria Short for photography and Andrew Fionda for use of his beautiful home. What Katie Did supplied all the wonderful stockings and Cornelia James supplied the elegant gloves that helped to bring the projects to life.

Finally, the biggest thank you of all goes to my very understanding family who put up with me through this process from start to finish. It turns out that I am not a natural-born writer but they still love me anyway.

Index

boning 55,57
bow tie blouse 77–78
bow tie blouse 77–83
bow tie blouse pattern 79
bra and girdle set 23–25
bra fitting 24
bra patterns 30
bullet bra making 32–34

chalk line skirt (town suit) 69–70, 73
chalk line skirt (town suit) pattern 71
cover belt 21
cover buttons 21
creating the look 113–123

detachable collar 91–92
detachable cuff 93
dress fitting 25

fabrics 20–21
fillers and falsies 39
fitting 20
french dart 80

girdle making 39–41
girdle pattern 31
girdles 28
gloves 114–116
gusset 89

haberdashery 21
ham 19
hand sewing needles 18
hand size chart 116
handbags 121–122

Haslam system of dress cutting 11–12
hat size chart 119
hats and hair 117–119
hip ruffle pattern 48
hook and eye tape 37
horsehair braid 47
House of Youth, Dior 51–52
housewife's kimono pattern 87
housewife's Kimono shirt 85–86
housewife's kimono blouse 85–93

jet pockets 65–67

longline bra making 36–37

mannequin 20
manteau making 109–111
manteau pattern 108
manteaux 103–111
measuring and fitting
moulage 13–14

'New Look', Dior 9
nylon 77

overlocker 18
overwire 34
overwire bra making 34–36

paper patterns 11
patch pocket 109–110
pattern abbreviations 14
personal measurement chart 24
petticoat 43

ruffles 43

scissors and shears 17–18
self neatening gathered skirt 95
self neatening gathered skirt pattern 97
self-neatening gathered skirt 95–101
sewing machine 18
shoes 123
shoulder pads 82,90
soft tailored jacket (town suit) 59–61
soft tailored jacket (town suit) pattern 62
steam iron 19
stockings 120
stockings size chart 121
stockists and suppliers 124
strapless cocktail dress 51–57
strapless cocktail dress 51
strapless cocktail dress pattern 53
suggested reading 125

taking measurements 23–24
tape measure 17
thimble 18
thread marking 78
tools and materials 17–21
town suit: chalk line skirt 69–75
town suit: soft tailored jacket 59–67
Twilfit 28–29

vintage patterns 13–14
Vogue patterns 11

waistband 75

Related Titles from Crowood

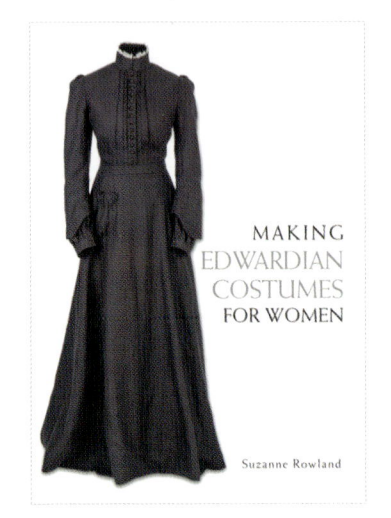

MAKING EDWARDIAN COSTUMES FOR WOMEN
Suzanne Rowland
ISBN: 978 1 78500 102 4

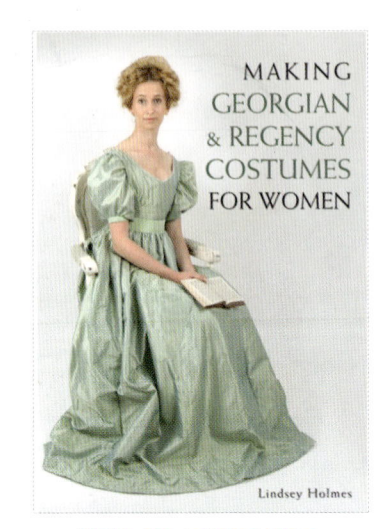

MAKING GEORGIAN & REGENCY COSTUMES FOR WOMEN
Lindsey Holmes
ISBN: 978 1 78500 070 6

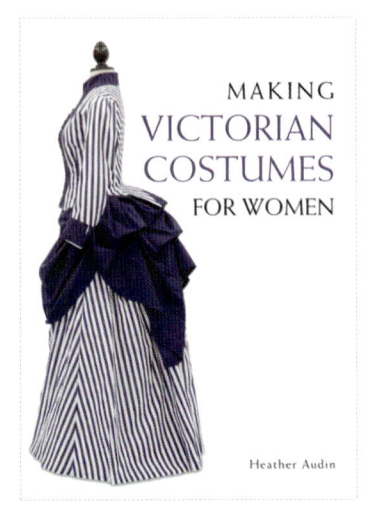

MAKING VICTORIAN COSTUMES FOR WOMEN
Heather Audin
ISBN: 978 1 78500 051 5

Making Vintage 1920s Clothes for Women
Suzanne Rowland
ISBN: 978 1 78500 339 4

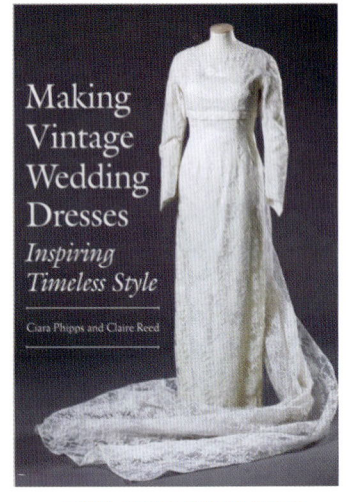

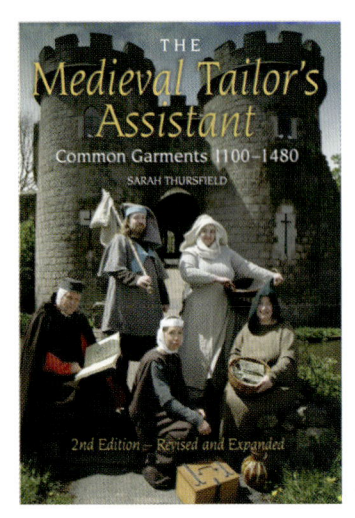

Making Vintage 1940s Clothes for Women
Sarah Magill
ISBN: 978 1 78500 310 3

Making Vintage Wedding Dresses
Inspiring Timeless Style
Ciara Phipps and Claire Reed
ISBN: 978 1 78500 312 7

The Medieval Tailor's Assistant
Common Garments 1100–1480
Sarah Thursfield
2nd Edition – Revised and Expanded
ISBN: 978 1 84797 834 9

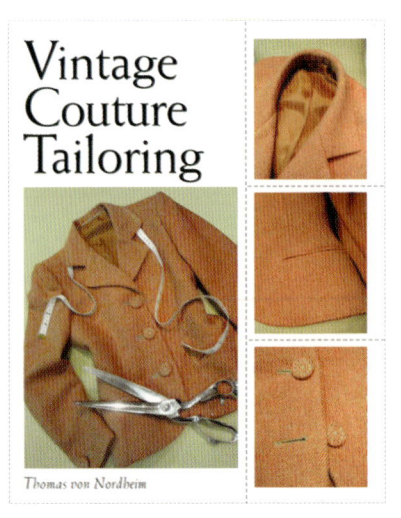

Vintage Couture Tailoring
Thomas von Nordheim
ISBN: 978 1 84797 373 3

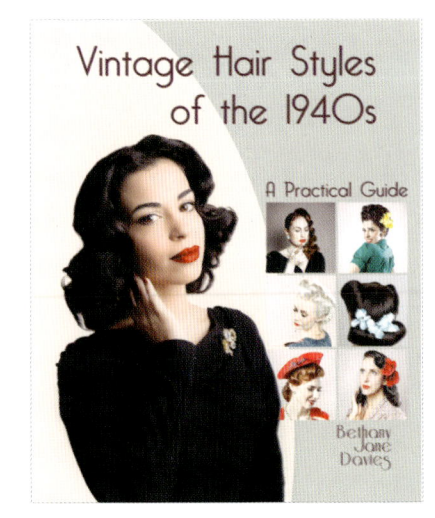

Vintage Hair Styles of the 1940s
A Practical Guide
Bethany Jane Davies
ISBN: 978 1 84797 832 5